Advance Praise for *Bumping Down Highways*

"…you will laugh, you may even get a tear or two as you join Jenni on her RV adventures as a single woman crisscrossing our great country. Young or old, new or experienced RV'er, there is something for everyone as Jenni grows in spirit and experience as she conquers America by RV. Certainly as a single person Jenni provides a great follow up to one of our school themes of 'Women –You CAN & Should Drive Your RV!' I am very proud to have been a part of her travels."

—Chuck Urwiller, RV Driving School.com

"*Bumping Down Highways* is a compelling story of an executive who traded her office for an RV yet continued her career without missing a beat and I couldn't put it down. I was inspired and envious at how she worked on corporate deals with America's majestic vistas and most scenic locations as a backdrop. Edwards' visually descriptive style helps the reader experience her day-to-day life in this inspiring ever-changing environment."

—Bob Higley, CEO Upliftv

BUMPING DOWN HIGHWAYS

From Boardrooms to Back Roads in an RV

JENNI RANEY EDWARDS

Post Hill
PRESS

A POST HILL PRESS BOOK
ISBN: 978-1-64293-207-2
ISBN (eBook): 978-1-64293-208-9

Bumping Down Highways:
From Boardrooms to Back Roads in an RV
© 2019 by Jenni Raney Edwards
All Rights Reserved

Cover art by Tricia Principe, principedesign.com

Cover Photo credit to Nathan Deremer at Deremer Studios
Special thanks to the City of Jacksonville for the use of Huguenot
Memorial Park

Post Hill Press
New York • Nashville
posthillpress.com

Published in the United States of America

To everyone who ever had a dream....
May the call of your dreams be stronger than your fears!

CONTENTS

INTRODUCTION

I climbed the corporate ladder and found success at every turn. I was chasing the traditional American Dream. I loved to travel (the "five-star hotel and dining" kind that you got to by airplane), and I had it all…except time for me and my family.

I saw dear friends die too young from cancer and co-workers die from heart attacks. To be honest, I was miserable in my job. It was the challenge of accomplishing something and helping other people that I really loved. Perhaps I got the definition of "success" all wrong.

When I was forced to temporarily leave my pretty beach condo, I needed a place to stay with my dogs, so I took a road trip from Florida to Oregon in my SUV. Carrying only the barest of necessities, I took my time, following detours. I fell in love with the road and simple lifestyle. I decided I was going to live my life *now*! I had no experience with RV life, but I jumped in with both feet. When I say no experience, I mean zip, zilch, nada, zero, none! Still, I decided to trade boardrooms for back roads and hit the road in an RV by myself. People thought I was crazy. Many said I couldn't do it or shouldn't do it. I have bumped down highways through forty-five states. Now I drive, and live in, a forty-foot motorhome, towing a car behind me, zigzagging across the country.

When people learn I am traveling the country alone in an RV, they think I am brave. That is about as far from the truth as you could get. The journey has been full of challenges and dangers. I am often scared, I just am not afraid to try. I made mistakes, learned lessons, and met amazing people along the way. I am here to tell you, no matter how crazy it may seem, you *can do anything*!

Life requires guts, courage, and vulnerability. I took it all one step further and did something even crazier. I had no experience writing a book, but I kept a journal along the way. Although I had no idea that people would be interested in my fears, triumphs, and raw emotions, after so many asked, I turned my journal into the story you are about to read. I hope that in these pages, you find the faith and courage to re-evaluate your definition of success, and that perhaps you will find the inspiration to do something you have only dreamed of!

I'm Jenni, and I'm a real person.

BEFORE THE JOURNEY

I climbed the corporate ladder at a large publicly traded company. Or maybe I snuck up the ladder, because it was rare that women had high-level positions. More hours, more travel, more money. I had the "things" I thought represented success. I had the big house, the Lexus convertible, the forty-seven little black dresses, the designer handbags and shoes. I rented a house on the beach for our annual vacation. I never stopped working. I was constantly on the phone, reading and responding to emails while the kids were on the beach. I chose the beach house because it had Wi-Fi, a printer, a fax machine, and was close enough to home in case I needed to go to the office. My job was demanding, and it was hard for me to find time for family and friends. I would apologize for missing this or that, claiming, "I am just so busy." I told myself I was working this hard to make life easier for my children.

I led a "glamorous" life—or so it appeared. I traveled so much that I flew first class at coach prices. I took weekend trips with my best friend, flying first class on my miles. We stayed at five-star hotels on points. I valet parked everywhere I could. I ate at expensive restaurants, usually tipping 50 percent or more. I paid more for clothes and shoes in small stores because I was too busy to shop. I realized that I was working eighty to a hundred hours a week to pay for *stuff*. My job was no longer enjoyable. I had polished my identity and felt like such a fraud. I just didn't see a way out.

At any given moment, you have the power to say "this is not how the story is going to end." Are you enjoying life? Doing the things you enjoy on a regular basis? I wasn't. I worked a lot, slept little, and spent time with family and friends even less. I sold my house at the beach and bought a tiny condo even closer to the beach.

I decided to write down some goals. The most important were spending more time with family and friends and traveling to places I had never been. And then I went back to work. Until a few weeks later, I came home from a trip to find that water had been pouring into my new beach condo. One call to the developer, and they said they would fix it. It was very bad. So bad that living there was impossible. My insurance company would pay for a hotel or a short stay somewhere. However, no one wanted to accept my big dog, Saint. Where could I go? What could I do?

I thought of the saying, "If God brings you to it, He will bring you through it." I woke up one morning, made a cup of coffee, and went outside to sit with my dog and my Bible. As I was praying, I felt like someone was there. I looked up at the chair on my left. I didn't see anyone, but I *knew* God was sitting there with me. I can't explain how I knew, but I knew. The words I heard were not out loud, but I heard them as if they were.

"I am here."

It was the most amazing experience I have ever had in my life. Thinking about it, I knew I couldn't tell anyone. Surely, they would think I had gone crazy due to stress or that I just dreamt it. I sat in the sun and thought, "Wow! God took the time to sit with me. Wow!" Eventually, I told my sister-in-law, knowing she wouldn't judge me and would give me her honest opinion. Until now, I have told very few people about my experience that day.

Think what you may, but I will never forget that special moment in time.

My son Tyler called with the perfect temporary solution. He and his girlfriend Andreea had just bought a house in Oregon that needed some sprucing up before they moved in. They suggested I drive out with the dogs, stay there, help them, and work from home. If I needed to travel, I could fly out from there.

I still had the challenge of where to stay along the way. I needed places that were safe and would allow both dogs. I started researching my options and found that Kampgrounds Of America (KOA) had campground locations all across the country. They even had small cabins that were dog friendly. It felt good to have a plan.

I drove across the country from Florida to Oregon in an SUV with my dogs and fell in love! I took my time. I took detours. I saw the sights. I stayed in KOA Kamper Kabins when I could find one or sometimes slept in the back of my SUV snuggled with the dogs. But *wow*! That was fun!

And that's how the story begins…

CHAPTER 1

THE LONELIEST ROAD IN AMERICA

AFTER asking many people what I should take on my crazy journey, my Acura MDX is packed with four cases of water, tea bags, dried fruit, nuts, a pillow, sleeping bag, extra blanket, five changes of clothes (or layers), a pair of flip flops, a pair of hiking boots, a few necessary toiletries, dog food, a small bag of "fat wood" to start campfires, a handgun, bear spray, and a knife. I also have my new KOA VKR (Value Kard Rewards) Membership and a KOA Guide. This is way outside my comfort zone, but it's temporary.

So many people are worried about me doing this alone and want me to call them each night it would take hours to touch base with them all. I throw in my battery powered "glamping" chandelier, promising to post a picture of it hanging at my location each night on Facebook as a compromise.

I leave my condo in Atlantic Beach later than I had planned, but I am determined to get on the road today. I am not planning to turn my radio on at all on this trip. I am going to take in the sights, play with my dogs, think about life, and talk to God along the way.

I drive until late and I am tired. Though it is going to be after closing when I arrive, I find a Georgia KOA in my guide that allows tent camping. I pull up to the Calhoun KOA and stop to read the availability board. I find a spot, fill out the envelope provided, and put money in it. I love that they trust people to do this. I drive along the main road to the back and park for a night of camping in the car.

I feed the dogs, walk them, and make our bed in the back of my SUV. I have a gun under my pillow that I know how to use but am not sure I could even pull the trigger if necessary. This is a long way from the life I have been living. Saint, my eighty-pound flat coated retriever, Emmi, my little Jack Russell, and I are snuggled into the back with our belongings piled around us. It's hot and humid. Saint cannot get comfortable and Emmi thinks that because he is moving around, it's time to play. It takes a bit for the dogs and I to settle into a spot, but we finally drift off to sleep.

At sunrise, I wake up to Emmi's soft, low, growl. I am so petrified I don't even want to open my eyes. My heartrate speeds up. I am shaking as I put my hand on the gun under my pillow. I am so afraid that I now know I could pull the trigger if I had to. I open my eyes slowly and sit up even slower, expecting to see someone staring in my window. I come face-to-face with a giant nesting Mother Goose just beyond the hood of my car. It was dark when we came in last night, so I didn't even notice her. Now I must manage packing up around her with two dogs, both of whom are barking at her incessantly. I make it fast, and we are back on the road before people start moving around.

After a rainy ride, it is late afternoon when we arrive at the Memphis KOA Journey in Marion, Arkansas. This is our first night in a KOA Kamper Kabin. I am impressed with the front porch, memory foam mattress, cable television, DVD player, microwave, and mini-fridge. Saint and Emmi even have their own Kamp K9 playground in back. Our chandelier is hung and our firepit is crackling in my fenced front yard. I am swaying gently in the porch swing with the pups relaxing at my feet. This is going to be a good trip.

We wake up with no alarm when the sun begins to peek through our windows. Both dogs are snuggled together in Saint's bed on the floor beside me. It feels good to not be in a hurry. Even with a mattress covered in plastic and using my sleeping bag for bed linens, I could get used to this.

Today we drive from west Arkansas to Kansas in constant rain. We have a cabin reserved in Goodland, Kansas. I get checked in and follow my directions to the cabins around back feeling more than a little anxious. I bump along the muddy road and see a young couple with a toddler and baby on the porch of the cabin next to mine. Their muddy yard is full of children's toys. It's a shock when it registers in my brain that this is their actual home. It's hard for me to comprehend living in such a tiny space alone, much less with a family.

This cabin is totally different than last night's. The door has a space along the bottom big enough for small critters to come in and doesn't even have a doorknob. Instead, it is like a barn with a board that slides over a wooden catch secured to the wall. There is nothing inside other than the wooden bed with a plastic mattress, a tiny desk, and a small unit jutting out of the wall blowing warm air. It's dirty, but it's dry. I won't be hanging the chandelier outside my cabin tonight. I did say I was looking forward to an adventure, right?

I get the few things inside that we need to sleep. It starts pouring and the wind is howling outside. I have most of my clothing layers on and am zipped into my sleeping bag with my blanket on top. If you don't hear from me tomorrow, I froze to death. The heater has a timer that lasts an hour and it is going to be 31 degrees tonight. Good thing I brought my sub-zero sleeping bag. I start worrying about my safety. I can't stop thinking about the creatures that could come in under the door. I consider just packing up and driving out, until there is a flash and crack of lightning. I close my eyes and pray myself to sleep instead.

We barely slept last night, but we survived. The storm continues to rage and I am nervous. I am in such a hurry to leave I decide to feed the dogs later. I pack up as fast as I can and get on the road. I don't even take time to say my morning prayer asking God to be with us and keep us from harm's way.

The storm is getting worse. The wind is blowing so hard I can barely stay in my lane. The rain is coming down in sheets so fast that my windshield wipers are useless. My hands are gripping the wheel and my eyes strain to see the white line on my right.

"BOOM!"

A bolt of lightning strikes right in front of me and I nearly run off the side of the road. Then there is another and another. The air is yellowish-gray around me. I am in Kansas, where Dorothy and Toto are from. They have tornados here. What if I am heading towards one? Now there's hail. Crap! Crap! Crap! I am shaking, and the dogs are both whining behind me.

It's time to break the "no radio" vow and find a weather report. I turn it on and the first voice I hear is a man saying, *"Welcome to this morning's sermon."* He begins to tell the story of Doubting Thomas. I did not even know this story came from the Bible until today. I think of how I forgot my prayer this morning, of how I turned on my radio instead of praying. The sermon is short and immediately goes off the air, leaving nothing but static on this station. I notice then that the storm has passed and I don't know when.

When we stop for lunch, I call the KOA in Carbondale, Colorado. I would like to stay two nights, but they are not yet open for the season. My heart sinks. I tell the woman how before I even left for this trip, I wanted to stay there. She tells me that no one is in the park, but she can leave a key and let me stay one night. She also warns me that there is still snow on the ground and tells me where I can find my key to the cabin. She has made my day.

I first see snow on the mountains in Applewood, Colorado and start the steady climb up, passing flashing signs warning of ice ahead and to "Proceed with Caution." I am nearly at the top when it starts to snow. Not just a few small flakes here and there, but *really* snowing. It does not take long before I think this might not be so exciting. My car is not equipped for snow and I don't know how to drive in it.

As I start down the steep, curvy mountain, I am seriously afraid of sliding off the side of it or crashing into someone else. I ask for God's help. I feel slightly calmer and focus on keeping my speed reduced enough that I only have to tap my brakes occasionally.

We made it down the mountain into Georgetown, Colorado where I am rewarded with a pristine blanket of white snow. We stop at the first rest area for a walk. It is absolutely gorgeous and not as cold as I imagined. The dogs are not sure what to think of all the white fluffy stuff and look funny walking through it.

There is even more snow on Copper Mountain. I stop to wander through it and take pictures of the winter wonderland spread out in front of me. The giant snowflakes look like goose feathers gently floating through the air to the ground. It's so peaceful. I find a frozen lake and walk cautiously around it. I hear a crack. I have gotten too close and the ice is breaking under me! Soon, I will be in the lake and trapped under the ice. Frantically, I slip, slide, and stumble in place, trying to get away. In my panicked state, I fall…on a stick. There is no ice under me, only a stick that broke when I stepped on it. I sit in the wet snow laughing at my silly concern and the spectacle I must have been. I climb up and sit at the edge on a rock in the sun to catch my breath and dry off. Now somewhat dry, and still shaking with laughter, I get back on the highway.

I take the exit for my riverside cabin and wind my way up the mountain. The sun is shining and it's beautiful! I arrive, find my key where it was promised, and go in search of my cabin. Colorado's Rocky Mountain majesty surrounds us in this gorgeous spot, spread along the banks of the Crystal River at the foot of Mount Sopris. My home for the night is just feet from the river.

I want to unpack then sit on the riverbank, but I don't want to leave the dogs in the cabin. I am going to try something new with my big old faithful dog, Saint. He never gets far from me, while Emmi would be off and running after the tiniest distraction. I attach Emmi's leash to Saint's collar, so he can be the babysitter, knowing he won't let her get in trouble. Emmi is exploring but can't go far because Saint is laying in the sun and not moving. This is perfect!

I go inside to explore my home for the night. I love the sound of the screen door slamming behind me. My rustic cabin has a fully equipped kitchen, bathroom, and even linens. I stop for a minute to listen. All I hear are birds singing and the river rushing by. And then it all evaporates.

My heart is racing, and I am afraid. There is a spider next to the kitchen sink. My greatest fear is spiders! While I know that this is the woods and that spiders live here, and my brain knows he is probably not going to hurt me, I am still petrified. I want to scream but am frozen in my tracks and the scream is trapped in my chest. I hear barking as Emmi's tugging on her leash and Saint's trying to keep her in check. This brings me out of my trance. I can handle this. I am going to apologize ahead of time to the house-keeper for leaving a spider trapped under a glass in the sink. It was a dance with my wood-carrying gloves on, but I got him.

Back outside, I set up camp. My chandelier is hung, and a fire is burning. The coolness of an early spring evening in the mountains has replaced the warmth of the sun. Saint and Emmi are sleeping peacefully at my feet. Listening to the sounds of nature, I absorb the calmness. Staying here with no one else is like having my own private camp in the mountains. It is perfect! When it's time for bed, I open the cabin door and latch the screen door. I climb into bed with Saint on the floor beside me and Emmi on the bed at my feet. I drift off to sleep listening to the sounds of the river running past us.

We wake up to the sound of birds singing. It's cold. I want to cling to this moment and stay snuggled in my warm bed. I need to get up. I peel back my blankets and *dang!* The cold air hits me hard! I rush to the bathroom before finding warmer clothes and the toilet seat is like ice.

I'm wearing warm clothes and coffee is brewing. I notice the spider running in circles under the glass. He actually isn't as big as I thought he was. I think of my best friend and how she would rescue him. I just don't have the guts to set him free. *Someone will free you soon, little guy.*

When I step outside with a hot cup of coffee in hand, I am greeted by warm, welcome sunshine and soothing sounds. The river is flowing, the birds are singing, the squirrels are chattering. My own slice of heaven. I can imagine being here forever.

While the dogs are inside eating breakfast, I sit down on the rocks beside the river and talk to God.

"Thank you, God, for the challenges at my condo that pushed me to do this. Thank you for creating such beauty for me to enjoy. Dear Lord, please lead me in the right direction and keep me safe on this journey."

We take one last walk around the property before packing up and heading out. I know that someday, I will be back.

I stop at the trail-lined Colorado National Monument and marvel at the red sandstone monoliths and canyons. A few hours later, we stop at a rest area. Emmi is so excited. There are little creatures scampering everywhere. They are so cute, darting from behind one rock, then another to peek around and see if we are watching. In the dry, rocky soil, wild flowers are growing. It reminds me that God works in mysterious ways. Not long ago, I was rushing from Point A to Point B. I never took time to notice the little things. If I was going on a trip, I flew. I had a packed schedule then got back on the plane to fly home.

I don't drive far before making another detour that I've read about, to Dragon Canyon. It's a bit hard to find, but it is absolutely breathtaking. Wild chrysanthemums are growing out of the rocky canyon walls. This is a fabulous place. I could spend an entire day here. I get back on the road, but only for a few minutes before I am pulling off at the next rest area. From here, I can see Ghost Rock and am in awe of the majestic views. I am literally standing on the edge of a cliff. *Wow!*

We aren't back on the road long when I see signs for Eagle Canyon and take another detour. There are no barricades between me and the canyon below. It is truly breathtaking. I understand why they built a rest stop and viewing area on the edge of this canyon. I stand close to the edge and slowly peek over the side. It's a long way down the flat, sheer wall to the bottom. This is impressive from the top, but even more impressive when I finally make it down into the canyon. I am standing at the bottom of what used to be the ancient inland sea. I decide I need to take more scenic routes.

After an amazing day of detours, our home tonight is the Ely KOA. There is a sign on the front door, "I survived Highway 50. The loneliest road in America!" The sign must be meant for those travelers who have come from the west. I get checked in and head off to get settled. Our cabin has a bed, bunks, and a desk. That's it. The mattresses are covered in plastic like all the others. From floor to ceiling it's all the same wood. As with all of these cabins, there is no shower or bathroom. We have a small porch and a dusty rock yard. It's a clean roof over our heads.

I unpack our bedding and clothes, then feed the pups. I am going to reward myself with a trip into town for Mexican food. The park owner tells me that I should try Margarita's Mexican Restaurant & Steak House. I find my way to the hostess and she seats me next to a funny Mexican man statue. He is right behind my chair. All through dinner, I feel like someone is watching me. I am miserably full, but the service and food were both amazing. It's been a long, fabulous day.

It's a new day. I am both excited and a bit nervous about this part of our journey. I will be driving through Nevada today, on Route 50. It is made up of large, desolate areas with few or no signs of civilization. I will cross several large desert valleys separated by numerous mountain ranges towering over the valley floors. When I was getting ready for this trip, I read something about this being a high mountain desert environment with open range highways. In several places I read the words, "Please be prepared." Today begins the part of my trip that is the main reason I have a gun, a knife, and mace. Not for people, but for survival, should I break down.

I don't see anything except the road ahead of me and the sand dunes beside me. Well, there was a sign back there that said seventy-seven miles to Eureka, but that's it. No trees, no bushes, no cars, no nothing. It's both peaceful and a little scary. Mentally, I run through the supplies I have and what I would do if I broke down. How long would it take for someone to find me?

A truck just passed me! I am not alone out here! As I drive, I imagine flying by a young rider racing his horse down the Pony Express trail to the next mail station. They only rode about seventy-five miles per day. That seems like nothing. I drive about five hundred miles per day.

There is a sign telling me that I am in Eureka, population 610. Just ahead, there is a bigger sign, "You are entering the *friendliest* town on the *loneliest* road in America." I drive seventy-one miles through the same flat, empty, nothingness, before I reach the "big city" of Austin, Nevada, population about two hundred people! Once upon a time, there were ten thousand people here. Now it's the true definition of a ghost town. I see what's left of a silver mine. Old rock and wood buildings still stand. I wonder why the two hundred people live here so far from civilization. I don't think I could do it.

Now for the longest part of this lonely road. It's 111 miles to Fallon through nothing but desert. A truck passes me and further along the road, the man is pulled over for what appears to be a bathroom break. At least I know that if I break down or have a flat tire, he will pass me.

I pass a lone, leafless tree. I must turn around and see this. One, because it's the only tree (or bush or weed) I have seen in hours, and two, it's clotted with hundreds of shoes hanging by their laces. With no one else on the road, it's easy to turn around in the middle of it. As I pull off onto the hot, dry, hard-packed dirt, the truck I passed zips by me. Now I am alone in the desert.

I have never seen anything like this tree. It is packed full of tennis shoes, hooker heels, horseshoes, and hiking boots, all hanging like Christmas ornaments. Would people really drive this far to throw their old shoes up in a tree? If not, why would they throw the shoes from their feet or luggage into the tree? I have a pair of flip-flops and a pair of hiking boots. I am not willing to part with either one. I try to get a cell signal to figure out what all this means. It only takes me a minute to know that isn't going to happen right here and now.

Beside the tree, there is a scraggly, dry old bush. I have been drinking a lot of water. I am the woman who even hovers over the cleanest gas station toilet. Now I decide that this is a good spot for my bathroom break. I dig out the toilet paper and a Ziplock bag to seal the paper in when I am finished. I get behind the bush and it hits me: with no leaves, it doesn't offer much privacy. I look up the road and down the road. The odds of anyone coming along are next to zero, but I also realize that if anyone does come from either direction, they will see me squatting behind the bush with my shorts around my ankles. The visual makes me decide against the bathroom break and I get back on the road.

I see what looks like snow ahead. As I get closer, everything is white and fluffy along the side of the road for miles ahead, only it's way too hot for snow. But it doesn't look like sand. I see an abandoned car with all of its doors open, sitting off to my left, way out in the middle of this white wonder, and tire tracks leading up to where the car could go no further. A memory of grade school geography class fills my brain. This is a salt flat! I could have never imagined then how incredibly beautiful this amazing sight would be.

There is a mountain in the distance rising out of the sand dunes. Then in just a minute, I see flashing lights and emergency vehicles ahead. "Traffic" is stopped (a truck, a van, and me coming from the east). On my left, a car appears to have rolled several times before coming to rest on its top in the dunes just off the road. An ambulance waits while emergency crews are working to get whoever is inside, out. I wonder how, with no people on the road, this could happen. It's a straight, flat road. One of the front tires is laying away from the car. Were they driving too fast and have a blowout? Did they fall asleep, run off the road, and wreck, causing the tire to come off? I am reminded that life can change in an instant. Whatever happened, we are now being signaled to move around the scene. I proceed with caution and a heartfelt sadness for the occupants of the overturned car.

Further ahead, there is a large body of water on the horizon. I must be getting tired. My eyes are playing tricks on me. This is impossible. I am in the desert. When I reach it, I stop to look, and see that I am not crazy. It is a large mass of water, but only an inch or two deep, across the top of the salt flat.

I made it to California! The scenery is different along this stretch of Highway 50. I am surprised at how quickly it changes from desert to tall trees and snow-topped mountains. My jaunt across 299 from Redding takes us through another mountain range on winding, redwood-tree-lined roads. It's a lovely drive all the way to McKinleyville.

Eight days ago, my two dogs and I left Atlantic Beach, Florida in my SUV, with only the essentials. My goal was to take each day as it came and eventually make it to my son's house in California. The only real plan was to stay in KOA Kamper Kabins, because I knew they would allow dogs. Online, there were photos of one cabin perched at the edge of a river in Carbondale, Colorado. I knew I wanted to stay in this one. Every evening, I looked at my KOA Campground Directory for a route with KOA's along the way. Each day, I went north and west. After lunch, I would pick one of the KOAs and call to see if they had a cabin available. I did this until I reached that one cabin on the river. From there, my goal was to get to the eastern part of Nevada for a night so that I could make it through the desert during the day. I went north and west until I reached that point. 3,315 miles, mostly with no cell service, and many amazing experiences later, I made it. I stepped out of my comfort zone and I did it!

After a few days of rest, the dogs and I are loaded back in my SUV, following my son and his girlfriend north. He just bought a house on the outskirts of a tiny town in Oregon. It needs "some work, but not much," he says.

It's a peaceful, winding drive up the 101, and an even curvier drive through the Jedediah Smith Redwoods State Park on the 199. I follow them through a checkpoint at the border and it isn't long before we are turning onto a narrow dirt road. We turn into the drive of an old white house that is set back off the road. The fence is overgrown with years of untended, wild climbing rose vines in full bloom. Before I even walk in the door, I know that I am going to love bringing this house back to life.

After a trip to Wal-Mart in the closest big town, I am settled into my rustic, temporary digs. I have an air mattress, a skillet, a pair of metal tongs, a teapot, a charcoal grill, and the few things I traveled with. There is no furniture, no heat or air. I bundle up on the cold nights in my sleeping bag, relying on the night's low temperatures to keep the house cool during the burning heat of the day. I learn my way around the neighboring towns, finding the people and places I will need over the next few months. It's been over twenty years since I set foot in a laundromat, but here I am, excited to have found it. I feel like a pack mule when I walk inside. The ten dollars in quarters, bleach, laundry detergent, and fabric softener in my bag weigh more than the other bag filled with the clothes, sheets, and towels I am washing. While the three loads wash and dry, I catch up on emails and talk to people coming in. This life is way different than the one I worked so hard to live. Yet, for some reason, I feel good.

The first dryer buzzes. I open the door and have to step back, overwhelmed by the strong smell of "weed" emitting from this machine that has now penetrated every piece of clothing I have brought with me. Mortified, I close the door as fast as I can and look around nervously to see who notices, sure everyone in the place can smell it too. I go find the manager and quietly tell her my predicament, "I have no idea why everything smells like this because I don't smoke pot." She laughs and says, "You must be new around here. It's not you and no one else will notice it." She goes on to tell me that the workers at all of the legal growers do their laundry here and everything smells like that. I have lived such a sheltered life. Good thing I brought my diffuser and Young Living essential oils with me. I decide not to fold my clothes. I will just hang them all up in the closet, close the door, and run the diffuser with Purification.

The local UPS Store allows me to use their internet and office so my consulting work can stay on track. The designs for my son's property are complete for the main house and the guest cottage, and the people at the local Illinois Valley Building Supply store have been a huge help. If they do not have what I need, my next stop is the mid-size Diamond Home Improvement about an hour away. Most of the materials are ordered and I am starting on the guest space out back first.

My days are long and hot as I work to transform the back cottage. I love my quiet, cool evenings outside. My stove is the portable charcoal grill and my dining room is one lone camp chair that has seen better days. I grill simple dinners and spend my evenings outside watching the sun set.

It's Mother's Day and the kids are here for the weekend. They have planned a special outing to the Oregon Caves National Monument and Preserve. We find the monument and get our tour passes. There is time for a little exploring and lunch before our tour starts. I feel like a kid full of nervous excitement. I have never been inside a cave and can't wait for the tour.

Only twelve other people and a guide are with us as we enter the dimly lit, forty-four-degree cave. Our guide leads us on an unforgettable journey through the Marble Halls of Oregon. We climb up and down over five hundred steep, uneven steps, making our way through the marble passages. Some of the ceilings are as low as forty-five inches and we have to stoop or duck crawl our way through. One of the passages opens into a massive room over two hundred feet below the surface. The rock walls are smooth in some areas and jagged in others. It's impossible to put the beauty of this cave into words.

In this room our tour guide turns the lights off. I feel a bit off balance and it takes a minute to adjust to the shock of utter, complete darkness. The damp air on my skin somehow feels colder than with the lights on. I imagine the sound of mice scurrying or bats flying. I can hear the breathing of the people around me, an occasional drip and its resulting echo, but nothing else. I take a deep breath and hold it. There isn't a smell. The only description I can think of is "pure." I want to sit here for hours and just absorb it. And then the lights come back on!

The cave experience is a lot like this journey out west. I was immersed into something that scared me because it was different. Once I conquered the fear, I learned to relax and enjoy the simplicity, realizing that young family I saw living in the cabin may have had the right idea. I find myself not wanting the lights to come back on, but I need to deal with some condo business and work back in Florida. Today Emmi and I are flying to Jacksonville and taking a detour through Texas to celebrate Father's Day with Daddy early.

Emmi and I made it back to Oregon from Florida last night. I still don't have a home to live in. No work has started on my condo and the developer won't return my calls. An attorney is handling it now.

Have you ever seen a handmade sign on the side of the road when you are driving? One that tells of a place you should visit? If you are like me, you usually drive right by without much thought. A month ago, we saw one of those signs. It didn't boast thrilling adventures, fast rides, or even a petting zoo. It simply said "Butterfly Pavilion." Today I am going back to the Cave Junction Butterfly Pavilion with Tyler and Andreea.

If you have never experienced standing amid thousands of butterflies, just close your eyes and imagine the whispering sound their wings make. Feel the tickle of tiny wings brush across your skin as they float by. If that's not enough, open your eyes. It is a cloud of color and soft motion. Wow! I am in love with this journey! Doing the simple things more often is truly life-changing.

CHAPTER 2

THE MOUNTAIN LION

CONTRACTORS are installing the final details to the main house. My work here is done and it's time to go home.

I am awake before daylight, excited to see more of our beautiful country. As I pull out of the drive, the sun peeks over the mountains, and soon it's like an explosion of color everywhere. Leaving Oregon this morning with such a stunning sunrise is the perfect way to start our trip back across the country.

I meander through the mountains along the Rogue River, then cross the border into California. I roll through Yreka, then I am in Weed, California. From the rest area here I can see the snow still on Mount Shasta. Once closer, I am treated with an incredible view of this snow-covered mountain. It's so stunning!

Just south of Sacramento, we are taking back roads along the Kern River. Ahead, I can see a pull-out area between the road and the river. Both dogs need a walk and I could use a break. I hope we can get down to the river from there.

We are in luck! From my windshield, I can see a path through the trees leading to the river. I step out of the car into bright, warm sunshine. There is no humidity and it is glorious! I stand motionless outside the car and hear the river flowing over the rocks. I breathe in the smell of heavenly, clean air. Saint and Emmi are barking excitedly. I open the back hatch of the Acura and they are both quivering with anticipation of the walk to come.

The path in front of us curves to the right and gently slopes a few feet to the river. The pups and I take a stroll along the edge of the Kern River. Saint stays close to me with plenty of slack in his leash, while Emmi is running along at the end of her leash, criss-crossing back and forth trying to find the critters who have been here before her. After a good walk, we find the perfect spot to sit and listen to nature.

The big, flat rock is rounded at the edges from years of water flowing over it when the river is full. I hear the melody of grass-hoppers trilling, birds singing, and water rushing by. I sit down on the cool, shaded rock with my knees tucked under my chin. Saint immediately flops down beside me, smiling with his tongue hanging out. He is watching the river roll by just beneath our feet, while Emmi chases whatever scurries across the rocks around us. The air is filled with the sounds of Emmi's echoing barks as she leaps up trying to catch the butterflies and dragonflies zipping over her head. Saint remains flat on the cool rock, watching her and wagging his tail.

Stretching out, I lay down and close my eyes. It's astonishing how much better you can hear with your eyes closed. The sounds of cars and busy life are non-existent here. The peacefulness is interrupted by a loud splash. I sit up quickly, thinking Emmi fell in the river, however, she's standing right beside me. Saint picks his head up and starts to growl. I look across the water and see what I think is a mountain lion at the edge of the trees. He's not watching us; something else has his attention. I hear another big splash to my right and my leg is yanked sideways when Emmi races to the end of her leash strapped to my ankle. She's barking viciously. It's a bear in the water not far away. Both the bear and the mountain lion look at us!

The big, flat rock we are on is fully exposed. Emmi won't stop barking. I pick her up. I don't know how fast I can run across the rocks carrying her, or if Saint will follow me. I remember the gun I have holstered on my side and reach for it. If I shoot, can I actually hit the bear or the mountain lion? How close do they have to be for me to shoot them? I'm not sure, but we have to get out of here!

My heart's racing and I can't breathe. It feels like I am suffocating. I can't move. Fear has me frozen and tears start to roll down my cheeks. I close my eyes. I am going to die today.

Saint's tail brushes against my leg and I open my eyes. I am shaking, and my cheeks are wet with tears, but Saint is wagging his tail. I look for the mountain lion, but he is gone. I look for the bear, but he isn't there either. I am confused. I try to wipe the cobwebs from my brain. It was just a dream. I must have fallen asleep. It was so vivid. I wonder for a moment why I had the dream. I try to unpack the parts, but today, they don't make sense. I stand, stretch, and take in my surroundings one more time before continuing with our journey.

After a fabulous, eleven-hour day, we are checked into the Lake Isabella/Kern River KOA in Weldon, California. The staff is super nice and shocked that I am making this journey alone. They even made sure I had an after-hours phone number and urged me to call if I needed anything. Somehow, they make the dusty, rock-filled park look clean and inviting. I have no idea how they keep all of that dust out of the cabins, but ours is immaculate and has a great view of the Sierra Mountains.

After a quick dinner, we go exploring. We walk past the playground and through the fence along the back of the park. Short, dry shrubs are scattered along the parched, dusty, flat ground. I have to be careful not to trip over the exposed rocks protruding out of the earth. When I look up, I am near the base of a mountain. It is by no means the highest mountain I have ever seen, but from here it stretches high above the surrounding land. I feel so small in comparison. Standing in its presence, I think of the challenges I have faced. They often seemed impossibly large. Today, I say, "Bring on the mountains!"

It's a new day. We are on the road in the Mojave Desert. Our drive takes us weaving through places in Southern California like Gap Canyon and Walker Pass. I keep seeing signs for Historic Route 66 and wonder where it leads. I take a detour just to say that I have driven along the Main Street of America. It takes only seconds to know this was not a good idea. "Bumpy" doesn't even begin to describe this road. It was probably in better shape as a wagon road in the mid-1800s. Today, it would have broken every wagon wheel that used this route.

I thought I was going to go somewhere, see something, but nope, it runs right alongside the interstate and the road is so poorly maintained it took me an hour to drive fifteen miles. No one, and I mean *no one* else is on the road with me. They are all happily buzzing along the highway to my left. I stop in the middle of the road, get out, and walk back a short distance. At least I will get a picture of the Route 66 emblem painted on the road behind my car before joining other travelers on the interstate.

It's 107 degrees when we stop for a break in Needles, California. People must have been dreaming when they named the few roads along the past two hundred miles things like River Road and Mountain Springs Road. I am glad I brought three cases of water with me. It is brutally hot and dry along this stretch.

I didn't think it could get hotter, but it's 113 degrees as I cross the Arizona border in Topock and stop to let the dogs out. When I open my door, it feels like I stuck my face in a hot oven. There is not a drop of moisture in the air and the burn is a shock.

I open the back hatch and both dogs excitedly start to move forward for their leashes. As fast as they moved forward, they back away. Saint never wants to leave my side and always does whatever I ask of him. It was as if they were afraid of something. Although I try everything short of dragging them out, they are not budging. It's too hot for them to even get out of the car. I don't blame them, it is even too hot for me.

I need to go to the bathroom, but I am faced with a conundrum. I cannot leave the dogs in the car in this heat. Even though the signs say, "No dogs in bathrooms," I have been taking them with me anyway. I could make them get out, but by the time I drag them across the parking lot, I will have peed my pants! There are some people with small children parked next to me. I introduce myself and ask if they would please watch my car while I leave it running so I can go to the bathroom. Relieved when they agree, I rush off, praying my car is here when I get back.

Coming out of the bathroom, I feel much better. Then my stomach sinks. I don't see my car *or* the people that were parked beside me. The panic must be written on my face. Someone asks, "Ma'am, are you okay?" I can't move. I hear him, but my brain is not registering enough to respond. Frantically, I look around. "Do you need help?" the man asks. That's when I notice I came out a different door. I am on the wrong side of the building.

"No, thank you. I don't think so," I say, and walk around the bench-flanked wall where I see my car. I apologize for taking so long and thank these nice people.

"No problem," the woman says, "Do something nice and it will come back to you. I am glad we were here to help." We talk for a few minutes about our trips then both get back on the road. The kindness of people on the road makes me feel like I have guardian angels all around me.

I had thought I would stop near the Grand Canyon tonight and see part of it tomorrow. I make calls looking for a cabin at one of the two KOAs close by, but even during the week they are booked. They both tell me that summer reservations are often booked six months to a year in advance. The closest one I can find is Holbrook, two hours further east of the Grand Canyon. I book it. I will have to plan the Grand Canyon trip another time.

Just outside of Winslow, Arizona there are signs for Meteor Crater. I take the exit hoping to see what is boasted as the best-preserved meteor impact site on Earth. I wind along the roads, following signs directing me there, but it's too late. They are closing soon. Things just are not going my way today. It probably doesn't help that I am tired, hot, and hungry. I should have taken this route on my way west, then the northern route home.

It takes another hour for me to get to the Holbrook/Petrified Forest KOA in Arizona. It's mostly just gravel and a few shade trees, but I am in the desert. The most important part is the staff are friendly, the air conditioner works, and my cabin is clean.

✧

Yesterday was a long, emotional, tiring day, but I slept well last night. The Petrified Forest National Park and Painted Desert are about twenty minutes east of us and you can drive through the entire park.

The pups and I arrive, pay our twenty-dollar entrance fee, and start out on the Painted Desert Rim Trail. It is a mile-long walk that hugs the edge of a windswept mesa with views of the rolling, multicolored landscape. The colors from just one viewpoint range from greens to grays to different shades of red. It's beyond amazing!

I have spent hours in the park and probably only just scratched the surface of everything to be seen and learned. This is definitely among the places I want to return. I loop back around towards the exit and the interstate.

I am zooming down the highway in the middle of nowhere and ahead on my left, I see what looks like an old Spanish-style, stone church at the top of a hill. It is surrounded by other structures that cascade down the hill in stair-step fashion. It's an odd sight to see out here. I pull over to learn more about it. When I stop, I sit in my car and stare. I need to write about what I see. I pull out a notebook and drop it. It lands with only the cover flipped open. The first thing written on this page is from about a year and a half ago. It's a Bible verse, Jeremiah 29:11—"For I know the plans I have for you, declares the Lord, plans to prosper you and not to harm you, plans to give you hope and a future." I read a bit further down the page and see another entry, "I feel like I need to sell my house. Get rid of all my things. Things are holding me back. I need to go somewhere."

Since it was written, I have sold my house and bought a condo. I did not get rid of all my things, but I did go somewhere with only a few of them. It's the adventure I am now on. When I actually think about it, I realize that circumstances forced me to go some-where. I learned on this trip that I don't need so many things. Rather than writing, I close the notebook. I get out of my car and read the sign posted in front of me, indicating this is the New Mexico San Josè de Laguna Mission. The old mission church has been a signpost for travelers in the past and makes me think hard about my life today. I am still thinking about my life as I merge back onto the highway.

We cross the Texas border and are soon at the Amarillo KOA. It's about ten miles off of the interstate, but it's easy to find. I am over-the-top excited to see green grass. On our way to Kamp K9, Saint tiptoes through it like he has never seen this strange green stuff before while Emmi is happily hopping through it like a rabbit.

Sitting on our cabin porch, I watch the sun until it dips below the horizon, and its light is nothing but a soft glow. It has been a sunny day. The high today was in the nineties, but it's funny how that's not bad. I guess it's all about what you are used to.

I wake up to the sun peeking through our windows. I lay quietly, listening to the campground waking up around us and smelling the aroma of fresh brewed coffee. I consider going to find the source of that incredibly rich smell that I can almost taste, but just can't seem to get motivated. I did not sleep well. Trains rolling through somewhere close by kept waking me up. I close my eyes and go back to sleep.

A few hours later, before I open my eyes, I feel like someone is watching me. Our cabin is full of light, but I don't see anyone else inside. I open them wider and see Saint resting his chin on the side of my bed, staring at me. The minute Emmi sees I am awake, she is bouncing across the bed. I guess they are both ready to go outside. I feed them a quick breakfast and we go for a walk.

Today should have been an eight-hour drive, but we hit horrific traffic in Dallas. We are going to arrive at the Shreveport/Bossier City KOA after dark and well past closing. Once we are out of the city, I stop for a break and call the park to ask if they can possibly leave a key to our cabin. The woman who answers the phone could not have been nicer. She said, "Don't you worry. No matter what time you arrive, just call and I will meet you at the office."

It's dark when I pull into the park. I am a wee bit concerned. There are several police cars with blue lights flashing in front. I stop where I am and call the number I was given earlier. No one answers. I leave a message and wonder what to do. I call again and again, no answer. I am about to leave when my phone rings. It's the camp's owner, full of apologies. She will be here in a few minutes. I am still nervous about staying with the eerie blue lights flashing through the trees, but I wait.

She is so sweet, and immediately puts me at ease. Apparently, guests from last night stole things, like the refrigerator, from the cabin they stayed in, but it was not noticed until early evening. I am expecting a small Kamper Kabin like the others I have been staying in, but she takes me over to a bigger cabin in the trees. We climb the steps to an old-fashioned screen door leading onto a cute porch. I know we are going to sleep well tonight.

Back on I-20 East, we are cruising along through mainly rural, hilly terrain. Once we are through Monroe, the road flattens. The only things that break it up are occasional curves. Gone are the days filled with exciting landscapes.

I exit the interstate just east of Jackson, Mississippi, and take 49 south down a four lane, bumpy, grass-divided highway. I am zipping along and pass a bunch of brightly painted old metal chairs which reminded me of sitting in the backyard with Granny and Poppa when I was a little girl. Then I am passing a parked truck full of watermelons. I can taste the sweetness in my mouth and imagine feeling the cold juice run down my chin and decide I have to go back. I hit my brakes and bounce off the road onto the shoulder with gravel flying everywhere. I wait for the dust billowing up behind me to settle before I make a U-turn.

Though a sign says, "Watermelons for sale," there is no one tending the truck. There is another sign reading, "Deck the Yard," and head towards the building ahead of me thinking perhaps the watermelons belong to them. The metal chairs in many colors are on my right as I make my way down the dirt drive. I get out with the dogs and totally laugh out loud at the sign in front of me. "Spring is Here! So excited I wet my plants!" I left the roadside yard and gift store in Florence, Mississippi with two watermelons.

Tonight, although we will go back to sleeping in tiny cabins with no bedding or bathrooms, our Gulf Shores cabin on the water makes up for it. I am excited when I pull up to see the breath-taking view we will have from our cabin tonight. I can't wait to get settled and take a look around. When I open my door it's hot with no breeze, though nothing like the furnace-hot heat of the southwestern desert. I remember wishing for moisture just a few days ago as I am immediately dripping wet. I seriously think that I am melting. Oh! And the bugs! They are everywhere. Is this really what they mean when they talk about warm southern welcomes?

I collect the dogs and we rush into our cabin to escape the heat and humidity. Once I cool off, I will unpack the car. I open the door and find it's stifling inside. The a/c is not on, even though it's the middle of the summer. Why on Earth would a campground not do this before someone checks in? I go to the window unit and switch it on. Nothing happens. I turn it off and back on. Still nothing. Feeling overwhelmed and in tears, I call the office. They will send someone as soon as they can. I tell them the door will be unlocked. We are going to dinner.

After dinner, we make our way back to our cabin on the water. I am going to be sure the air conditioner is working before I get the dogs out and unpack. I hold my breath as I open the door, flooded with relief when a cold blast of air hits me.

Traversing across the panhandle on the long, flat empty stretch of I-10, I reflect on my past months' journey. I think about it all the way to Atlantic Beach, Florida. Besides becoming a mom, this adventure has been the most amazing experience of my life. I wish it didn't have to end.

MISS DAISY

In the beginning, I had thought my trip west was merely the solution to a temporary problem. I believed that I would return home and resume a normal life. However, I am here, repairs are not finished, and I still cannot live in the condo. My attorney says, "This won't take long. I am sure they will settle."

I need a temporary home. Several times along my trip I thought it would have been nice to have a small camper. I already miss being on the road and know I want to travel more. Wouldn't it be fun to spend the rest of the summer in a camper in the woods or on a lake?

There are a lot of campers for sale. I decide to buy a nineteen-foot Shasta Airflyte camper and picked out my piece of real estate in Hannah Park for the summer. I am very excited about my temporary vacation home.

I am going to spend the summer in a trailer. My family and friends move between being shocked and thinking I am crazy. Some of the conversations go a little like this....

"You, in a trailer park?"

"No. I will be in an RV Park."

"In a big fancy coach?"

"No. A tiny retro camper."

Tiny living is good for the soul. Besides, it's only temporary. I have a lot to learn about sewer systems and amps, but I can do this!

I am driving across town to pick up my adorable yellow and white Retro Remake Shasta camper by Forest River. I have affectionately named Miss Daisy. I am not nervous about pulling the camper behind me, but I am nervous about backing her into our spot among the trees by myself. Now I wish I had asked for help. Hopefully someone will take pity on me.

I did it! I got Miss Daisy here and parked her! Help did come. I am so grateful for my best friend, Hope, who guided me straight in. Now we have another challenge; neither one of us can figure out how to work the stabilizer jacks. Another camper is walking by and Hope flags him down. He handles the task like a pro, then asks, "Can I bring my wife back by to see this? She would love it." She became one of the many who stopped and asked for a tour.

It's time to get organized inside and decorate. I am concerned about weight, but I need to stock my new tiny home with the essentials. List in hand, I am off to Target first, then Bed, Bath & Beyond. I am in search of an inspiration that will be the base of my future color scheme. This is the hardest part. It takes hours. My seat cushions and curtains are already sunny yellow and white. I find a quilt with yellows, oranges, pinks, and greens and think *this is it*. It's the first thing that goes into my cart.

After my shopping is done, I buy a welcome mat that says, "My Happy Place." For the bedroom, I have a thick, fluffy mattress topper, my quilt, one set of one thousand thread count white sheets, and two pillows. For the bathroom I have two thick fluffy white towels. For the kitchen, four plastic plates, four retro-looking plastic "glasses," and real silverware—four forks, four knives, four spoons, two coffee cups, one plastic spatula, one grill spatula, one small saucepan and skillet, two pot holders, two dish towels, and two sponges. My splurges are an electric teapot and a handheld mixer. For the dining room, I have four placemats and four cloth napkins. Why do I tell you all of this? Because I don't need much to live tiny, but I do need the things to be pretty and to match.

Miss Daisy came with a cute black and white striped awning. Today I am going to install it. I drag the bag out of my storage compartment under the camper. The bag is the kind that a camper chair fits in, only taller, the awning rolled tight inside. I loosen the drawstring and turn the bag upside down, thinking it will slide out. Nothing happens. I lift it higher to try and shake the stuff out. This thing isn't light, and each time I lift it to shake, it gets heavier and heavier. One last hard shake and my bag is as light as a feather. I am caught off guard, lose my balance, and land hard on my rear end as everything flies out across my campsite with a clatter of metal poles. My first thought is that I hope no one saw me. The second is that there is no way this is ever going back into the same bag.

I pick up all the pieces and roll out the awning. I don't see any directions, and it does not appear self-explanatory. Sitting on the ground with the awning partially laid across my lap, poles scattered around, and pieces of rope in impossible tangles all around me, I look up at the side of the camper where the awning is supposed to attach. I hope no one is watching me. I have a nine-foot by seven-foot heavy sheet of vinyl stretched across my lap and I look like I am waiting for a wind to come along, snatch the thing up, and magically attach it to Miss Daisy. No magic happens, and no light bulb comes on. The wind would be nice though.

Plan B. YouTube. But where is my phone? I am crawling around on the ground under the giant sheet of vinyl until I can barely breathe. I can just imagine the little old woman camping across the road, telling her husband, "Honey, I think there is a bear tangled in that lady's awning." Triumphant, I emerge dripping with sweat. I found my phone. I do a quick search and find the video I am looking for. Now I am an expert.

The awning is stretched out across the ground. The edge of the awning is wrapped around the hard piece of tubing. All that I have to do is guide the tubing through the track at the top of the camper. Piece of cake. I pick up the awning, grasping the corner where the tubing starts, and climb the ladder with it. It easily goes right into the track. My left arm is stretched out lifting the awning so the awning-wrapped plastic tubing will continue to move into the track straight. With my right hand, I am pulling the tubing through the track, with the awning sliding across the top of my head. I pull it about two feet and feel good about my quick progress, until I can't reach any further. I climb down the ladder, move it over a few feet, and climb back up. Grasping the tubing with my right hand, I pull. It doesn't budge. I tug. It doesn't budge. I yank. It still doesn't budge.

I climb down, move the ladder back to its starting point, and climb up under the awning to investigate. It's crimped at the edge because the tubing is not entering the track straight. Rather than pulling it through, maybe I can push it through. It works! I am about halfway there. The heavy vinyl over my head has created a sauna and has me smooshed flat against the wall of the camper. I feel like I am suffocating, and my arms feel like jelly. No matter what I try, I cannot get it to move any further.

There is not enough room in this little camper for two people. Why would they design something that takes two people to install? Feeling defeated, I climb down the ladder and out from under the heavy mass with tears rolling down my cheeks.

I wanted to be self-sufficient and do this myself, but I need help. I call my friend Rach. She will be here in twenty minutes. When she arrives, it's a quick and easy job. We are both sweating under the awning/sauna, but it takes less time to finish than it did for her to drive here. We stand back to admire our success and I understand how blessed I am. There is always someone willing to help me, if I just ask.

My toilet isn't draining like it should. On my way out, I make a mental note to check it out when I get back.

I took my first trip to Camping World today. Something *must* be wrong with me. I bought a t-shirt with something printed on it.

It's after dark when I get home. Of course, I have to go to the bathroom first thing. The toilet won't flush at all. Dang! I forgot all about checking on it. Google, here I come! I found several posts saying turn water supply off and pour boiling water into the toilet. Sounded like an easy enough thing to try, but by now it is nearing midnight and I want to go to bed. I don't want to be boiling pot after pot of water. I will deal with it in the morning. I put my PJs on, snuggled into bed, and am soon sleeping.

In the middle of the night, I sit straight up in bed thinking, *Did you open the drains when you connected the sewer?* Here I go, out into the dark in my pajamas with a flashlight, praying I don't run into an armadillo or worse, a giant man-eating spider. Both drain valves are closed. I pull the handles and *whoosh!* Water is flowing.

First crisis averted. If you can't laugh at yourself, you must not be living right.

Yesterday, I came home to my awning pole stakes ripped out of the ground by a storm. When I turned into the campsite and my headlights hit Miss Daisy, all that I could see was the black-and-white-striped awning plastered to her side and blocking the door.

I got the awning re-staked, the camper leveled, and all of the mud away from the front door. The weather alert on my iPad goes off seconds before I hear the distant rumble of thunder. It is only mid-afternoon and already dark. The wind is picking up and pushing heavy black clouds across the sky towards us. Leaves and pine needles are like missiles flying at me, stinging my skin as they hit. I wish there was a way to secure the awning without taking it off the Shasta, but there's no time to do either. I dart back inside and close the door.

Within minutes, wind is slamming against our tiny home. It's literally rocking and dishes are rattling in the cabinets. Limbs are snapping from the big trees all around me. Before the first drop of rain falls, I hear a crack of lightning and then see the giant flash. Everything goes dark. The power is out. Saint is whining, and Emmi is barking. Neither helps the incredible fear I am trying to control. The rain starts falling with a vengeance. In place of the soothing sound of raindrops on a tin roof I love, it's like a million bullets pounding over our heads. Lightning strikes are hitting everything around us like javelins hurtling from the sky. If the wind doesn't blow Miss Daisy over, a tree is going to fall on her roof and crush us. What was I thinking? I shouldn't be here, but I can't get out now.

Thwack! A different sound gets my attention. I peek out the window that I have been trying to stay away from. The tent stakes holding down the awning poles have been yanked from the ground. The poles were launched through the air into the trees on our other side as the awning flipped up and spread across our roof.

Grabbing Emmi, I climb in bed and draw the covers over us. Saint lays on the floor beneath the edge of the bed beside me. I close my eyes and pray that this will be over soon. Somehow, I fall asleep.

I am jolted awake by a noise. Thankfully, it's only the beep of the microwave as the power comes back on. The storm has passed, and the sun is shining. I track down the awning stakes and clean up the mess outside. Miraculously, nothing is damaged. I need to find another place to park Miss Daisy. One where there is less mud, fewer spiders, and more people.

My friends Mary and Michael invited me out to Flamingo Lake RV Resort for an evening of dinner and live music a few weeks ago. It's because of them that I will move to the RV Resort and have a paved spot on the lake. It's the perfect place to spend the rest of the summer.

Everything is stowed away. Thank goodness for backup cameras. I even got her hitched up all by myself. This is actually easy once you get the hang of it. I merge onto I-295 and in just a few minutes I am on the Dames Point Bridge. I love this bridge. This cable-stayed bridge was actually the inspiration behind my company logos. Now it scares the crap out of me. The main span is 10,640 feet long and is 175 feet above the St. Johns River at its tallest point. The wind can be brutal.

I remind myself that fear is just the feeling of perceived danger. I tell myself fear is meant to protect me from legitimate threats. This situation is far from life or death, and I have the most incredible co-pilot. There is no way I am going to let it stop me now. Gripping the steering wheel and driving slower than a turtle might cross the bridge, I throw up a prayer and make it safely across.

By the time I pull Miss Daisy into Flamingo Lake, I feel quite proud of myself. I am excited about my new temporary home. I walk into the office with a smile on my face, ready to check in and get settled. Now I just have to wait for the escort they have called. Being new to this and having to find my own way to the previous site, I have no idea what to expect. He not only leads me to my site, but he guides me into the space so easily I feel like a pro.

I am settled into my monthly spot and discover after just a few days that RV living is a great equalizer. I had a house in a community with an HOA. One where you drove your car into the garage then closed the door before even getting out. Here, I found a different kind of community. One where people took time for those around them, where it didn't matter where you were from, what your job was, or what you had. I want this life.

Not everyone who knocks on your door in a campground is going to kill you. My two dogs do not understand this. I had locked up, turned out the lights, and climbed into bed when there was a soft knock on the door. Emmi launches off the bed, jumps over Saint, and races to the door barking like someone is going to eat us. Of course, this puts Saint on alert and he joins the verbal alarm. I am trying to get out of bed and climb over the wiggling, barking mass of fur to get to the door. I get the door open and Saint stands behind me waiting, while Emmi rockets out the door and stops just outside in front of me with her "don't come any closer or I will attack" stance. When she notices it is just the sweet little old lady from a few doors down, she goes back to bed.

CHAPTER 4

THE BEAST

THOUGH I adore Miss Daisy, it has been months and there are still no condo repairs. She would have been perfect for trips across the country, but a bathroom that consists of a toilet with a shower head over it isn't working for me every day. She was not designed for long-term living. The a/c has a hard time keeping up and the condensation from it is making a mess. I love not being responsible for yardwork, not paying monthly utility bills, and I don't miss the daily drama of neighbors angry with me over suing the people who sold the leaking homes to us. What if you could have your own home and not have to deal with any of those things? Even better, what if you could take your house with you wherever you went? Would you do it? If I am going to do this long-term, I will need a bigger camper. My consulting company is doing well. I hired people smarter than I am to do the majority of the consulting work for my GPS contracts. I pay them more, but it means I can work less. Between this, my taking on small consulting projects that I can do from the road, and my rental properties, I should be able to afford a life on the road in my RV. If it's not enough, I am young, I can go back to work. Who knows? Maybe along the way I will get the opportunity to make the dream of having my own TV show a reality. For now, I will take it one day at a time. I want to enjoy life now, before it's too late.

I head out to see what RV I can find.

I walk through the larger, pull-behind campers, but don't see the perfect one in my budget. Then I walk into a used Forest River Wildcat fifth wheel. Oh wow! It feels good to spread out a little! A real shower, a true vanity sink, and a washer/dryer combo! It has a U-shaped kitchen with a full-size sink and plenty of counter space. It even has an oven I can bake in. There is a big screen TV in the living room over the realistic-looking electric fireplace, an actual dinette table with chairs, recliners, and a sectional sofa that makes out into a bed. The bedroom has a queen size bed and a closet. I will no longer have to pull out my bed each night and push it back in to use the bathroom. And there is a bonus...you push a button to extend and retract the awning. I am sold!

Every time I think I have all of my ducks in a row, one of them waddles off in another direction. It's pouring rain and my fifth wheel is being delivered today. In and out the door I go, from Miss Daisy to the gazebo on my deck, carrying bins. The gazebo has zippered screens and fabric walls, so everything will stay dry. It doesn't take long, because I am living a simpler life with fewer things. Still, I am soaked to the bone from walking just the few steps each trip. From my hair to my bare feet, water drips off of me.

I still have to hook up Miss Daisy in the rain and tow her across the park. I get better each time I do this, but it's only the fourth time, so I am a bit slow. Task completed, I am not only wet, but muddy too. I dig through bins in search of a towel and some clean, dry clothes. I exchange "rain-soaked" for the dampness caused by humidity and wait for my new home.

My phone rings. They are in the park! I excitedly watch the Wildcat coming up the road. The delivery driver backs my new home into the narrow site that seemed so much larger with my little Shasta in it. He is now going to get Miss Daisy, and I am left with the guy, who promised to help me get set up.

The rain is still constant; I am so glad I have help. His idea of help is to walk with an umbrella over his head around to the sewer hook-up side and give me my first instruction, "Hook your sewer hose there, then connect it to the drain pipe over there." I am slightly taken aback at him standing over there on the pavement trying to keep his shoes dry and holding an umbrella over his head.

"Okay," I say. "I will connect it from the camper. Can you connect it to the drain?"

"There is no way I am touching your honey pot," he replies.

I am shocked by his response, and a little offended. I stood in the rain for twenty minutes this morning making sure it was completely cleaned out. I even flushed some bleach through it after the line was rinsed. But okay, he doesn't know this, and I am tired of standing in the rain.

"Fair enough. Could you hook up the electric?" I ask.

"I don't want to ruin my shoes in the wet grass."

I stop in my tracks with water dripping off my nose and one end of the sewer hose in my hands. I am hot and tired of working in the rain, so I am a little short when I reply, "What exactly are you going to help me do?"

I get the patronizing look and response of, "Women and stress." Then he walks away.

I just experienced my first lesson in learning that if I am going to live this life, I am going to have to figure it out myself. It's a hard lesson. I drop everything, go back around, sit on my steps, and cry. This is how my neighbor Lynn finds me when she gets home from work.

"Oh, girl. Come on, we've got this. I will help you." I am overwhelmed with gratitude. As I wipe my running nose on the bottom of my t-shirt, another neighbor, Scott, walks up. I see the panic on his face when he rushes towards me, certain something bad has happened.

I realize how silly I am being and laugh. "No. It's just me being a girl."

He helps me up from the steps and tells me, "The three of us will do it together." Scott, still in his work clothes, handles everything outside, while Lynn helps me figure out how the slides work. In less than thirty minutes, everything is connected, my things are all put away inside, and I know how everything works. Neither one of them left until everything was done and they were sure I was okay.

Standing here in my spacious RV that feels more like a home, I feel blessed. Six months ago, I was faced with not being able to live in my home at the beach. A week later, I was presented with a solution that also helped my son and taught me many things. I came back to Florida thinking that life would resume as it was before I left. I learned that God wasn't finished with me yet. I still couldn't live in my condo. Thinking it wouldn't be long before everything was resolved, I bought a little camper. It took longer than I thought. With the attitude of *I can do anything,* I found another solution. I just keep following what's next. Today, when I was at the end of my rope, help arrived. I am sure there will be other days, other moments like this one. My faith may be different than yours, but right now I am reminded of a saying I have heard a thousand times: "Faith is about trusting God, even when you don't know his plan."

I am settled into life in an RV Park but am getting antsy. I have this fabulous camper I want to use for more than just my home. I want to travel. For weeks, I have been searching for a truck that will pull the Wildcat. Today I found it. My new chariot is a white F-250 Super Duty crew cab with the fifth wheel hitch already installed. In just a few weeks, I will make my first trip.

My RV neighbors helped me connect the truck to the Beast (as I decided to name it) last night. I have been given a million tips and instructions. This morning, several are here making sure every-thing is connected and stowed correctly. They are all worried about me pulling this beast down the road by myself for the first time. I don't tell them that my heart is hammering in my chest as they guide me out of the site and onto the road. I do not tell them that I am afraid; I assure them that I will be fine. I smile and wave as I pull down the road. With the dogs in the back seat, and my niece Caroline in the front passenger seat, we are headed south for Thanksgiving.

I have talked to my brother, and have a route planned on back roads. I think this will be easier. I can go slow and there won't be much traffic. First, we have to get on the interstate for a bit. Daddy is in his truck, following behind us, as I merge onto I-295. I took the ease of merging onto an interstate for granted. As I approach, I see cars, trucks and semis coming over the hill in both lanes towards me. My blinker is on, but no one is moving over. Afraid to jump in, I am crawling along and am almost off the pavement. Thankfully, Daddy sees my predicament and merges into traffic, forcing people to move over and allowing me to get in. I became cognizant of exactly how big the beast behind me is. I keep looking in my rearview mirror only to see the huge Wildcat logo rising out of the bed of my truck and high above me. Though I can see down both sides of the Wildcat in my extended side mirrors, I can see nothing behind me. Getting up to a respectable speed, even for this scared female behind the wheel, takes a bit. I am only a few miles into my journey when I crest a small hill. Instantly, I feel the heaviness shoving me down the other side. I did not expect this. What if I can't slow down? I am quickly on flat ground and all is well, but now I have another fear added to my growing list.

I have been driving less than ten minutes and don't think I can do this. I have always believed I could do anything that comes my way, but I want to turn around. I have battling conversations in my head. *If you turn around, you admit you can't. If you don't keep going, you will never know you can.* I don't do failure, but still I worry that I cannot get us there safely. I have no idea what I am doing. *Believe you can, and you will.*

I keep going.

Along the next twenty miles, I practice speeding up and slowing down and I start to relax. I learn that besides the weight, the fifth wheel is easier to pull than Miss Daisy because there is no swaying.

Exiting the interstate, we start south on back roads, with red lights and small-town traffic along the way. I am good until I see a sign for the narrow bridge ahead. I'm in full-blown panic mode when I see how long and tall it is, then I hear my brother's voice,

"It doesn't matter how big the thing behind you is. Just watch the road up ahead of you."

I tell Caroline, "I am afraid. Talk to me." She says silly things that make no sense and soon has me laughing. I am glad she is with me. We are now safely across the bridge that wasn't as big as I thought it was.

We roll on down the back roads laughing and talking. I am glad I kept going. People are snaking in a line, backed up behind me, but that's okay. I am getting the hang of this. I am still cautious, but it's not as hard as I first thought.

We made it to Groveland and are tooling down the long drive towards the house and our parking spot. No one is home. My next "first" lies in front of me. I have to back the Beast in. The good news is that I have plenty of room and am not by myself. It takes several tries, but with Daddy and Caroline's help, I manage. I have electric and water, just no sewer. My holding tanks get to do their job. I will just have to be careful with the amount of water I use. We are connected, the slides and awning are out. This is home for a few days.

The drive home is uneventful and easier than my drive a few days ago. I can actually think about what a great trip this was and how I loved spending time with all of the family. Thanksgiving is usually at my house, but the lack of a livable home made that hard. I am so grateful for my brother Buddy and sister-in-law Connie hosting this year.

Back at the Flamingo, I have to manage backing into my narrow site between the deck and the power connection. Making it even more difficult is the narrow road I have to accomplish the stunt from. The six men giving me different directions are not making it any easier. I am frustrated and scared half to death. If I had a husband, I would not have even tried. Lynn, being the amazing woman she is, noticed my concern. Though it was his day off, she went over and brought one of the park escorts, Mr. Fred, back with her.

When he walked up to my window I asked, "Would you do this for me?"

I did not get the "yes" I expected.

He calmly tells me, "You can do this. I will show you. Ignore everyone else and just listen to me." With his hand on the truck door at my open window, never leaving my side, he talked me through every inch and turn of my wheels. I am in and straight. I am learning that we can do way more than we think we can.

December has been fabulous. I have Christmas lights up outside and decorated a little tree inside. For so many years, I got so wrapped up in the rat race of buying gifts and doing all of the cooking myself that I missed out on what the holidays are really about. Time with my family, my friends, and my neighbors. This year I enjoyed simple things like Christmas caroling through a campground in a golf cart parade with Daddy. I spent many cool evenings outside by a fire, roasting marshmallows and laughing with my neighbors.

Today I am headed south with the pups in the back seat and the Wildcat behind us. I am both more confident and afraid of the unknown as I pull out of the park. This trip I will be pulling the

Beast down Interstate 95, from Jacksonville to Lake Worth, just south of West Palm Beach. I will listen to the advice of taking it slow and staying in the right lane. My brother tells me that people merging onto the interstate will either wait or get out of my way, and that I am bigger than they are.

Once I get over my initial worries, I learn that interstate driving is actually easier than on two-lane country roads. Until I am in West Palm and must change lanes to stay on my route. I reduce my speed, riding in my lane a few minutes with my blinker on. No one is getting over. The people behind me are flying around me then jumping back in front of me. I remember I am bigger than they are, and I can do this. I speed up some and slowly start moving over into the lane on my left. People get out of my way.

A woman in a tiny sportscar is merging onto the interstate from a ramp on my left. Instead of speeding up or slowing down, she is riding steady along my side. Her lane is about to end, and she is motioning for me to move over. There is no way I can. Traffic to my right is moving, but near bumper-to-bumper. The best I can do is take my foot off of the gas. She jerks across the lane in front of me and hits her brakes. Stopping before I hit her isn't going to be easy. I imagine plowing over her and leaving the sportscar pancake flat on the road behind me. I am simultaneously standing on the brakes and working the trailer brake. It's her lucky day.

I am moving. As I start to let out the breath I was holding, I see brake lights and cars just ahead swerving out of the lane I am in. Some go left, others go right. By the time I know why, it's almost too late. There is a full-size semi-truck tire in my lane. If I hit it, I am going to wreck, and probably cause others to wreck. I start moving right, faster than I would prefer. I am praying people get the idea and move over. Another catastrophe averted. I am tired and shaking. I want this day to be over. Just in time, Siri tells me I only have one mile before my exit. I am less than ten minutes from the campground.

I turn into the entrance at John Prince Park Campground, then call my daughter. She and her boyfriend will meet me at my site. I am checked in. There are no pull-through sites available and there are no escorts. I warn the woman that this is only my second trip, and I have never backed in by myself.

"I am sure you will be fine," she responds. "If you need help, the man next to your site is really nice."

I find the site, but it is angled in the wrong direction. I make several failed attempts, but trees are in my way. After looking at my map, I decide to loop around and come at it from another direction. As I come back around the corner, I see that my daughter Amber and her boyfriend Dave have arrived. They are talking to an older gentleman. I stop to tell them where I need to be. I start getting conflicting instructions from different people on how to back into the site. I know they are all just trying to help. I feel like this is a new reality show called, "How many people does it take to park a fifth wheel?"

I am backed in and notice that the power is on the wrong side of the camper and my cord is not long enough to reach. My neighbor tells us of a place that might have an extension. We put the dogs in the back and I jump in the car. When we talked on the phone, the owner of the store was certain we wouldn't make it before five thirty. Two hundred and twelve dollars later, I have what I need, and we are working through traffic on the way back to camp.

When we get back, my neighbor was also worried that we would not make it in time. He has tracked down extensions and already has the Wildcat plugged in. I am learning that RVers are a community like no other.

After I feed the dogs and shower, I am driving over to meet Amber and Dave at his family's home. I am excited that they have invited me to spend the holidays with them.

It's late when I get home after an enjoyable evening. When I climb into my own bed, it feels good. I drift off to sleep, thinking that I truly like being able travel and always have everything with me.

Last night, Amber requested a red velvet cake for Christmas dinner. I go in search of a grocery store to get the few things I don't already have. I love to make cakes. However, baking in a camper is sometimes challenging. I pull the layers out of the oven and am reminded that level is a thing of the past. This cake will either need a lot of trimming or a lot of cream cheese frosting. At least it will taste good!

It takes me most of the day to finish my somewhat lopsided masterpiece. I arrive for Christmas Eve dinner just as steaks are going on the grill.

Christmas Day is perfect. It's sunny and warm here in South Florida. Dave's entire family is here. Everyone gives each other small, useful gifts. As the scarves, socks, and other trinkets are exchanged, they were so thoughtful to also include me. Amber and Dave had special Christmas ornaments made for me. They are small cardboard cut-outs of Saint and Emmi painted in watercolors.

I love them! The day is exactly as Christmas should be. It's full of food, fun, and laughter, with guests stopping by throughout the day. I feel so blessed to have been a part of the Chodos family celebration over the past few days.

It's the day after Christmas and I am packing up to go home. I back up and connect the Beast to the truck with the help of my neighbor. I get everything disconnected and my slides are in. My neighbor has told me how to find the dump station. I start the truck and put her in drive. As I begin rolling forward, I hear him yelling, "Wait! Wait! Wait!" I hit my brakes to see what is wrong. I was about to drive down the road with my awning out! I am so embarrassed. This is about the dumbest thing that I could forget.

Compared to this, my drive home is easy and uneventful.

CHAPTER 5

FROM PRADAS TO FLIP-FLOPS

THE winter has been hard for me. My faithful old companion Saint crossed over the rainbow bridge, leaving a huge hole in my heart. I ran out of propane twice and woke up certain I would freeze to death. The tanks are heavy and too high up for me to change them myself. More than a few times I forgot to leave water dripping and my hose froze. My condo issues didn't get resolved. I started a home renovation and Tiny House business that grew quickly, but I continued to make the forty-five-minute trek across the river to my office at the beach each day.

Today I realized, I am doing it again, working non-stop. I am pushing the reset button! It's my life and I get to change the way the story goes.

I clear out my closets, keep a pair of Spanx and just one of the forty-seven little black dresses (because a woman never knows when she might get asked out on a date). I keep two of nearly one hundred designer handbags. The two hundred pairs of shoes are whittled down to only a few pairs. Most of what's left are flip-flops. The Pradas and Louboutins are all gone, my furniture is gone, even the art is gone. Everything I don't need has either been sold or given away. The hardest thing to give up was the old office chair I spent so many hours working in. Honestly, I could not have done it all without my astounding assistant Brittany!

Just before my birthday, my sister Rebecca asked if I would like to swim with manatees at Crystal River since my minimalist lifestyle doesn't have room for *things*. Spring break is going to be a blast. We have reservations at Crystal Isles, one of the Encore RV Resorts. My niece Caroline is spending the night so that she can ride with me to Crystal River.

The Beast is hooked to the truck for my first RV adventure this year. I have checked and double-checked everything. I roll out of the park way more confident than I was when Caroline took my first trip with me.

As we pull through the gates of Crystal Isles, it appears to be a nice place. We park outside the office, which looks brand new, to check in. There are no escorts, but I should be okay getting parked since I have a pull-through site. Caroline is directing me through the park, following the sharpie drawn route on our map. Our site is ahead on the right and I pass it because the way it is angled, I need to come from the other side. Now someone is driving towards me, yelling that I am going the wrong way. I back up so they can pass, then I try to get in, but the turn is too sharp. Caroline gets out to help me back up. She has zero experience in this department. Up and back. Up and back. Turn this way, then that way. I get out to survey my situation. I have myself in a pretty big jam. Shaking and close to tears, I call the office for help. It's not gonna happen. I take a deep breath and look around. An older couple riding by on their bicycles stops and offers their assistance.

"I needed to get in the spot from the other side but they yelled at me for going the wrong way and I backed up to get out of their way and I'm stuck too close to this tree and..." I gush.

The man lays his bicycle down and says, "There are no one-way roads here. Come on. Take a breath and get back in the truck. We will help you."

Soon we are out of our pickle, circled around the loop, and tucked into our site.

I am determined that we are going to have fun. Caroline helps me find places that rent pontoon boats. The first one I call has availability for tomorrow, and we are booked for a half day.

I still have my chandelier. It is hung and dancing in the breeze, and the somewhat cock-eyed picnic table is covered with a decorative tablecloth. The citronella candles flickering down the whole length will keep the biting insects at bay, we hope.

Everyone is up early. The cooler is packed with sandwiches, and the fishing gear is loaded. Our pontoon boat is waiting for us at Adventure Center Marina, less than ten minutes from our campground.

We're all aboard, even Emmi in her new West Coast Marine life jacket. My brother-in-law David guides the boat effortlessly out of its slip and up the canal towards Kings Bay. It is going to be an awesome day. We have over six hundred acres of water to explore here in the Bay.

We see birds diving into the water at the edge of a little island and figure it will be the perfect fishing spot. We drop anchor and ready our fishing gear. The hooks are baited and in the water. Now we wait. My nephew Trey and I are sitting together and in just minutes, he has a bite. He sets the hook and starts reeling, then yanks the rod back. His fish comes flying out of the water, right at me. I duck just before his catch smacks me in the face and lands in the boat at my feet. Emmi barks excitedly while Trey dances around the boat, trying to grab the flopping fish. The next fish is his too. Before he gets this one to the boat, a bird flies over and snatches it right out of the water. Several more small fish are landed before we have lunch and pull anchor. We may not be going home with dinner, but it was definitely the most humorous fishing trip!

On our second day, we are swimming with manatees. We show up at 6:30 a.m. while it is still dark and climb into our wetsuits, not an easy feat. We watch a manatee safety video warning us not to touch the manatees before climbing into our boat. The animals have not had the same "passive observation" briefing. This was made evident as soon as we got in the water just around the corner from the Plantation on Crystal River. We all jumped into the water with our noodles as flotation devices. Our captain swam out first then called us over. We dog-paddled/floated over in the direction of the manatees. What I experienced when I got there was incredible. A manatee swam right up to me—nose to nose. As I tried not to scare her or touch her, she swam forward under me. I had to put my hands down on her back as she moved so close that she was touching me from my chest to my feet, then stopped. She rolled over and the captain told me it was okay. She just wanted me to rub her belly.

It was incredible to be so close to these gentle giants. They don't have teeth except molars for grinding, can grow up to about thirteen feet long, and can easily weigh twelve hundred pounds. This trip defines the saying, "It's not things we remember, it's moments." Thank you, Rebecca, David, Trey, and Caroline, for a birthday present I will never forget!

CHAPTER 6

RUNAWAY TRUCK RAMP

BACK at the Flamingo, I am getting ready for travel. I bought a new tailgate that I hope will make getting hitched by myself easier. My RV park friends, Rex and Tony, get it installed and want to make sure I get hooked up correctly. I think I am lined up straight. I start backing the truck towards the Wildcat. My first try is too far to the left. My second try, too far to the right. Tony asks if I have any duct tape. I have no idea why he wants it, but I break out my new bright pink roll. He laughs and shakes his head. He adds a strip of my pink duct tape to the top of the toolbox in my truck and another to the hitch on the Wildcat. I just have to line up the two as I back up. I start backing up, using his advice. I am almost there, but have to push the gas harder to make it over a little hill. I stop, afraid I will hit the fifth wheel too hard and push it into the lake behind me if I go in reverse too fast.

Rex encourages me, "You are fine. You've got this." I press my foot harder on the gas and *bang!* I stop.

"No, no, no," Tony says, "It was just the two pieces of metal connecting. Come back another inch." My third try is a success!

My biggest trip so far starts today. I was hooked up last night so all I have to do is disconnect power and water then pull in my slides. I push the button for the slides. The bedroom slide is in, dinette slide comes in, the big slide starts in and stops. I push the button for it to go back out, then to come in again. It stops short about three inches. It continues to try, but it's not moving. Releasing the button, I go outside to look. Nothing seems wrong. Back in I go. This has never happened before. I push and hold the "In" button for a minute...and *pop!* I have no idea what just happened. It sounded like wood breaking but the slide closes. I search everywhere to see what broke. To get to the living area with the slides in, I have to climb up and over the kitchen counter onto the couch. On my hands and knees under the dinette, I find the source. Somehow, one of the storage drawers under the couch got hung up on the opposing slide. The pressure popped the drawer front off.

I finally leave Flamingo Lake RV Resort with Emmi tucked into the passenger seat. I drive down Interstate 95 South straight through downtown Jacksonville to Interstate 10 West. The first few hours are a breeze.

I *thought* I was halfway through my six-hour drive for the day, but get caught in Atlanta traffic. The roads around Atlanta are beating the crap out of us. I am going slow, but I feel every bump as if it is a huge crater. Emmi makes a quick retreat to the floorboard behind my seat. Remind me *not* to go through Atlanta ever again.

We make it to our home for the night, Allatoona Lake RV Park. It's a pretty place, set way back off of the interstate, gated and quiet. At check-in, the guy at the desk gives me a map to find my spot. Wait, no escorts? My heart begins to pound but I don't want them to think I am the crazy woman who has no idea what she is doing.

When he sees the Beast outside, he takes back the map. "Actually, you really should not follow the map I gave you. There is a low limb in that direction that could tear up your fifth wheel." He draws the new route in pen, then hands it back. "This should be easier, just be careful."

I am on my own. Now my heart is pounding. By the time I get back in my truck I am shaking. I sit still a minute fighting off the panic. "Dear God, help me. Please do not let me tear anything up on my rig."

Side note: Since God is in the business of answering prayers, you should be careful what you pray for.

Breathe in, breathe out. Breathe in, breath out. I've got this! I can do this!

I put the truck in drive and am ready to tackle my first challenge. I've got to make a tight right turn around the office and get through the electric gate. I have to be close enough to the keypad to punch in the code, but also straight enough not to plow over anything and make it through the narrow gate. I think I have it, but I cannot reach the keypad from inside my truck. I stretch, but can't reach it. I know they must be watching from inside and laughing. Do I back up and try again? I decide that might be worse. What if I get out to enter the gate code and I am not close enough or straight enough to get through the narrow gate? I put my truck in park, hop out, and enter the code with the biggest fake smile.

The gate opens as I get back in the truck. Slowly, very slowly, I creep through the gate using my mirrors. This would be so much easier if I could get my heart rate down and quit shaking. I just know that I am going to embarrass myself by either ripping the gate off its track or scraping all of the paint off one side of the Beast. I sigh in relief when I look in the mirror and see the gate closing behind me.

I try to drive and at the same time pay attention to the route drawn out for me. Who decided that this was a good idea? A) Hand a person who has never been to your park a map of your park with a faint pen drawing showing them where to go. B) Assume that the happy camper will not run into a tree or another RV as they are looking down trying to read their map.

My spot is ahead and I have not run over anything. It's a pull-through, but I am coming at it from the wrong direction. If you have been in many campgrounds or RV Parks, you know that pull-through sites are usually angled so it is easy for the driver to easily veer off to pull into the site. When they leave, they just keep going out, making only a possible slight turn. The roads and sites are designed for this pull-through process, something that never crossed my mind before I headed towards my spot going against the intended direction. So now here I am, looking at my assigned location and realizing I have to make a sharp forty-five-degree angle turn back to the left. For someone with greater experience than I have, this might not be such a big deal.

The park is virtually empty and the campers I do see don't have cars or trucks parked by them. At least no one will be watching me. I stop in the middle of the road, get out, and consider my options. It is not going to be easy, but what else is there to do but try? I swing wide as I pull forward and make a sweeping turn.

There are so many things to watch at the same time, like the giant pine tree in front of me. I definitely don't want to hit that, so I turn harder, having to watch the front of the fifth wheel so that it does not get hung up on the toolbox in the back of my truck. If it clears that, I have to make sure it doesn't crash into the cab of the truck.

I crawl along, watching the back of the trailer so it doesn't hit the power pole and power box. That would be bad. I am in, but not even close to straight. Now my right side is blind. I straighten my wheel, pull further through, and into the road ahead. I am still not exactly straight and need to back up. I turn my wheel the other direction and put the truck in reverse, trying to straighten out a bit more. I am feeling pretty good about this. Inching along, I meet some minor resistance. Thinking it's a bump, I press harder on the gas. *Pop!* And then the sound of gushing water.

I know immediately what it is. I had totally forgotten about keeping an eye out for the water connection on my blind side. I get out to assess the damage. The Beast is okay, but the water line is snapped off at the ground. Of all the things that could come to my mind, I remember I only prayed that God wouldn't let me damage my rig. I laugh at my mistake.

I call the office, "Hello, this is Bob. Can I help you?"

"Yes. This is Jenni. I just checked in a few minutes ago. I might need a little help. Site 56 has just sprung a leak." I find the cut-off valve for the water and turn it off.

"No problem, I will send someone right over."

Jim comes bumping through on his golf cart right away. I apologize profusely, rambling on about being new at this and offer to help if he has an extra shovel.

Jim says, "You don't need to help and don't worry. This park was not built for fifth wheels and the hook-ups are on the wrong end. Trees are all close to the pads so that the front of the campers these sites were meant for get shade. Problem is, you can't put your slides out if you park where you are supposed to on the pad."

I feel a little better but admit to him that this is my second time running over a water line.

Jim responds, "I see men who have been pulling trailers for a long time do the same thing all the time. Let's just get you moved over to another spot so you can take a break and enjoy the day." He shifts me to the next spot over. In just a few minutes, I am parked straight.

I left the Beast hitched to the truck last night since it was a short stay. I am up early, with water and power disconnected. Emmi is in the truck while I pull the slides in. The slides won't come in at all! I don't even hear the slide motor running. My camping friends Pete and Jana live not too far away. I hope they can help me.

In the interim, I call Good Sam Roadside Assistance and am advised that an RV mechanic should be here by ten thirty. While I wait, I hit the internet, Google and YouTube. I learn that my slides are probably operated by a hydraulic pump and go through the suggestions I find. Check the breaker inside—it's on. Check the fuse—I pull it out and accidently drop it inside the compartment where my fingers can't reach. Out to my toolbox to get needle-nose pliers. After a few times of dropping it as I had to get around corners, I get it out and it's good.

Now I am trying to find the area that gives access to manually operate the slides. Bill, the mechanic is late. He calls at eleven and says he is on his way. I find the hidden compartment and tool just as he arrives. He is deaf and hard to understand. He continues to ask me where things are that I don't know the answers to. He checks the breaker and fuse, although I told him I had already done that. Then he tries, after I tell him how, to manually bring the slides in, but says there is a problem and he doesn't have the right tools.

I ask, "Sir, could it be the batteries?"

"No, they would have charged while you were connected to power all night. It's because you are not level."

For an hour now, he has done a lot of walking to and from his van and repeating steps that I have already tried. I have less and less faith in him knowing any more than I do about what he is doing. He proceeds to start jacking up the trailer—enough to pick my truck up, which is still attached, and making me nervous. The park manager arrives to say that a group of RVers needs my site. One of the men from the group of campers (another Jim) is with him. We all agree that this "RV mechanic" doesn't know what he is doing. I go back to Bill. "Sir, please stop and lower my trailer. You have done enough."

He looks at me like I must be kidding and asks, "Why? You don't want me to fix it?"

I tell him, "No," and try to explain that I am uncomfortable with what he is doing. "The hitch in the bed of my truck is not meant to hold my truck in the air. If it had to do with being level, the slides would make some kind of noise when I pushed the button. They do nothing."

He grumbles, "You owe me for my time," and starts packing up. He hands me an invoice for $120, which I pay, though annoyed, just to get him out of here.

It is hot and sticky out. I need to get out of this site because the incoming group has the entire row. I remember reading something about not unhooking your truck until after you are level with your slides out. The reason was because you may have to move to accommodate slides. It said that you could leave your slides out as long as you had a spotter. I ask the park manager where the closest truly pull-through, level site is. He points over close to the bath house.

I ask, "Can you give me just a few minutes?" Now I have like ten men standing around watching and waiting. I walk down to this site and call a mobile repair guy from home on my way. "Can I drive with my slides out if I am going a really short distance and very slowly?" I ask.

I tell him why and he says, "Yes. Just go slow, be careful, and make sure you have people watching all of your sides." I thank him and head back up the hill.

I tell these men what I plan to do, show them the direction I am going to take, and tell the park manager I will need that spot for the night. They follow along beside me as I creep along. I ease into this new perfectly level spot, put my stabilizer jacks down, plug into power, and disconnect the truck.

The park manager asks if I need anything else. I ask if he has a battery tester. He calls maintenance and has them bring one by. I call my next stop to cancel my reservation before maintenance arrives with the tester. Sure enough, the batteries are four years old and D-E-A-D, dead. He leaves a charger with me as well. Of course, I don't know how to use it, but I do not tell him that. I Google it.

Once the battery has started charging, I go inside to cool off. I put ice in the sink, add a few drops of peppermint essential oil, a towel, and some cold water. I wring out the towel, wipe my face, arms, and neck with the iced peppermint water, then place the cool damp towel around my neck and dig out my favorite cold Fentimans Rose Lemonade.

While I sit enjoying my cold drink, in comes more of the RV group. I hear a noise that sounds like a retractable cord being pulled in too fast. I look up just in time to see the snapped cable line zipping through the air. The man has also caught the power line with the antenna of his fifth wheel and is seconds from snapping it as well. I take off, waving my arms, yelling, and racing across the park to get his attention. Just as the power line pulls tight, he sees me and stops. He gets out, looks, thanks me, and backs up. Major crisis averted.

I get one slide all the way in, but not as fast as it should, then the batteries die. I am hot, frustrated, and dripping sweat. I disconnect the cables from all the batteries and load them into my truck. Holy cow these things are heavy! Back to my phone to find the nearest auto parts store. Pep Boys it is.

At Pep Boys, I purchase new batteries, a power tester, and a charger.

I get back to my site and back in as close to the battery compartment as possible. I don't want to carry these heavy things very far. I set the batteries in and then…I am such an idiot! I did not think to take a picture of all the different cable connections. Feeling defeated, I want to give up. More than anything, I just want to cry. I can't give up. This is only my second day. With the help of YouTube, Google, and Facebook, I start connecting. I am so afraid of shorting out and frying everything in my rig. Just one more connection that pulls them all together. I cross my fingers and hope I got it right. Nothing sparks, and just like that, everything works. Thanks to my FB friends and a big thanks to you, Chris, for the final connection advice. I *did* it!

It takes a few tries, but I hitch the Beast to the truck by myself for the very first time. I am continuing north from Allatoona Landing Resort a day late. I am a bit worried about crossing Monteagle Mountain. This will be my first time pulling something behind me going through the mountains, and I am not sure what to expect. I am at the base, climbing up at 30 mph. My truck is handling the load well. I make it to the top and have to survive making it through a 5 percent grade coming down. It's scary, but not as bad as I thought it would be. The truck does what it was built to do. After some time, I am at the bottom, without riding the brakes.

My next challenge is the pouring-rain thunderstorm that has come out of nowhere. I can barely see the road in front of me. Your beliefs may be different than mine, but that's okay. I am glad that God is my co-pilot. I don't think I have ever had such a long conversation with Him. I talk to Him all the way through the buckets of rain pouring down my windshield. The flashes of light caused by each jagged bolt of lightning are blinding. It's hard not to close my eyes, as I am already anticipating the crack of thunder that immediately follows.

I pull off at Exit 81 in Murfreesboro, Tennessee and stop at the Pilot Travel Center for gas. Just so you know, it's not exactly RV friendly. It's tough to get in and even harder to get out. After filling my tank, I realize there is not enough room for me to pull forward and make the turn without plowing over the pump to my left. I am not super excited about backing this thing up. It's even worse when there are moving objects all around me. I have no idea how to get out of this jam. I see two young landscape guys and ask them for help. They are nice enough to stay behind me and block traffic as I creep backwards. Then they move up in front of me so that I can get out without running over anything.

I weave through downtown Nashville and merging city traffic a bit white-knuckled, but without a challenge. As I cross into Kentucky, I find a rest area that Emmi and I can take a nice walk in. Behind the rest area are acres of corn fields with an old barn peeking through. It looks like something that should be on canvas.

I am glad we took that relaxing break, because I-24 is rough from the state line all the way through Exit 40, where we pull off for gas at another Pilot. I am happy to see that this one appears to be easy to get in and out of. Bonus—the outside lane pump is available! As I get back on the road, I am feeling fairly confident. Sort of like life…when it's easy, we feel good. But when things get tight or the journey is a bit bumpy, our confidence tends to suffer. As I drive along, thinking, watching the scenery, and talking to God, I am relaxed as I head over a big bridge when *wham!* We caught a gust of wind crossing the Ohio River into Illinois. My truck and fifth wheel are both shoved sideways. That certainly brought me to attention.

With only nineteen miles to Interstate 57, traffic stops. I don't mean crawls—stops completely. The interstate is closed ahead because of a major accident. There's no way around except where State Police are detouring at the next exit into Vienna, Illinois, a tiny, two-lane town. For twenty minutes, I don't move an inch. Of course, I have been drinking a lot of water and have to use the bathroom. Like now. Oh, the joys of age. My truck is in park in the middle of the interstate and I consider getting out and running back to the fifth wheel to use the bathroom. What if traffic starts moving? Probably a bad idea. Then I think of the years I sold adult diapers to nursing homes and wish I was wearing one. It's getting that bad.

After a long time, we are moving. I make it off the interstate and take the first left into McDonald's. Am I going to make it? Will there even be a place I can park? I round the corner behind McDonald's and there are two empty spaces for buses. I don't have time to line up and park in one, so I take them both. There's no time to go inside. I unlatch my seatbelt and move as fast as possible around to the fifth wheel's door. As I unlock it, I am praying I don't wet my pants. At least I have water in my tanks and clean clothes inside. My eyes are watering. I get the door unlocked and climb in. I made it!

Now to figure out how to get across the road and back into the line of detoured traffic. As I sit and ponder, a trucker stops, honks his horn, and waves me out in front of him. I am certain that Vienna has never seen traffic, much less a back-up like this in their little town.

Heading down Highway 37 to who knows where, there is a sign with a truck on a very steep hill. Guess what that means? Cresting the hill at 55 mph, I see what looks like a giant roller-coaster—straight down and straight back up. I am probably going too fast. At least the road is straight. All that I can do is pray as I rocket down the hill. I am at the bottom and shoot up the other side. Slowing down, I think of what happens to a rollercoaster at this point. I don't want to roll backwards. I quickly put my foot on the gas.

Three and a half hours from the point where I-57 was only nineteen miles away, I eventually make it back to the interstate. After being delayed replacing my batteries, I had thought I would make up part of the eight-hour drive I missed yesterday. My day just got longer. I call the next park and cancel my reservation. This is becoming a habit.

This interstate has potholes big enough to lose my truck in. I continue north then head west through St. Louis, Missouri before dark. About nine thirty I start looking for a rest area to sleep in, but this highway doesn't have any right off the interstate. I pull off at a truck parking area, but it is full. I keep going. Finally, a rest area, but it's full too. A few exits up there is a Pilot. Seems like a good choice, but as I pull in and around, I notice this is not only a truck stop, but a loud casino and strip club. *Not* where I am going to sleep!

At 11:30 p.m., after fifteen and a half hours of driving, I am exhausted. I pull into Love's Travel Center at the same exit and snug in between two big trucks for the night. With the noise of running semis outside, it takes us a long time to go to sleep. Emmi keeps growling at the foot of the bed. Still, it feels amazing to climb into my own bed.

I wake up before daylight. Emmi and I sit on the steps of the Wildcat and watch early morning life at a truck stop. I fill the truck's gas tank before continuing west. Next thing I know, we are going north on 29 in the pouring rain through downtown Kansas City. I was supposed to take the bypass, but because I can barely see, I missed it. I just remembered that I forgot to change "Day 4" on my GPS and I was eventually going to be heading in the wrong direction. Quickly juggling directions between my iPhone, iPad, and GPS, I drive down the interstate. I am so glad Siri listens to me and can give quick directions, and even more excited that my new GPS also listens to voice commands.

It rains most of the way to Iowa Highway 2. I am stopping for gas at the Pilot there. Other than being very busy, it was easy getting into the station. Three pumps per lane, so I line up to wait behind a van. The woman is having a challenge with her "pre-pay" and had to go into the store three times. In the meantime, people kept pulling around me for the pumps in front of her. Two gentlemen on motorcycles did the same. I get out to talk with them. They were kind enough to block the space for me until the woman in the van was finished and I could pull up. We chatted about them heading to Sturgis and they are concerned about me crossing the country by myself, pulling the Beast.

Another guy getting fuel has a broken passenger window on his truck. He was trying to get plastic on it by wrapping it around and shutting the door. The wind was giving him fits. It's hard not to laugh, but I feel sorry for him. I offer the big shaved head, covered in tattoos guy my pink duct tape. He thanked me for the offer, but declined. My tank is filled and I look around to see how I am going to get out. Oops! Big trucks getting diesel have blocked what I thought was going to be plenty of room to pull forward, turn around, and easily exit back out. My new biker friends said to get as close to the semi as possible then cut sharp left. Done and out!

Just as I pull back out onto Highway 2, my GPS says forty-nine miles to my next exit. I am on a bumpy two-lane road.

"Um. God? This is what I am supposed to do for the next forty-nine miles? And the speed limit is 45 mph?"

Be careful what you ask God for. The road quickly turned into four *bumpy* lanes with a speed limit of 65 mph. I am lucky to do

50. Babump, babump, babump! Nine miles to go and there is a traffic light. On a highway! Seven miles to go and another traffic light. Six miles to go and another, and another! I am in the middle of a small town. I guess that's what they do here on a highway. I make it to 77 North, then I-80 West. We take a rest area break in Nebraska, about an hour and a half from tonight's destination in North Platte.

It's after five when we reach our exit to Holiday RV Park. After ten hours of driving today, I made up the rest of the time lost doing RV repairs on Day Two. The woman checking me in says, "There are no escorts, but you have a pull-through site that is easy to navigate." So far, I definitely stink at this pulling in with no help, but here goes. I get close to my site and I see a tree at the edge that I have to get around and a car in the road on my left that is going to make it extremely difficult for me to swing wide and miss it. People stop what they are doing to watch me. You would think they might consider moving their car or offer some assistance, but nope, they are happy to just watch the show.

I take a second for a quick chat with God not to let me make a complete fool of myself and swing as wide as I can. I have about three inches between me and a garbage can on the left back end of the fifth wheel. I am probably only two inches from the car before I make the sharp right. I tell myself to ignore the people, and to watch where I am going. I make it in, straight as an arrow. I have a huge smile on my face and am feeling proud as I thank God for the help and climb out of the truck. I am only here one night, so I'm not disconnecting the truck. I connect the power, hook up water and sewer lines, put out my slides, and turn on the a/c. I even put out my awning, lay my welcome mat at the foot of the steps, and set Wilbur the flying pig out on my picnic table.

When Emmi and I sit down to relax, a little dog shows up to visit. She went right up my steps and sat down by the door. A few minutes later, my neighbor arrives to find her. After visiting for a bit, Beverly and her friend John invite me to dinner. Hot dogs, baked beans, and shrimp cocktail are the perfect RV Park meal. I had such a good time getting to know them. The coach they are in is hers, and *she* drives it. We exchange numbers, I invite them to visit at Flamingo Lake, and they invite me to their ranch in Missouri. Walking back home for the night, I am aware of fireflies all around me. I needed the joy of this evening with nice people and this was a perfect way to end it.

I am getting ready to leave Holiday RV and doing my "pre-flight" walk around. I notice one of my slide awnings is disconnected from its track and hanging down. I go in search of a ladder, which I found at the office. The guy working there asks, "Where is your husband?" He appears concerned when I tell him that I am traveling by myself.

"I will let you borrow a ladder, but I can't help you," he tells me.

I had not asked him to, but that's okay. Do unto others.... On the trek back carrying the six-foot painters' ladder, I see a guy outside his RV and ask if he has any experience with slide awnings. He follows along to hear the story of the lone woman traveler. We pick up the seventy-five-year-old retired fireman-turned-rancher on our way by. Once they get a good look, we find that both screws holding the bracket in place are missing. Yesterday's bumpy ride must have shaken them loose and out. I pull out my "box 'o screws and stuff" (feeling proud that I even had one of these) to find something that would work. Then made a note to self: I need a bigger selection of RV-type screws. The fireman went to see what he had in his more appropriate collection. I'm not feeling so proud now, but I learned something new. All set and ready to head out after I return the ladder.

The two bikers tent-camped across from me are watching closely as I finagle my way out. They look impressed when I clear all of the obstacles around my "easy to navigate" site without hitting anything.

I-80 West is a bit bumpy to start, but it clears up quickly. I am getting extremely concerned over this 5 percent grade descent for five miles I have to survive later today. I call my best friend for some details on the exact location. Like knowing where exactly it is, is going to make me feel any less worried. The information she finds says the decline starts in Laramie and that there is a rest area just before. I plan to stop before that in Cheyenne. I alternate between praying and worrying, trying to stay calm. I start seeing sunflowers growing along the side of the road. They are so pretty I forget my worries. I am still seeing cornfields this far north and wonder who eats all of this corn?

Just after the 80/76 junction there is a sign, "Freeway ends ahead." What?! Now I am on a two-lane road for eight miles as I begin to climb. A little further and another sign, "Freeway ends ahead." Another eight miles of two-lane road. Speed limit 65, but not this girl. As I continue to climb, I am backing truckers up for miles. I exit onto Highway J and stop at Love's for gas.

I am back on I-80 heading west and the terrain is drastically starting to change. It's gray out and misting rain. I am starting to worry about having to head down this mountain on wet roads. Back to praying. God sends another distraction. I see a neat flat, wooden, coyote up high on some rocks with an American flag blowing in the wind. The coyote is howling at the moon. I think how beautiful this is and about how blessed I am to be living in a country where I am free to make this trip. Then...here come the bumps again and back down to two lanes. I have a concrete wall on my left and a guardrail on my right, no shoulder on either side. This is a twelve-mile stretch with the right half of my lane grooved. It makes me want to move left, but there is a concrete barrier in my way. I encounter several more of these similar stretches. In between, I have more sunflowers to look at along the way.

I see lots of turbines. To me, that means wind. Within seconds my new GPS dings an alert, "*Vertical winds ahead.*" At first it scares me, since winds have blasted me off and on throughout the day. Then I relax. None are so strong that I am afraid of being blown off the road, only bumped and nudged a bit. I learn to watch the wind socks along the way. It really is the best and easiest way to know the direction and strength of the winds.

My mind goes back to that mountain. I am seriously worried about the 5 percent grade descent. Maybe I should just turn around. I tell myself that it would be okay to not go on. I have already accomplished something that many thought I couldn't do. I don't want to give up, but I am scared. I talk to God about it. I remember a Facebook post from my brother this morning telling me, "You will be fine. Just take it slow." And then up pops another field of sunflowers, my sign to keep going. I start seeing snow fences along the roadside as I continue to climb. Cars are passing me at high speeds, and even trucks at times. The speed limit is mostly 75 mph. Depending on where I am, I'm somewhere between 45 and 60 mph.

I pull off on Exit 367 for gas and a sandwich at the Pilot in Cheyenne. It is easy to get in, with an angled pump island and direct access to exit the station. I pull out, then circle back in to park and eat lunch, partly to delay going over that mountain not far ahead. The fear I have about this 5 percent descent is increasingly real—my neighbor last night told me that Monteagle Mountain was nothing compared to this—and more so as I Google suggestions on crossing big mountains. Turn off your air conditioner, open your windows, and whatever you do, don't burn your brakes up.

I pray. "God, thank you for letting me take this journey. Thank you for letting me see and do so much. God, I still have so much to see and so much to do for you. If this is the day that I meet you face-to-face, I hope I have done enough. I am not ready to die. Please help me make it down this mountain without hurting anyone. I am faithful that with you as my co-pilot, I can do this."

I am reminded of Philippians 4:13: "I can do all things through Christ who strengthens me." Delaying isn't going to get this over any faster or make me feel any better. I am so upset that I can't eat anyway. As I am pulling out, I think I will stop at that rest area Hope told me about just before the descent. I wonder how much it would cost to hire someone at the rest area to drive my truck down the mountain? I am scared! Like gut-wrenching, cold-sweat scared.

I just saw a sign reading, "5 percent grade ahead" with that picture of a truck sitting at a forty-five-degree angle pointing down. I thought that the descent started in Laramie? Crap! I am not ready!!! Deep breath. I don't have a choice now.

"Okay God, we've got this."

Now the fear hits me extremely hard. Recalling the story of Doubting Thomas from the Bible, I apologize for my lack of faith. I remember my daughter believing I could do anything when she was little. I thought of the story about Jesus in the boat sleeping. As I crested the highest point in Wyoming at 45 mph, I say, "Jesus, I have faith. I am ready."

Within seconds, I go from 45 to 46, to 47 to 48 to 49 to 50 mph. The truck is in tow/haul mode, but the engine is not holding back all of this weight. I am tapping my brakes. (Don't burn up your brakes.) I am working the brake controller. Work, work, working it...51, 52, 53, 54 mph. Things are not going well. I am gripping the steering wheel and tapping the brakes, working the brake controller faster. It is screaming. 55, 56, 57, 58, 59, 60! My mind is racing with all of the available options, but my speed keeps increasing. None of the options are good, and all I can see is more mountain. God, my co-pilot, must be sleeping. I think I am going to die! 60 mph may not seem fast to most, but when you are careening down a mountain gaining speed at about 1 mph/second with a massive curve ahead, this is a life-or-death situation. Especially when you are pulling a thirty-eight-foot fifth wheel behind you.

I am considering the run-a-way truck ramp ahead so I don't hurt anyone else. I was relying on God to do this. Is this really how it ends? Tears well up in my eyes and I am about to be sick. I think, *what if I wet my pants?* What if this is how they find me? Dead, covered with puke, and I wet my pants? I have to get His attention.

"*God!* Where are you?!"

As I hit 61 mph, I hear a calm voice in my head say, "Put your foot on the brake now." I do as the voice says. If I burn up the brakes, so be it. I am not going down without a fight. I put my foot down and pushed hard, just for a second. Immediately, it was like a parachute grabbed me and pulled me back. The truck shifted into lower gear and slowed me down. Within seconds, I am at 55 mph.

Now I still have three miles to go, but my faith is back. Through Him I can. Thank you, God! Now just two more miles. One mile to go. I am going to make it!

I am suddenly aware of being soaked in sweat and every muscle in my body hurts. I see the sign for Laramie. The 5 percent grade *ends* here, it doesn't *start* here! The excitement I feel is just as great as the fear I felt a few minutes ago. I thank God again, and laugh at myself for seriously thinking God was sleeping and not paying attention. I want to shout for joy! *We did it!*

Emmi comes out of her hiding spot, hops up front onto the center console, and sits down. After looking at me for a minute, she stretches over to lick my hand. If you know me and dogs, they are *not* allowed to lick me. This was such a sweet and gentle gesture it made me smile.

A few miles up, we pull off at the next rest area for a much-needed potty break and walk. It is actually just a big gravel spot. I now know that what I previously thought were snow fences were actually tumbleweed guards. Now I see snow fences. In this dry, rocky terrain, I also see yellow wildflowers and purple flowers nestled in thistles growing. The biggest dandelions I have ever seen, at least four inches in diameter, are everywhere. I am reminded that even without water and nutrient-rich soil, flowers can grow, life can exist. No matter how "prickly" the situation, there is something good. This reminder will stay with me after I leave.

I weave through parked vehicles who stopped wherever they wanted in this gravel spot and it isn't even making me nervous. I am getting better at this.

It's mid-afternoon when we arrive at the Journey KOA in Rawlins, our destination for the night. It was only a seven-hour drive today, but I am worn out. I am escorted to a great pull-through site and I didn't run over anything. It's level front to back but not completely level side-to-side. I need to figure out how to pull the tires up on block pads without help. It's not off much. I am just going to live with it.

Not long after hooking everything up, the owner comes by concerned about the dripping water at the spigot on my site. "Water is a luxury around here. Do you mind if I take a look?" I am embarrassed. I did not even think of the tiny drip as a problem. "Of course! Thank you!" He turns the water off, saying, "I will be right back." He returns with a new gasket seal for my hose, a pressure reducer, and a Y adaptor. He shows me how to connect everything, explains what everything does, and then tells me that they are a gift. "Take them all with you when you leave."

The young couple next to me are in a newer Wildcat fifth wheel. They are on their way to Mount Rushmore with their two children and little dog. The man is shocked that I am doing this by myself. He keeps saying he can't believe I actually made it this far. He spooks me about the mountains I still have to cross. He says that what I experienced today was nothing compared to what I will see further along. I do more research before I go to bed. I wonder why there is no map with locations and grade data. I dig and dig, but find nothing. I do learn that there is an old saying among truckers: "There are two kinds of drivers—those who've been in trouble on a mountain and those who will be." I find a blog that mentions an app called Mountain Directory. I pay and download it. The app is not fancy, but gives me more information than I can find anywhere else. I feel much better as I drift off to sleep.

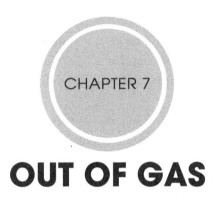

OUT OF GAS

I am getting ready to leave and having problems with the same darn slide. This time, the rubber seal at the top has worked its way partially out. I tuck it into the offending slide for now and add some pink duct tape as an extra precaution.

Idaho Falls, here we come! It's sixty-six degrees and sunny, with no humidity. Shortly after we cross the Continental Divide, elevation 7,000 feet, the road shifts to two lanes for twelve miles. Some lateral winds, but otherwise a smooth glide downhill. We stop in Wamsutta for gas, then cross the other side of the Continental Divide, elevation 6,993 feet. While in Wamsutta, I was reviewing the road ahead on my new app. I had to make a route decision. Option A was to continue on the Good Sam-suggested route that would take me up 191 North, to 89 South, to 26 West. This route has a 6 percent grade descent for only two miles on 26, but it has *miles* of 45 mph curves with mountains on one side of the highway and a drop-off into the Snake River on the other. Though I am sure it is beautiful, I would not see it. I would be white knuckled with my eyes glued to the road. Option B provided by my new RV GPS would have me take Exit 66 further west on 80 onto 30 West towards Kemmerer, Wyoming. This route has just one 5 percent grade descent that is five miles long. I decide that I made it through yesterday and I am more afraid of those curves. I choose Option B.

The day is gorgeous, and the scenery is spectacular. About fifteen miles east of Green River, Wyoming, I notice that rubber seal I had tucked in this morning has started to come out of the track more. Since I tucked it in and taped it, it resembles a lasso at the back corner of the Wildcat. The lasso continues to get bigger and bigger as I go. There is no place to stop. I am sure people around me are wondering what this is all about. Praying for an exit, I see a tunnel ahead. Now I am a wee bit panicked, because I have no idea how tall it is. I was too busy watching the lasso and road, and I must have missed the sign. There is nowhere to go but through. What if I am too tall? I don't worry long because I have another distraction. Just before I was either entering the tunnel or crashing into it, that lasso became a massively long rope when it came "untucked." Like a bullwhip, it is flapping and snapping in the wind. Oh God! Please don't let it hit anyone! I reduce my speed to about 45 mph and turn my flashers on. I make it through the tunnel without bringing the mountain down on top of me. It was silly to worry about being too tall. I did not even think about the fact that I was on an interstate and truckers had been passing me. As I come out of the Green River Tunnel, I see that there is probably not an exit close by, unless it was dug into the side of the mountain.

I meander through the curves with my bullwhip snapping in the wind and take the next exit, whose sign reads, "No services" then "No parking on ramp." I get to the foot of the ramp as far to the right as possible and park anyway. There is no sign of civilization and no possible way to turn the Beast around if I turn right or left.

I get out to examine the situation. The wind is blowing so hard it is tough to catch the bullwhip-turned-snake. I catch it and try to pull it all the way out. Better than hurting someone or losing it. Of course, that would be too easy. I tug and pull, pull and tug. How can this thing just slide out on its own and yet, no matter how hard I try, I cannot pull it out?

Next solution—break out the pink duct tape. The problem with this is, I have to let go of the evasive snake. I am so glad that no one is around to see this. Woman on the side of the road, long red hair flying in the wind, holding pink duct tape in one hand and trying to catch this long piece of rubber whipping around over her head with the other hand. I finally catch it again, but can't see because my hair is flying in my face. I have a hair tie on my wrist, but my hands are full. Duct tape now between my knees, snake in my left hand, I use my teeth to pull hair tie up over my right thumb, use the same hand to capture all of this flying hair without letting go of the rubber seal, and pull it into some kind of ponytail, knot, or something, while also trying not to drop the duct tape, which will roll down the hill. That accomplished, now I have to figure out how to tear the duct tape and attach the bullwhip to the fifth wheel. With knees, teeth, and tape, I accomplish this and I am laughing but back on the road as if nothing ever happened.

I merge onto Highway 30 West and soon am not sure about my choice. It's a two-lane road with nothing in sight. But here I go, bumping down another highway, talking to God, and thinking about my life and how thrilled I am to have the opportunity to take this journey. Not long after I cross into Idaho, the scenery changes drastically. I have not seen a cornfield all day, only rocks, dirt, dead brown grass, and more rocks. Now it's *green*. And wouldn't you know, I see another cornfield.

About thirteen miles from Cokeville, my rubber snake begins to uncoil, ready to strike at any second. Next thing I know, it's flapping in the wind behind me. I stop at the Pilot in Cokeville for gas and more duct tape repairs. It's much easier since the wind is calmer. The Wildcat is being held together by pink duct tape. I need to buy some more soon so I don't run out.

I check my map to review the remainder of today's route and realize that my Aunt Sandy and Uncle Roger live not far from here in Montpelier. I call them to tell them where I am and where I am going. This is the first part of the trip where I will be at one campground for a few days. I need to get there before dark and set up, but I want to plan a day to see them. They are busy tomorrow, but we plan to spend the day together on Wednesday.

As I am driving through the tiny town of Montpelier, my mind is a thousand miles away as I think of the time I spent here as a little girl. Someone pulls alongside me and is furiously honking their horn. Coming abruptly out of my daydream, "Oh no! What now?" I turn my head and see it is my uncle and aunt! They point to the side of the road and we both pull over.

After exchanging huge hugs, Uncle Roger says, "You were this close! There was no way we were going to miss you. We thought at the very least we could give you a big hug on your way through."

You have no idea how special that made me feel! For someone to care enough about me to jump in their car and catch up to me simply to give me a hug on the side of the road on my way through their town. Wow! I don't know that I deserve such love. I spent a big part of my life too busy to think about spending time with my family, and they do this. Once again, I am grateful for this journey. I remember living here when I was about seven or eight years old, while Daddy worked in Idaho. I promise to come spend the day with them on Wednesday and after one more hug, ease back onto the road, passing through small towns I remember from my early childhood.

Ten miles up the road is the next mountain to contend with. I am a little concerned but not really worried. After yesterday's near-death experience, I should be shaking in my boots, but today my faith will remain steady. As I start the incline, I move into the right lane. When I reach the top, I am going 35 mph and head down. When I approach 45 mph, I use the trailer brake controller a few times to keep me under 50 mph. When I reach 50 mph, I put my foot slowly, but firmly on the brake and then let go. The truck downshifts and I coast the rest of the way down at about 50 mph. I reach the bottom in Lava Hot Springs and am so excited.

"Thank you, God, for being patient with me."

Wham! I relaxed too soon. We are not on flat, level ground yet and the wind is blowing like crazy, nearly shoving me off the road. It's constant, shaking the Beast behind me and sometimes literally slamming into us as if it is something solid. Emmi is in the back seat, standing on her hind legs. She is looking out the passenger window towards the trailer, growling and barking, like she just saw something following us. She will not calm down. We make it to I-15 North. I am glad to be back on a four-lane highway. The winds calm down about twenty miles up the road, and Emmi settles into her bed as if nothing happened.

I pull into Snake River RV Park and Campground. I am checked in and have an escort to my pull-through site. I get hooked up to power, water, and sewer. I even set up home inside. I am sitting still for a few days. I meet the neighbors facing me. They seemed friendly until I finished setting up and sat down with their crew. Immediately, I know I am not welcome. All of the RVers have been friendly and helpful so far. Oh well, you win some and lose some. Emmi and I are off for a good night's sleep. We don't have to pull our house anywhere tomorrow.

When I wake up, it's dark outside and chilly inside. I turn on the fireplace, make coffee, and feed Emmi. Then we go for a walk. It's nice not to be in a hurry today. Next on my agenda is to find a mobile RV repair guy. I call EC RV Mobile Repair, the one that the park suggested, and he agrees to come by this morning and rid me of my pink duct tape.

I am on my way to Bear World. I check out the petting zoo, get licked by a mama doe, meet her twins, chat with a pair of mallard ducks, and dance with a peacock. I got a private tour of the bear habitat and even got to help feed them. These creatures strong enough to tear a man to shreds seem so calm and friendly from the safety of a truck. Watching them play in the forest was the perfect end to my day. I grab a homemade strawberry milkshake and head back to camp for the night.

I wake up excited to see family in Montpelier today, but get a message from Uncle Roger saying, "Change of plans. Rick (my cousin) is not feeling well." I am bummed, but so glad I got to see them for a few minutes yesterday. I decide that I am still going. I want to see the small towns I lived in for a year when I was a little girl. First stop, Hell's Half Acre Trail, a very cool island of lava. I spend hours hiking around and reading the info signs.

I want to stop at Lava Hot Springs next. Years ago, we came here to swim in the hot, steamy water. I want to experience that again. Pulling off at the exit, I am saddened by the fact that it is now a tourist attraction with giant water slides. I decide I want to keep my memories the way they were. I loop around what has become a tourist town and get back on the highway.

In Soda Springs I stop at an A&W. This was different too. The A&W that I remember was a drive-in and where I had my first root beer float. You pulled into a lane and parked, and teenagers on roller skates came out to take your order and serve you. That A&W has been replaced with a gas station that includes an A&W walk-up counter inside. Even with modernization, they still make their own root beer. I order a float in a glass mug. When the young girl hands the frosty mug to me, I can smell the sweetness. I take my first long, cold sip. I feel the tickle of bubbles from the root beer combined with the silky cool smoothness of the ice cream and can't even describe the bliss. Wow! I just stand here and savor the flavors and memories, grateful that some things haven't changed. I drive on.

I see a sign telling me that I am in Georgetown. I don't immediately remember the name, but I know that I have been here. I see a post office and know where I am. I used to walk to this post office from my Grandma and Grandpa's house. I pull over and call Daddy to ask for directions from here to the log house Grandpa built so many years ago. When I find it, the memories flood in and tears fill my eyes. I can see Grandpa with the logs he cut from trees and hand scraped to build this house. As I walked around to talk to the man in the driveway, I see all of the artifacts Grandma and Grandpa collected on their many journeys, still lovingly placed along the walkway so many years ago. The clothesline that Grandpa built out of logs for Grandma still stands. I can still see her sheets blowing in the breeze and remember what they smelled like. Such sweet, sweet memories.

In Montpelier, my Uncle Van meets me for a tour. I see "M" Hill and the old drive-in theatre that is now just an empty field. As children, we would lay in the backyard watching the movies without sound. I drive by the old pharmacy, where when I was sick, we got "pink medicine." It is still open, but the big chain grocery store is quickly putting them out of business. I see the bakery across the street, where we would walk over and get a creampuff while we waited for my medicine. The building and sign are still there, but the bakery is closed. The big grocery store has everything. Heading back to camp, I am grateful for the sweet, memory-filled day.

Today I am leaving Emmi at home and driving to Yellowstone since I am not so sure it is "pup safe." I enter the park at the west gate and pull over to look at my map. Heading north, I hike through a valley along the side of a river. I watch an entire flock of Canadian geese swimming and frolicking in the water. I take a trail to Gibbon Falls and stare at the beauty of the water cascading down and crashing over rocks along its way. On Roaring Mountain, I listen to steam escaping from the mountains from the narrow vents in the Earth. In Angel Terrace, I walked along the edge of thermal areas where the ground is only a thin crust above boiling hot springs and scalding mud. The sights I saw are some of the most beautiful I have ever seen. The main road inside is basically a circle with trails and roads leading off of it. Inside that circle is over two million acres. I had never imagined how big it was. In six hours, I barely scratched the surface of only a quarter of it. I exit the park at the north entrance. The Montana back roads on my way back to camp are breathtaking. This is one of the places I will return.

One of the top things on my list was to go horseback riding in Montana. It was not as easy as I thought it would be. Most places want to book groups, or at least couples. Last night, I got a call from one of the barns I spoke with. Another group agreed to let me ride with them. I'm in!

I arrive at the barn with my boots on and Nikon camera hanging around my neck. It has been years since I sat on the back of a horse. I always loved to ride and am beyond excited about it today.

I jump out of the truck and just stand here taking everything in. It's the smell that hits me first. The sweet aroma of fresh hay brings back memories. I take a breath into my nose. I smell old leather mixed with new, then I detect the heavenly undertones of the horses before I even hear their low whinnying sounds. It smells like a mix of fresh honey and dust and sweat. If you have never experienced it, you won't understand. It's glorious!

I get checked in and meet my group outside. Our guide sorts through each individual's riding skills and assigns an appropriate horse. My horse is Dorothy. The minute I am handed her reins, I am immediately in love. Her shiny coat is almost the exact color of red as my hair. Dorothy nuzzles into my neck and exhales a deep fluttering breath through her nose. It's like, "Yeah, I feel better now."

I am in my own little world. I stretch up to put my foot into the stirrup and easily swing my other leg over her back. I wiggle my rear in the saddle to get a feel for it and test the length of my stirrups. I pull one foot out and adjust the too-short stirrup. It's only now that I understand everyone is being instructed to stand on a wooden block to mount their horses. I guess I got ahead of things a bit and am embarrassed. I pledge to listen to my guide from here on out.

It's cool and sunny when we start out. I am bringing up the rear, our guide leading us down the long drive and across the highway. We are in a field full of tall, swaying grass at the foot of a gently sloping mountain. I get to know my horse and how she will best respond to commands. In this field, Dorothy does everything I ask. I hope she does the same when we begin climbing that mountain.

The trails start easy and then become more challenging as the ride progresses. The forest we are riding through is full of beauty. It's shady here beneath the trees. Where the sun peeks through, there are pretty flowers sprinkled across the ground in patches. From afar, they look like throw rugs scattered around on the dried leaves and pine needles. Butterflies and bees share the sweet nectar, while the birds sing all around us.

As we climb higher, I lean forward to duck under low tree limbs and thank Dorothy for not raking my legs across their rough trunks. At times, rocks skitter down the path towards us from the other riders. With a few words of encouragement, my horse keeps climbing and never loses her footing. The view is incredible!

Our trip back is slower. The horses are getting tired and some of the passes are crazy steep. My stomach muscles are getting a workout as I lean back to help Dorothy balance. I lay flat on my back at times to make it under some of the limbs. Even in the shade, it is getting warm.

Back at the barn, I feel the muscles in my thighs as I dismount. It doesn't hurt, it feels good. I am sad the ride is over and drive away, already dreaming of another ride.

The thought of flying down a mountain still freaks me out a bit. To dodge them, it's a longer route, but I am staying on interstates through Idaho today. I head south down to I-86 West. The sparsely populated region winding along the Snake River is an easy drive. It takes the actual passage through Massacre Rocks that settlers did in the mid-1800s. Driving through, I think how hard this trip would have been for horse-drawn wagons. Compared to theirs, my trip is easy.

Near Jerome, I see a billboard advertising a Flying J. I need a bathroom break and gas and decide to stop. The station is easy to get in and out of. The cashier inside is impressed with my bravery and suggests that I stop to see the local sights, especially Shoshone Falls! We chat a minute and I tell him, "Maybe next time."

Just as I cross the border into Oregon, I get off at the exit for my campground. I need gas and see stations, but I am tired. I will get fuel tomorrow on my way out.

When I pull up to Vale Trails RV Park, I am worried. The office sits back off of the road in the middle of a big dusty, gray gravel parking lot and not many campers are here. I remind myself it's simply a place to sleep for the night. I park and go into the office/ general store looking for the nice lady I talked to yesterday. My second impression isn't any better than the first. The place is disorganized and a general mess. I don't see anyone around as I walk up to the counter.

Just as I step up, I hear her friendly voice coming through the door between the living quarters and the office. The same woman I talked to yesterday greets me as if I am family that she is excited to see. I quickly forget my first and second impressions as she talks non-stop about how inspired she is by my traveling across the country alone. She tells me that she and her husband just bought this park. They are in the process of cleaning it up and have plans for updating it. They have a pull-through site for me close to the office that will be easy to get into and straight out in the morning.

She calls her husband to escort me out and around to the back entrance and into my site, then recommends I try Chabelitas

Taqueria Mexican restaurant in town for dinner. I thank her for the suggestion and tell her that I am not unhooking tonight. Vale, Oregon may be tiny, but they sure are friendly. She tells me that when I am settled to just call her and she will give me a ride.

My fabulous chauffer delivers me to the restaurant's front door and takes me inside to meet the owner. He has me sit at the bar so he can be sure I am taken care of. Now I am getting treated like a queen, and the owner himself waits on me. Dinner was phenomenal, and I enjoyed chatting with several of the locals who popped in for dinner. I am miserably full, so I decide to make the short walk back to camp in lieu of calling for a ride.

I enjoyed myself so much I make reservations to stay here on my way back east. Drifting off to sleep, I think I would love to do what they are doing. I would enjoy owning a campground.

Emmi and I take a walk before unplugging and heading out. The hardest part of my trip today will be the steep mountains and curvy roads. I have reservations at Diamond Lake RV Park. My best friend and her husband loved this park and suggested I stay there. Tyler and Andreea are even going to join me there for a few days after we take our Rogue River jet boat ride tomorrow. I plug the next RV park address into my GPS for directions and pull out of Vale Trails.

I soon discover that I am not heading back towards the interstate. I am making this next part of my journey via back roads. I am enjoying the ride along Route 20 up and down, curving one way, then another, nothing in sight but farms and fields of sweet corn and sugar beets. As I start climbing into the mountains, I remember that I need gas and check my gauge to see how many miles I have to an empty tank. It says fifty. I just saw a sign saying that the next town, Buchanan, was thirty-five miles away. It will be close, but I should be fine. Or so I thought. I become more and more nervous about not making it to a gas station. Driving through the mountains and fighting lateral winds, that expected number of miles I could make it on this tank of gas continues to drop fast. I am across Drinkwater Pass. My gauge says that I am down to about ten miles' worth of fuel left. I saw a sign telling me that says Stinking Water Pass is ahead, but I don't remember how many miles. From there, I will still be six miles from Buchanan. There is no way I will make it. I am going to run out of gas in the middle of nowhere. As this reality sinks in, I see a turn out on the side of the road. I pull off and stop.

I am glad I have Good Sam Roadside Assistance. I will just call for help. I pick up my phone and find I have zero cell service. I get out to take Emmi for a walk and hope that someone might come along to help me. No luck with that. It takes a while, but I get a few bars of service and call my 800 roadside assistance number. I feel much better when a friendly voice answers. She asks what my problem is. I feel like a real idiot when I have to tell her that I have run out of gas. She tells me not to worry, they can send someone with a gallon of gas. There is no charge except to pay for the gas. While I am wondering if a gallon will get me far enough, I lose my cell signal and the call drops.

It takes twenty minutes before I get a signal and can get through. The first thing that I am asked is my phone number in case we get disconnected. This time I make it through my story and the woman on the other end asks where I am. I tell her, "Somewhere heading west on Route 20, in Oregon between Drinkwater Pass and Stinking Water Pass." After a few minutes she says, "I don't see a city with either of those names." I try to explain that they are not cities, they are mountain passes, but she is not getting it.

"I don't see anything like this on Interstate 20. Can you give me a landmark?" she asks.

I tell her I am not on Interstate 20, I am on Route 20 and there are no landmarks. I am at the top of a mountain at a pull-off somewhere heading west on Route 20 in Oregon between Drinkwater Pass and Stinking Water Pass. I can tell that she is getting frustrated and ask her where she is—Dallas, Texas. A city girl. No wonder she doesn't get it. I pull out my road atlas to try and figure out what else I can tell her. The next town is Buchanan. I tell her this and ask her to just find a service provider in that town, then simply relay the directions I gave. At that moment, I lose my cell signal and the call drops. I pray she is doing what I asked, otherwise, it's going to be a long walk to town.

A half hour passes, and I have not been able to get a cell signal since the last call dropped. I am about to start walking when a car comes over the hill and turns in behind me. A woman in a McDonald's uniform gets out and says that her husband has a gallon of gas for me. My Good Sam lady came through!

My rescuers tell me I still have a little gas in the tank and the extra gallon should get me the seven miles to Buchanan. They will stay in front of me just in case. As we pull into the town, my gauge says, "zero miles to empty." I am coming to a red light and see the gas station ahead at the same crossroad. No one is coming. I run the red light and coast into the tiny gas station on fumes.

I am back on Route 20 heading west towards Burns, Oregon in the wind and rain. I see a sign boasting Dick Raney Ranch and wonder if we are related. I am on straight two-lane blacktop with a few easy curves and in "open range" territory. I see miles and miles of cattle.

Going through the Badlands, completely relaxed and probably not paying enough attention because it is so easy...*Dang! Dang! Dang!* I totally forgot I was on top of a mountain with the Beast behind me. I am now flying down it too fast.

Don't panic...foot on the brake hard, but don't leave it there. My engine pulls me back a bit. Work the trailer brake, then press my brakes one more time and I am good. Just about the time I see a sign telling me about the slow lane and another incline ahead, I am heading up and see signs warning of the steep descent that comes after. Nothing like God reminding me to keep my head in the game.

I take my exit onto 27th Street and have to take a horrible, bumpy roundabout to get on US 97 South. There should be rules on how these roads are constructed. And who even decided that roundabouts were a good idea anyway? I make it around without running over anything and my teeth have not rattled out of my head.

I am in the Umpqua National Forest and getting close to Diamond Lake when I turn onto Highway 138. It's absolutely gorgeous driving through the giant redwood trees with the sun peeking through the branches. Then I smell fire. As I crest the next hill, I am confronted with a thick wall of smoke ahead. Lots of smoke. I stop in the middle of the road trying to decide if I should keep going. I don't see flames. Do I dare chance it? I take a picture and consider going through. I am going to get closer and check it out. It's thick but not as bad as I had thought from a distance. I make it through to the other side and keep going. Firefighters working hard to control the forest fire, but no one stops me or suggests that I turn around. I keep going.

I make it to the campground at Diamond Lake. There is no smoke here, but the fires are not far away. The woman in the office says that the fire marshal had been here earlier today and assures me that the campground is safe.

When I find the spot I have been assigned on the map, I am worried. It's not a pull-through.

"I requested a pull-through," I told the woman. "I am new at this and not very good at backing in."

"Not to worry, I will call an escort for you," she promised.

I am worried anyway. I follow the man on the golf cart as we wind around the park. We arrive at my home for the next few days (if the woods around us don't go up in flames) and it is the most horrible site ever. It does not look long enough, and I have to back in with trees all around it.

My escort tells me, "It is going to be tough getting in here."

Really? I have almost zero experience backing up this Beast and I can see that.

"Give me a minute," he says. "Let me go ask the person in the site next to you if he will move his car. There is no way you can get in around it."

My escort tells me to pull further up so that my tail is just past the site, then turn my wheels sharply to the left and start backing up.

"*Stop!*" he shouts, and thinking I'm about to hit a tree, I slam on my brakes.

Back to his calm voice, he says, "Turn the wheel to your right and pull forward a bit. Okay. Easy. Easy. Keep going. Easy." I am certain I am going to hit the tree in front of me. He has me back up, then pull forward again. It takes a while and a lot of pulling forward then backing up again. He asks me to stop, then calls someone else on his radio.

The next guy shows up, hops out of his golf cart, and comes over to my window. "Don't worry. I have been doing this for years. We will have you parked in no time." I have serious doubts. He has me go around the circle and come from the opposite direction. I try to get him to park it for me. "No, ma'am. You can do this." He was right. It took some effort, but I was parked in less than five minutes. Off they both go on their golf carts. I plug in the electric, put the jacks down, and put the slides out. a/c is on and I do the best I could walking Emmi. The chipmunks are getting great pleasure in playing peek-a-boo with her.

I try to disconnect the rig from the hitch in my truck. No matter how much I tug, push, or pull, I cannot get it to release. I look around for help. I don't see anyone outside, so I approach the nearest fifth wheel I see. I knock on the door, explain my problem to the man who answers, and ask if he would mind helping me.

"Not at all," he said.

When we return to my site, the guy can't get the trailer to release from the hitch either. He tells me to start the truck and put it in reverse. Thinking perhaps I did not hear him correctly I asked, "You want me to back up with my jacks down?" He says, "Yes, just go easy. It will be fine. You'll see." I am certain I have asked a crazy man to help me. The truck is in reverse and my foot is shaking as I take it off the brake. I am afraid to put my foot on the gas. I imagine the jacks bending and the fifth wheel crashing into the tree behind me.

I look out my window at him and ask, "Are you sure?" I get the "Come on, lady, you asked for my help!" look and he calmly tells me yes. I put my foot on the gas and gently press down...a little more and I hear metal hitting metal. My heart skips a few beats and I put my foot on the brake. I am afraid to look back.

I hear a few more noises and then he tells me to pull forward. I do as he asks and hear a soft click as the hitch rocks backwards. I learned something new and am disconnected. Thank you! Thank you! Thank you!

After talking to Tyler, I decide I will drive tonight so I don't have to wake up so early. We will all come back tomorrow night for a few days of hiking. I pack a bag, put Emmi in the truck, and wind my way out of the campground at six o'clock.

I am on a two-lane road winding through the trees. The curves get sharper, and now I am headed down a steep decline with a narrow ninety-degree turn ahead. I don't think that I could make this drive with the fifth wheel behind me. I am barely around the curve when I see smoke ahead. As I get closer to the smoke, flames are lapping close to the road. Exhausted looking firemen, covered in soot, carrying axes and all sorts of other equipment, are coming out of the woods. I slow to a crawl, wondering if they are going to turn me around. A man waves me on through. I have never seen anything like this. The mountain is on fire and they are encouraging me to keep driving into it? While I keep going, I am worried that I should not have left the fifth wheel behind. I alternate between worrying about these switchback curves, the mountain being on fire and leaving everything I own behind, certain it will be a pile of ashes when I get back tomorrow night. But I keep driving.

In a flash, I remember I need gas and panic when I check my gas gauge, wondering how far the next gas station is. I know that I am on a mountain in the middle of nowhere, but I hope it's not far. I see a sign advertising food and gas just a few miles ahead. I am in luck! I make the turn when I see the next sign and begin another long, winding drive. I pass the pizza place that was mentioned on the sign, but I don't see a gas station, fearing I have wasted my precious gas on a wild goose chase. And now I have to use the bathroom. I can just imagine squatting in the woods with flames all around me. About the time I am ready to accept defeat and turn around, I see a lone island with two gas pumps on the right side of the road ahead. Another thought flits across my mind—*What if I cannot get gas because of the fire?* I pull into the station between the pump and the tiny old wooden building that serves as the store. The passenger side of my truck is barely six feet from the building.

A smiling old man comes through the door and around to me as I am getting out. At first I think that he is coming to tell me that I can't get gas. Then I remember this is Oregon. They pump gas for you. I first ask him to fill it up, then ask for directions to the restroom.

I follow his directions around the back of the building that could easily have been here a hundred years. The door is closed. I knock. No answer. I gently push the door open and see that the light is off. I reach in to turn the light on and want to turn back around. I tell myself that it's a long way to go before I am off of this mountain. There is no way I can wait. This is better than fire under my rear. It's tiny, but I am in. I turn around to close and lock the door, which doesn't latch or lock. I don't want to sit on the toilet seat, but I also need to figure out how to keep the door closed. I think about those fabulous bathrooms in the fancy restaurants and five-star hotels of my previous life. They were nice, but not much of an adventure.

I roll up my pant legs so they won't touch the floor, line the toilet seat with toilet paper, pull my pants down, and balance precariously with one foot on the floor and the other against the door. Oh! If only my Corporate America friends could see me now. It's touch and go for a minute, but I manage and am out the door as fast as possible.

I pay for my gas and tip the guy for pumping it, then make my way back to the main two-lane road. It's nine at night when I arrive in Cave Junction. As soon as I step through the door of the house, I smell amazing food. It smells like Granny's house. Andreea has chicken and dumplings bubbling on the stove for me. I did not even know I was hungry, but my mouth is watering. I wash my face, hands, and arms before devouring the entire bowl she puts in front of me. It's a perfect ending to my very long day.

I booked a jet boat ride in Grants Pass on the Rogue River to Hell's Gate for today. We are up early and the three of us are excited about the day. It's cool and sunny when we arrive. The weather is perfect for a day on the water. We get checked in and follow the directions down to a dock where we will board our boat. There are about twenty-five other people in our jet boat with us as we leave the dock for a thirty-six-mile trip. It's a leisurely ride down the river, taking in the sights and learning the river's history. Wildlife is all around us. There is even a majestic bald eagle soaring over our heads.

We tour Hellgate Canyon with its hundred-foot-high cliffs made famous by the cliff-jumping scene in *Butch Cassidy and the Sundance Kid* and Meryl Streep in *River Wild*. We see the location where John Wayne and Katherine Hepburn filmed *Rooster Cogburn*.

We hear more about the history of the Rogue Valley before stopping for lunch at the OK Corral. We are seated on an open-air deck overlooking the river and have an incredible view since the lodge is perched high above the water.

The trip back is a blast. We are zipping along the Rogue River and skimming across the surface as our captain spins us in circles. We are moving fast and as he makes the turn, it feels like the spin is in slow motion, a wave of water spraying up over us. We all duck down fast, trying not to get drenched. Too late. The sun is shining, but the water is cold, and the wind is chilly now that we are wet. Still, we all want to do it again. Even as an adult, there is something exciting about the thrill of being splashed on a fast-moving water ride.

We slow down as we enter the residential area then pull up to the dock. Hellgate Jetboat Excursions is definitely something I would do again *and* recommend.

The kids and I talk about getting the dogs and heading out to the campground. The fires are still burning around Diamond Lake and the smoke will only get worse. We decide I will stay here.

I THINK I CAN

I wake up this morning to sunshine and birds singing around me. It's time to go back to pick up my rig at Diamond Lake. That's if it is still there and did not burn to the ground.

The drive back is beautiful. The smell of charred wood still burns my nose, but the wind must have changed directions. I don't see much smoke and the flames are no longer on the side of the road. I stop at the same gas station in Prospect to fill up my tank. It does not seem nearly as far back in the woods today.

At the campground everything is fine. I am thankful the place did not go up in flames while I was gone. I pull in my slides, then disconnect the water, sewer, and electric that I never used. My pink duct tape on the tool box and nose of the Wildcat are my guides as I back up. I hear the sweet sound of "click." I am connected on my first try. I am nervous about the drive out, but I want to make it back to Vale Trails before dark and still see some sights along the way.

On US 20 I have to take a detour. I make it through the first roundabout and then another before getting back on 20. Between Bend and Burns, the road is mostly 135 miles of lonely highway stretching across the sagebrush. Its most memorable features are signs warning "No gas next 74 miles." The hamlets of Millican and Hampton are collections of abandoned businesses that seem to indicate people lived there just long enough to go broke.

Despite the sagebrush and juniper landscape that is the one constant of the Great Sandy Desert, the area still has some cool sights. From a turnout on the highway at Dry River Canyon, I can see mountain goats. Just west of Burns is the Bureau of Land Management's Wild Horse Corral where the federal government collects wild horses to put up for adoption.

The city of Burns is clearly struggling with economic hardship. I stop at the Chevron for gas, and it's super easy to get in and out. Have I mentioned how much I love Oregon gas stations? They are required to pump gas for you. It's a straight shot from Burns across the Harney Valley to Buchanan, in the foothills of the Stinkingwater Mountains. This time, I have plenty of gas.

After Buchanan the road leaves the desert, crosses the Malheur River, and winds toward Vale. Coming back east along this route was much easier than going west. For today, this is as far as I will travel. I have arrived back at Vale Trails in Vale, Oregon.

It has been less than a week since I was at this sad-looking park. I pull into the big dusty lot in front of the office, and I already see an improvement. Things are tidier and cleaner out front. When I climb out of the truck, the owner's son recognizes me and waves with a big smile.

A bell chimes when I open the office door and I immediately notice everything in the store is organized and looks much better. The giant, welcoming hug I get makes me feel like I am visiting family. The proprietor is chattering ninety miles an hour, asking about my trip, what I think of the things they have done since

I was last here, and telling me they are cooking steaks tonight with friends.

"You will be there, right?" she asks.

"Of course I will. Thank you!"

Once I am parked in my site, my escort starts telling the other men with us how I had traveled across the country by myself. While they are talking about how impressed they are, these three go to work hooking up my electric, water, and sewer.

Dinner is absolutely incredible. We have steak, baked potatoes, salad, and the most fabulous berry pie with fresh whipped cream that I have possibly ever tasted. We sit on their back patio talking until well after dark. Full and sleepy, I head back to my rig with a promise to come back. I am so glad I came back.

It's late morning when I leave Vale. I stop at the Love's to have an attendant fill my tank one more time in Oregon. The guy pumping gas, Zac, is smiling and chatting. He tells me about his kids and how much he loves being a dad. He also tells me he was not supposed to work today, but his alternator went out and he was picking up an extra shift. I thank him, wish him luck, and tip him what I normally would before going in to pay for my gas. I remember the hard times I had as a young mom so many years ago. I also remember so many people helping me. I ask the manager inside if she will give him an extra twenty dollars from me, but to please wait until I leave. As I am pulling out, the manager goes out with the twenty for Zac. I witness the biggest smile in my side mirror. It's not much, but I hope it helps. I am going to miss people pumping my gas.

I ease onto Interstate 84 East and it isn't long before I cross the Idaho border. My goal for the night is Wyoming. I follow the Oregon Trail through Boise, and pull off on Exit 62 at the rest area. I love the rest area signs that tell you the history of where you are. I think of the covered wagons as original RVs, people traveling from east to west with everything they owned banging and rattling around inside the covered wagons. Life was simple compared to our lives today, but definitely not easy.

After my short history lesson, I am barely back on the interstate when a UPS semi-truck pulling three trailers blasts past me. It scares the living daylights out of me! Once my heart rate returns to normal, I think what an idiot he is. Being confident is one thing, but being over confident will get someone killed. There is no way he could stop that truck if someone did not see him coming and pulled in front of him. I can only imagine what would happen if he swerved with three trailers behind him.

I start passing the wind turbines and I am in awe. These giant, majestic looking poles with airplane propellers on top are pretty darn incredible. It's interesting to think that once upon a time people harnessed the energy of wind with windmills. As power lines snaked across the country, the farmers' windmills became a rare sight. Our country grew, and we became greedy with our resources. Now harnessing the energy of wind is back. I think it is interesting how history repeats itself.

The smell of fresh-cut grass brings me out of my thoughts of the past. For as long as I can remember, this clean aroma is my favorite. I take a long, deep breath, savoring the smell…then I smell the dairy farm ahead before I even see it. I roll up my window and turn the air conditioner off as fast as I can, but it's too late. The horrible stench of too much urine mixed with the mud under hundreds, thousands of cows' feet, burns my nose. I try to hold my breath. It doesn't help. It's terrible. Sometimes, life stinks. Literally!

In the city of Twin Falls, I stop for gas at the Flying J Truck Stop. When I make the easy turn into the station and up to the pump, I recognize I was at this same station on my way west. I fill my tank then go inside to grab a sandwich. The male cashier asked if I did anything fun today. I told him about my trip and he asked if I had seen Shoshone Falls.

"Can I get in *and* out?" I asked, pointing to the Beast.

He looked across the lot and responded, "Well sort of."

I'm going for it!

I follow the signs directing me to the falls. Soon I am on practically narrow, single lane, bumpy roads, turning first left, then right, and back left. I make a left at the next sign onto an even bumpier dirt road. People coming towards me have to pull over in the grass until I pass. I spot a small paved parking lot ahead with a toll booth in the middle. I pull up and ask the gate attendant if she thinks I can make it into the park. She tells me that others have done it in the past. Not often, but they have done it. She encourages me when she says, "*You* can do it. I have faith in you!"

I pay my fee and the gate arm raises to let me through. The road is paved, but barely two narrow lanes wide. I make the first curve around to my right and can see the waterfalls in the distance ahead on my left. I can only look for a second, because now I am headed down a steep mountain with the Wildcat behind me. Turn wheel left! Turn right! Turn left! Turn right! There is no guardrail on my driver side and only a mountain jutting straight up out of the road on my right.

Breathe, just go slow and look straight in front of you following the road.

After my last sharp left turn hugging the mountain to my right, the ground levels out some and I see a large parking lot in front of me. I pull into a long spot so Emmi and I can get out. I made it!

There is a cliff ahead of me with a warning sign, "Danger: Stay off of rocks." I head towards it and see a small gravel path winding up the hill. There are some small waterfalls from here and think how pretty they are. Just a bit further up, a lot of people are in the large grassy area below. I backtrack to figure out how to get down there. As I near the bottom and come around the corner, I catch glimpses of larger waterfalls through the brush and trees. When I reach the grassy area, I could never have been prepared for what I am witnessing. I stand rooted to my spot as Emmi tugs at her leash. I cannot move and am not sure that I could even speak. Over twenty thousand cubic feet of water per second is pouring over a series of rapids split by tiny islands before plunging over a vertical horseshoe cliff 212 feet high and 925 feet wide. The falls split into five or six smaller falls, the ones I saw from above, and there is a massive fall at the northernmost section. I can finally move again and walk toward steep stairs leading to a platform. From here, I stand in the bright sun and feel the cool spray of water. There are rainbows everywhere. I take lots of pictures, then find someone to take one of Emmi and I with our backs to the falls. So far, this has been the most incredible sight along my journey.

We climb back up the hill to my truck and prepare to traverse the narrow road snaking up the mountain ahead of us. The only good news is that I don't have to worry about flying too fast down the mountain. The bad news is that my side is against the mountain and I cannot see the cliff with no guardrail to my right. I am trying to keep looking straight out at the road, but I hear gravel falling and am worried that each time I turn left, my back end is going to get too close to the cliff. I can see it happening. The back begins to slide, then pulls the truck back with it, plunging Emmi and me to our deaths, all because I wanted to see some waterfalls. It's just my fear talking. I go slow. I see the line of people up ahead waiting for me so they can drive down. I make it up the mountain alive and stop in the parking lot to catch my breath. I spent hours here, but it was worth taking the detour to Shoshone Falls.

I am back on the interstate that is down to two lanes because of construction. Posted speed limits are 70 and 80 miles an hour. I am now brave enough to drive 55, even 60 on straight roads, but there is a long line of cars behind me. They are just going to have to wait to pass me when the road widens back up. As the highway opens to four lanes, people are flying around me on the straightaway. The speed limit drops to 75 mph as the road ahead gets curvy. I am driving 50 mph and the other vehicles continue to pass me. I experience long, steep climbs and long, easy declines. I am doing well and speeding up to 65 mph on straightaways...until the wind hits me. I battle the wind a few more miles before taking Exit 357 to the Flying J Truck Stop for gas and a bathroom break. It was easy pulling in, but there is a semi blocking my forward path and I have to back up to get out. I am so proud! I managed this one on my own.

I am still on I-84 East and the road is horrible! Bump! Bang! Bang! Bump! Then *Kaboom*! I hit the biggest hole so far, an alarm goes off, and "trailer disconnected" is the warning flashing in front of me!

I am at the edge of a city in Utah with six to eight lanes of traffic heading east with me. I am not in the right lane and need to quickly get over to the shoulder of the road before my trailer comes loose and kills someone. My blinker on, I put my foot on the brake and try to move over. People are flying around me on both sides. I think I am going to be sick.

"Dear God, help me!"

I start gradually moving over. Other cars swerve, but I *have* to get off of the road right now. I make it to the shoulder with my fifth wheel still behind me. I put the truck in park, turn on my flashers, and press the emergency brake. I am shaking uncontrollably. Cars are flying so fast past me that my truck shakes too. I just sit still while I calm down. Everything is okay.

I open my door a crack and squeeze out of my truck. When I get to the back of the truck and open my tailgate, I know what that warning actually meant. I start laughing uncontrollably. There are no electronics on the hitch itself. There is no way the truck would have known if the actual fifth wheel had disconnected from the hitch. It was the power plug connecting the trailer lights to the truck lights that was disconnected. I totally overreacted. This is why people did not know I was trying to change lanes. My blinkers were not working on the trailer! I am plugged back in and have to just start moving into traffic to merge back onto the interstate.

I am on I-80 East now in Wyoming. The curves ahead are so sharp the speed limit drops from 80 mph to 55 mph. It doesn't even matter because now I am creeping up the mountain on a long, steep climb. I work hard to manage 45 mph going up one after another. The down sides are easy; none are steep.

I make it to Fort Bridger RV Park right before nine o'clock. I called earlier to let them know I would be late. The camp host waited for me and even escorted me to my spot. It was the largest, easiest pull-through spot I have encountered so far. The site was in the grass, but perfectly level. For a park so easily accessed from I-80, it's very quiet. I am exhausted. I get connected to power and water, then pop the slides out before feeding Emmi.

The steep climbs and steady declines today would have been easy if the roads were not so dang bumpy. My stomach muscles hurt. After a shower, I am hungry, and I want steak. I don't eat steak often, but that's what I want. Maybe my daughter and her fiancé will let me take them to a nice restaurant when I get there.

It's late morning when I pull out of Fort Bridger RV Camp and back on the interstate, continuing east. My goal today is to make it through Wyoming and conquer the mountain that made me think I was going to die on my way west. I hope to spend the night in Nebraska.

I-80 East is now a sea of bumps. I try changing lanes, but it doesn't help. Every bump reminds me of the challenges I have had in life. The landscape around me is indescribably beautiful. There is something good in every difficult moment. In my life, that has always been the case. You just have to look for it and recognize the good in the bad. No matter how bad it is, be grateful for what you have and where you are.

I climb, climb, climb, and coast down over and over. I pass an old Landau motorhome going down the road. It brings back memories of my grandmother. I wonder if that's where I get my wandering spirit. She remarried, and she and her new husband bought a decommissioned Frito-Lay truck and converted it into a small RV. They drove across the country in it together. I remember them stopping in East Texas to visit when I was a little girl. I thought it was the coolest thing ever. Later, she bought a forty-seven-foot sailboat. They sailed up and down the coast from Maine to the Bahamas. She and her husband got caught in a storm off the southern coast of Florida and she fell and broke her hip. While my grandmother was in the hospital, her husband died. She donated the boat to the Sea Scouts and bought a Landau. It was a top-of-the-line motorhome when she bought it. She moved in, hired a driver, and toured the country before settling in our driveway for the last year of her life. I am a little sad, but also thankful for the inspiration.

The road has gotten boring. There is nothing exciting, nothing new. It's not ugly or bad, just a boring drive now. I think this is the same as life. You can sleep through it or use the easy times to accomplish something.

I need to stop for gas and do payroll. I take Exit 209 and pull into the Flying J. It's not easy getting out. I have to back up, then make a sharp left. I hear a crash, but have no idea what I hit. I get out and walk all the way around the Beast. It wasn't me! I get back in and drive over to the big truck parking area, drag out my laptop, and press the power button. Nothing happens, my laptop battery is dead. I need to find electricity. I am in Carbon, Wyoming at Fort Steele, searching for electricity. All I find is a sign that warns me to be careful of rattlesnakes. Moving on!

I am on a new interstate as smooth as butter for several miles, then hit patches of bumps in between the smooth blacktop sections. I wonder who coordinated this project, or if the workers got lazy. I hit wind as I start a steep climb at 40 mph. It's about forty-five miles to Laramie and the mountain I thought would kill me when I came through headed in the other direction. The several large herds of deer I see over the next thirty miles give me something else to think about.

I stop in Laramie in search of power. It's also a good excuse to delay going over that mountain again. I see a sign for KOA. I hope they will let me rent a spot for an hour. I will just plug in and get my work done. I pull up in front of the office and leave my truck running with the air conditioner on so Emmi does not get too hot. When I get out of the truck, the heat hits me like a physical force. It's hard to explain. It's like there is no air at all, like opening a hot oven and getting your face too close when you reach inside. I open the door to the office and a cold blast of air hits me. This is much better. I am greeted with a friendly smile from the young girl at the counter. I present my request to rent a spot for an hour. She looks confused, so I explain that my laptop has died and I need to get some work done. She excuses herself for minute.

When she returns, she says, "You can just leave your rig parked where it is and use our power over at the table by the coffee pot. If you need our Wi-Fi, just let me know." This service is why I *love* KOA Campgrounds! I express my undying gratitude and go grab my things. It takes me less than an hour to finish and I am back on the road.

I am climbing at 35–45 mph. I am a bit nervous, but doing okay. I turn off the a/c and roll down my windows. The passing lane ends and the speed limit drops from 65 to 45 with no other notice before I hit the top and start going down. This time I know what to do.

"God, just stay close."

I press the brake hard one time and the engine roars, but grabs and pulls me back. I coast a bit, reaching 50 mph, then press the brake. Another roar and I am back to 45 mph. A few more times and I am at the bottom. I owned that mountain!

It's 7:20 p.m. when I drive into my campground in Nebraska for the night, a clean and pretty park. When I walk inside the office, it resembles an old lady's house. It's dark and drab, with a long row of glass cases filled with too many old, dusty knick-knacks. It's not that the people who owned it are unfriendly, I just don't feel comfortable. The woman sitting on a stool behind the cases pulls up my reservation, and after changing her mind several times, assigns a site to me. She tells me her son will escort me.

I had requested a pull-through, but my escort leads me to a side spot. I remind him that I am new at this and the spot does not look easy to maneuver into. He is a little short when he tells me he knows what he is doing, if I will just listen. At least I do not have to back in. It takes me a few tries and I can tell that he is getting frustrated with me. I am in good enough, as long as they do not park anyone else in front of me.

I am hooked up with my slides and awning out before dark. I get a cold Rose Lemonade and pull out a chair. I lean back in my chair with Emmi curled up in my lap to relax and enjoy the quiet, peaceful evening.

We are awake before daylight. The first thing I do is look out to see if someone has parked in front of me or behind me. We are good. I will be able to get out. I don't want to hang around this morning. I get all of the essentials taken care of and pull out. I stop to fill up my tank at the Gulf station on the corner right at the entrance ramp to I-80 East, an easy in and out.

The road is mostly flat and bumpy this morning. There are some hills every now and then, otherwise smooth sailing for now. I am looking forward to visiting the new friends I met when I was headed west.

Five miles from Interstate 29 South, the road I am on becomes a two-lane road through town, with construction, red lights, and 35 mph speed zones. It's not the first time I have experienced this on my journey. It just makes no sense to me.

Out of nowhere, *Bang!* I hit a bump I did not see coming. It interrupted Emmi's nap. She picks her head up from the seat beside me and looks at me like it was my fault. I am in Kansas City and have no idea what the speed limit is. Just as I wonder, I see a sign; 65 mph. I'm doing sixty, so I am good. For a minute, anyway. The road is now crazy, with crazy drivers to match. They are flying past me on both sides. The car in front of me swerves right. *Crap!* There is a semi-truck tire in the middle of the road! I don't have time or room to change lanes. I pray I can line it up with the middle of my truck and not tear anything up. I hear a loud thump. I can only imagine the damage that I have done, but I cannot stop here.

I get onto Interstate 49 South and take the next exit with a Flying J so I can get gas and check everything out. Another pump lane that is easy to get in and out of, or perhaps I am just getting better at it. I start the pump, grab a blanket out of the back seat, and climb under my truck. People are staring, but no one offers to help. No damage here, so I go back to crawl around under the fifth wheel. Nothing twisted, bent, torn, or missing.

I am barely back on the interstate when *thump!* I am sure this almost gave me a heart attack. I swear I heard the thump before I saw the bird that bounced off of my windshield. Out loud, I say, "Didn't his mama teach him not to dart into traffic?" I get another look from Emmi as if her human has totally lost it.

I call my friend Bev to let her know I am getting close. She gave me different directions than Siri. I am glad I called her since Siri wants me to turn right on a dirt road with tall weeds down the middle and tree limbs hanging into it. I am winding along back roads, completely enjoying the scenery when Emmi rockets out of her seat, barking ferociously. She's running from the front seat to the back seat, lunging at the window. I have no idea what is wrong, but this is not normal.

Then I know she must have smelled them before I saw them. It's just horses.

I turn left into the long drive where several deer are grazing in the field to my right. This does not phase Emmi. I know that I am on the right ranch, because John is mowing the side of the drive. We made it! I drive up the long lane to a big farmhouse on the hill in the trees. Bev is waiting on the porch for me.

John installed an RV pad across from the house for Barb's Class A not long after they met. It has water and electric. This is where I am supposed to park, but it's on my right. I need to be facing the other direction. I look ahead, surveying my options for turning around. The house and yard with plentiful trees are on my left. I cannot turn around there. Beyond that is a pole barn that houses farm equipment. Then there is a gate to the pasture just after the equipment storage area. I could possibly pull all the way up to the gate, back up, and turn around. I am getting better at backing up, but I don't love the idea. I honestly don't want to embarrass myself either. Across from the open gate area is a horse barn set back a bit. Just up on my right before the barn is an open grassy area. I ask John how soft the grassy area was. If it's hard enough to handle my weight, I think I can swing wide left in front of his equipment and turn around there. I can tell that he's worried about my navigating the turn by the look of concern on his face, but he tells me it can handle my weight.

Then he heads off ahead of me to move the wagon he pulls behind his tractor so I don't run over anything. I know I can make the turn without damaging anything, but let him go anyway. I cautiously drive forward, make the wide swing left, and turn right. I make a bumpy loop through the grass with plenty of room to spare before easing back onto the lane in the opposite direction.

Now that I am facing in the right direction, I have to pull alongside a retaining wall that runs across in front of where I will be parked. This turns out to be a bigger challenge than turning around. I pull forward but am not close enough. I back up to try again. Closer, but not straight enough. I try listening to John's guidance, but there is not enough room for me to pull forward. I have to back up. I am afraid that at this angle, the front tire of my truck is going to fall off of the retaining wall. John seems antsy, like he wants me to do it, but he is getting impatient. He is being very sweet. I can just tell by watching him. John has probably done this a thousand times and it's easy for him. Sometimes a girl's gotta recognize the benefit and let someone help her. I ask him, "Would you mind doing it?" From the relieved expression on his face, those simple words made his day.

I am parked and hooked to power and water in minutes.

Emmi is excited to see their dogs, Abigail and Poppy. She would love to get off of her leash and explore, like her friends are allowed to do. I just can't do it. If she sees a squirrel, she will be off and running. It's happened too many times. John keeps trying to assure me that she would be fine. Against my better judgement, I give in and Emmi is free. She runs and plays close by with the other two dogs. Still, I follow close by and John keeps telling me to stop worrying. The moment I relax and let my guard down, Emmi takes off at a full-out run. I call her, but already know she won't hear me. She is like a tiny thoroughbred: nose stretched out, ears back and slicing through the wind as she races around the equipment barn, with a huge doggy grin on her face.

John is a cowboy. His lungs and heart are not what they used to be. He has wranglers and cowboy boots on. None of these are good for running, but he takes off anyway. He heads in one direction while I kick off my flip-flops and head the other. He is behind her as Emmi flies around the building. I pray she doesn't keep going and head out into the cow pasture. If she comes back around, I can cut her off. Here she comes, darting back and forth, dodging Bev and I like a running back intent on making a touch-down. She miscalculates in an attempt to cut past Bev. I snatch her up as John comes heaving around the other side of the building saying, "Dang! I have never seen a little dog run like that!"

For dinner Bev serves the manicotti onto our plates and I slather real butter on my warm bread. Before I take my first bite, my mouth is watering, and I am starving. It tastes even better than it smells. I am full and instantly sleepy. I help clean up and take Emmi for a walk (on her leash!) before calling it a night.

It's a clear, blue sky, sunshiny day when I wake up. I can't wait to explore the ranch today. The sun is already blazing hot when we hop on the four-wheeler. We are going out into the pasture to check on the cows. A heifer is lying in the hot sun while the rest of the herd is across the pasture grazing in the shade under the trees. Although we try to get her up, no amount of coaxing gets her to move. She will surely die in this burning heat with no water. I am tenderhearted when it comes to animals. John, the cattle rancher says, "She will get up when she gets too hot. We'll check on her when we come back through."

Reluctantly, I get back on the four-wheeler.

We take a tour of the entire ranch. I enjoy it all but am preoccupied with worry for the cow we left baking in the hot sun. As promised, John drives back to the pasture to check on her. She is still down, covered in flies and breathing heavily. After another failed attempt at getting her up, John now appears concerned too. I suggest we go get one of the small rubber feed pans and a bucket of water from the barn. It should be low enough that she can get a drink lying down.

We get what we need and drive back to the pasture. I pray she is thirsty enough after one sip to get up and follow the water bowl if I place it just out of her reach. I have on jeans, but of course this Florida girl is wearing flip-flops. John pours water from the bucket into the pan. I carry it over and put it right in front of her head. She takes a drink. I step back and plant my feet on either side of the pan and pull it away from her. She is a big girl. She struggles to get up and follow the water. I know that she could hurt me if she knocks me down and lands on me. She lurches forward and is down again. I feel soft mush between my toes and discover I have just stepped in a fresh pile of cow poop. This is among one of the many reasons one should not wear flip-flops on a working ranch.

I wash my feet and put on boots before we go out to brush and feed the horses. The horses are coming in through the back of the barn when I walk in from the front. I take a deep breath, inhaling the sweet scent of hay and horses. I love this smell and miss it. For the briefest of moments, I wish I could live on a farm again, though I know I could not handle all the work by myself. The odds of finding a rancher close to my age with land and a Class A are slim to none. One of the horses hangs his head over the rail and gently snorts a breath into my hair. I let the dream drift away and enjoy what I have right now.

CHAPTER 9

OH POOP!

I open my eyes as the sun begins to peek through the blinds. I sit up, yawn, stretch, and climb out of bed. Emmi and I are going for a walk down the lane along the tree line. The birds are singing, the sun is shining, and I am enjoying the leisurely stroll. I hear water trickling and peer through the tall grass to find a stream. I love the sound. What a great way to wake up.

John, Bev, and I say our goodbyes and promise to see each other soon. Driving down the lane towards the road, I take one more look around this beautiful place. We pass through the gate at the end of the lane and turn left on our way to Tennessee, taking our time down the two-lane country roads crossing several narrow, single-lane old bridges along the way. We drive along beside pastures of horses and cows with fields of soybeans, corn, and hay in between. When a mama and baby deer cross the road ahead of us, I stop in the middle of the road to watch them pass.

"Thank you, God, for this incredible journey."

While we are rolling up and down hills on this two-lane country road, I wish there was a shoulder big enough to accommodate us. I would love to take pictures of the old barns. Some are in good shape, while others are collapsing with age. The tiny towns on my route each have at least one old church beside the road.

We are stopped in the town of Avilla, Missouri. It has the Avilla Post Office, which I learn was built in 1914 or 1915—depends who you ask—and was formerly the bank. I am sucked into the Wild West as I listen to the story of how the Bank of Avilla was robbed by the Irish O'Malley Gang on May 18, 1932. They kidnapped the cashier, Ivy Russell, who was left unharmed on the side of the road near Carthage. This story is so interesting that I will have to do some research on the demise of the Irish O'Malley Gang, but will save that for a rainy day. The bank closed here in 1944 and was empty until 1952, when it became the Post Office.

There is Bernie's Bar, which used to be Flo's Tavern, next to an oddly constructed stone building that was once a grocery store and is now boarded up. The odd stone building shares a wall with the two-story wood Victorian-style building built in 1885. It was the most impressive building in Avilla and also the IOOF (Independent Order of Odd Fellows) meeting hall called the Odd Fellows Lodge. Both the Odd Fellows and the Free Masons formed chapters here in about 1870.

Such a lot of history in what appears to be a ghost town now. After I pull back onto the country road, I am glad I stopped and learned their story.

Route 66 is closed ahead. I have to detour onto another narrow two-lane country road, with signs warning of horses pulling carts and "fresh eggs for sale." Along this short stretch of road, the barns are larger than the houses they tower over. Life may be hard work for these people, but maybe they have the right idea.

I merge onto 44 East around Springfield, Missouri, turn on one road, then another, and another. Finally, I am on a decent four-lane divided highway. There are crossovers, traffic lights, and small-town pharmacies here and there.

I am approaching a small gas station ahead. There is an old man holding a little girl's hand. She may be four or five years old, with lots of curly blonde hair. She has an ice cream in her free hand. When I am almost to them, the old man says something to her. She gets a big smile on her face, switches the ice cream to her hand shared with the old man, and excitedly waves to me. She is still waving in my side mirror as I pass them. People should wave more often. I used to walk along the side of the road we lived on with my own grandpa so many years ago, him spending real time with me and teaching me things. I remember him asking me as an adult if I knew how to never hit my fingers with the hammer when I was driving a nail. I thought hard, trying to remember if he had taught me this. Eventually, I said no. His response still makes me laugh. "Never hold the nail. Have someone else hold it." He laughed and laughed at his joke. My grandpa is gone, but I am reminded of how blessed I am to have had him spend so much time with me. I am grateful for that old man behind me spending time with this little girl. Maybe because of it, she will grow up to be an amazing woman who continues to make a difference in the lives of others.

I stop for gas at Lucky's Country Store. You know it's a true country store when you see a front porch and men sitting in chairs watching the day go by. It's easy to get in, but a tight left to circle out. The men on the porch watch as I barely skim past the parked car on my right. If this were the South, those men would have jumped up to move the car in my way or direct me through. Instead, one shouts out "You got it, girl!" Either I look like I know what I am doing, or they just have more faith in my abilities than I do myself.

I still have about an hour until the complete solar eclipse. I climb steep rolling hills up and down, one right after another. I encounter 55–60 mph and even some 45–50 mph all the way through the hills. As the temperature begins to drop and the sky gets darker, it looks the same as when a storm is coming. I really want to watch the eclipse. There is no traffic. It's kind of eerie. I am guessing everyone else stopped a long time ago to watch. I am looking for an exit, but there isn't one. I should have stayed at the country store. I am now looking for a shoulder big enough and safe enough for me to pull over and watch from the side of the road. It is not going to happen. There are temporary signs saying not to stop on the side of the road and police officers everywhere to keep it from happening. Everything around me goes dark as I drive through the eclipse above me.

My road becomes Interstate 57 North for a bit. I am taking Exit 12 so I can stop at the Flying J for gas. As I come off of the interstate, someone zips around me on the shoulder to my right at the same time I am turning right into the gas station. When I see them in my mirror, it's too late. I slam on my brakes. I can just imagine everything in the fifth wheel behind me crashing forward and finding a pile of destruction when I open the door. They are moving so fast I just know they are going to collide with me. I hold my breath and brace for impact. I hear gravel flying. The car swerves around in front of me and bounces back onto the road.

There is no doubt in my mind that a guardian angel is watching over me.

This station is super busy. It's not hard getting up to the pump, it's getting out that has me concerned. The only way out is the driveway behind me I came in through. I have to manage a tight U-turn that appears impossible. I get out to view the situation and a couple on a motorcycle suggests I pull forward as far as possible then back up while turning my wheel. They will help watch my back so I don't hit the pump behind me. I am nervous as I back up an inch at a time. The man signals for me to stop and turn my wheel sharply to the left as I drive forward making the U-turn. I move slowly. My thoughts are everywhere. "What if I hit the pump? Pray. Trust God. But I can't see what's on my right at this angle. Have faith." Cars and motorcycles are zipping around me. The eclipse is over and suddenly everyone is in a hurry to move on with their day. I make it out and back on the road without a scratch.

There is a bridge ahead. I feel the anxiety creeping in because bridges scare me. To make matters worse, the left lane is closed, making my path really narrow. I try to relax, knowing that if I am gripping the wheel, it will be even harder to cross. I am at the foot of the bridge, and I'm sure there is no way I will fit. I know in my brain that if it was truly too narrow, there would have been a sign. What if there was and it blew away? I slow down to a crawl. I am shaking as I grip the wheel and watch behind me through both side mirrors. I am way too close to the edge. The smallest gust of wind will push me into the guardrail, throw me over the side, and I'll fall to my death in the water below. My fate could be different if I hit the rail, overcorrect, and end up wrecking in a tangle of metal. I struggle to calm myself.

"God?" I whisper through my tears. I am reminded of Philippians 3:13: "Brethren, I count not myself to have apprehended: but this one thing I do, forgetting those things which are behind, and reaching forth unto those things which are before." I should stop looking behind me and look ahead, beyond the place I am in. I do this and my fears dissolve. Coasting across to the end of the bridge, I think this is more than just a lesson in pulling the Beast behind me across a narrow bridge. Life is the same. We often get tangled up in a problem and cannot find our way out because we look behind us instead of ahead.

I have to cross another bridge when I reach the Illinois State Line. Concrete barricades move me into another narrow space across the bridge. It's a tight squeeze, but I make it across without damage or another moment of panic. Now another bridge as I cross the Ohio River on I-24 East into Kentucky. This one was easy. I just kept my eyes on the road ahead.

I am not having any luck finding a place to spend the night. Everyone is booked all the way through Nashville and beyond. Apparently this was the best path for watching today's eclipse, and campgrounds have been booked for months. As I cross the Tennessee State Line, it's getting dark. There are deer in the road that I don't see until they are almost right in front of me. I have no idea how, but thankfully I manage to get around them without hitting one.

I love Nashville, but seriously, I hope to never drive through it pulling the Beast behind me again. About forty miles east of Nashville, I pull off at the Pilot Travel Stop in Gordonsville, hoping to find a spot to sleep for the night around back with the truckers. I am in luck! There is a long opening along the edge of the parking lot. I slide in and get situated for the night.

It is hot and muggy. I can't sleep. With no power, I cannot run the a/c. Without the slides open, I cannot open windows to get a cross breeze. It's miserable. I wish I had gotten my battery-powered camping fan out of storage before leaving Jacksonville.

It's 5:30 a.m. when I wake drenched in sweat. I have tossed and turned all night and am exhausted. I decide to give up on sleep in favor of dry clothes and getting outside where at least there might be some air.

Emmi and I hop in the truck with the cold air conditioner blasting. We are ready to hit the road as soon as we pull up to the pump for gas. Ahead, a truck and camper are occupying the spot I need to be in. It's the only pump I can get into from this angle without going out and down the road before coming back. They have been there a while. Surely, they will be done in a few minutes. I ease out of my space and get as far left as possible so that I am in line and out of the way. I pull as far forward as I can, right against the curb by the store, where cars leaving the pumps can still get out. I wait for five minutes and this truck with the camper is in no hurry. I go inside the store to see if anyone knows where the people pulling the camper are. I find out that they broke down there last night and are not going anywhere anytime soon. I am going to have to get gas further down the road.

I get back in the truck and start to leave. I look in my right-side mirror before easing out toward the exit. A semi-truck is coming from the back parking lot, planning to squeeze between me and another big truck on the far right. I don't think there is enough room for him. I turn on my blinker to let him know that

I will get out of his way. He keeps coming. I flash my lights. He keeps coming. He pulls alongside me, just inches from the side of the Wildcat. I put the truck back in park, watch my mirror, and hold my breath. His window is even with mine now. I glance over at this young, angry driver. With a bright red face, he is shaking his fist and ranting. He looks like he is either going to have a stroke or a heart attack. All I can do is shrug and stick my tongue out. He creeps forward, trying to get by without hitting me. If he had let me go ahead of him, he would already be out of the lot and on the highway.

I am low on gas, but out and back on the interstate. I keep watching for the next truck stop. I see a sign for Love's at Exit 280. Small-town truck stops are not set up for morning school and work traffic. There is a traffic light where I need to turn, but people are so backed up that only one or two trucks get through before the light turns red. It seems like an eternity before I make it into the station and up to the pump.

I thought getting in was bad. I am back at the light waiting to turn right. My light turns green, but traffic is stop-and-go for miles and cars are blocking the intersection. I wait through three lights the same way. This is the country, and people are supposed to be laid back. This is the South, people are supposed to be polite. Why are these people so rude? I am tired from lack of sleep, beginning to get hangry, and darn near road rage. This southern girl is done being nice. My light is still red, but the second there is a foot of space, I start pulling out. I am bigger than they are. They will just have to hit me or wait. The driver lays on his horn, but I keep going.

I am heading up a steep mountain behind a semi. 35 mph is about all we can manage before we hit the peak and start down the other side. Now I have to work at keeping my speed below 45 mph. Climb up, roll down. Climb up, roll down. It took me long enough, but I am getting the hang of this!

It's noon. I am still driving through Tennessee when I hear someone honking beside me. I pull over. The other rubber seal over my passenger side slide is coming out. Pink duct tape to the rescue! It's much easier to secure it without the wind.

I make it across the French Broad River bridge alive. I am hanging with the truckers. Only one has passed me. I go through a tunnel, then drive through thirty miles of steep, up and down, curvy switchbacks through the Great Smoky Mountains into North Carolina. The scenery is green and absolutely gorgeous. I go through another tunnel. Pulling the Beast is getting easier!

I am still on I-40 East, just past Asheville, North Carolina. It's different here than it was in the west where I was surprised by mountains. I start seeing signs telling me I am going down a mountain soon and that the speed limit is 35 mph ahead. As I start down, there are flashing signs overhead warning me when I am going too fast. I have to make it six miles through intense curves all the way down. Each one is easier than the last.

I am only a mile down when I see brake lights and smoke pouring up from the road, and the semi swerves. He is several cars ahead of me, but I am trying to slow down enough to stop if I need to. He swerves right when the road makes a sharp curve left. He hits the guardrail. Sparks flying, he yanks the wheel left, dragging part of the guardrail with him. I watch in horror as his trailer keeps sliding right over the side of the mountain. It's like a slow motion video. There he is, hanging by a thread, his cab tangled in the guardrail and his trailer dangling over the side of a mountain. Cars are all pulling over to help. I am still going too fast to get off the road and stop, so I move into the left lane and keep going, praying he gets out alive.

The truck driver surely had more skill and experience than me, and still, he wasn't ready. I know the fear he felt when he was losing control. I can't imagine what went through his mind when the cab of his truck struck the guardrail, or when he tried to regain control and the trailer swung around and went over the side before he was able to stop.

Live life, never give up, and take every second chance you are given. Do the things you have dreamed of doing before it's too late.

Another mile down, a Jeep Cherokee pulling a small utility trailer has plowed through the guardrail and into the trees. It must have happened mere minutes before. Cars are stopped on the side of the road with people getting out and running toward the Jeep. I merge left and pray. I pray the rest of the way down the mountain.

I feel a rush of excitement and accomplishment when I reach the bottom. I also thank God for getting me through it. I now know my fear of that first 6 percent grade decline for five miles less than a month ago was justified. Today, I conquered another one.

I am getting close to Winston-Salem when I find myself in the middle of rush-hour traffic. A small car jumps in front of me and hits his brakes.

"Lord, help me stop!"

Before I hit it, the car jerks into the next lane. We are all soon at a crawl, then stopped. I am only eighteen miles from my exit and we are going nowhere. Apparently, there is a bad wreck ahead. We inch along for a bit then stop, inch along then stop. I am stopped on the interstate only ten miles from my exit for ten minutes straight! After six bottles of water in three hours, I am grateful for the bathroom in the Beast behind me! I pull over onto the shoulder and take advantage of my traveling bathroom.

I call the RV Park to let someone know it is going to be after five when I arrive. The sweet, sweet lady is going to wait for me. I wait for traffic to start moving and turn on my blinker. Immediately, someone flashes their lights. They are going to let me in. I am now rolling along at the posted speed limit. Four miles from my exit, the rubber seal over my slide is coming out further. Let it fly. I am not stopping until I get to Clemmons!

The minute I pass through Tanglewood's gates, I am welcomed by the majestic oaks overlooking the entrance, and lining the road. At 5:10 p.m., I roll into the drive at the Tanglewood Park office. I am greeted by a friendly face inside the office. She hands me my packet and gives me directions to the back of the property where the RV Park is located. I am to stop at the camp host's site. They will lead me to Site 9.

I wind my way back through the park on a narrow road. Trees tower over the road along the way, then open to a large dog park on one side and a big green grassy field on the other. I find the camp host and tell him that backing into a spot is not one of my best skills.

"Don't worry," he says, "I have been doing this for years. Just listen to my directions and you will be fine." Twenty minutes later, I am getting out of the truck and letting him try. I don't feel like such an idiot when it takes him another twenty minutes with another guy's help. I learn that this is the hardest spot in the park to back into and just as hard to get level.

I plug into the electric, turn on the air, and open the slides. Back out to hook up water and the sewer line. I have my sewer line stretched out and connected to the drain. I remove the cap to connect the drain line to the fifth wheel. I discover too late that the bumpy road has wiggled the valve pull for my black water holding tank open. In a gush, my black water holding tank half-empties on the ground and over my flip-flop-clad feet before I can get the valve closed. If I did not need a shower before, I definitely do now! I connect the sewer line and stand up, wondering if anyone saw this crappy situation just occur. I start laughing, and as hard as I try, I cannot stop. Every time I think I have it under control, the laughter bubbles anew. Not so long ago, this would have upset me.

I finally manage to clean up the ground, rinse myself off with frigid water from the hose, and drop my stinky flip-flops in the trash. I wish I could take my clothes off outside and do the same with them. Probably not a good idea. If only Corporate America could see me now. After a much-needed hot shower, I am on my way to meet my daughter and her boyfriend for that steak dinner they promised me.

I am leaving Tanglewood Park in Clemmons, North Carolina today. I am pulling out with rubber seals tied to the back ladder and pink duct tape adorning the Wildcat, but I am going home.

Sometimes Siri is great with directions, and sometimes, not so much. She tells me to turn left out of the park onto 158. It gets me where I am going, but soon I find she has led me to a narrow roundabout just ahead. I am barely crawling along so I can yield to others and make my turn into it. No one is letting me in, and people actually sped up when they saw me coming. I stop and wait. There is a line behind me and still, I wait. Where did all of these people come from? I am not in the city and it's after nine o'clock. I eventually decide I am bigger than they are and start to slowly inch my way out into oncoming traffic. Surely, they won't hit me. The first few swerve around me. The others don't have a choice. It's stop or hit me. I get into the loop and take the first right onto 801. From there I take I-40 West to I-775.

I am doing more than "bumping" down the highway. It's more like banging, because I cannot avoid the massive craters in the road. Traffic is now at turtle speed and I encounter stupid people. It's the nicest word I can think of to describe them. They are jumping in front of me and the semi-trucks. Don't they know we leave space in front of us on purpose so we have room to stop without hitting the vehicles in front of us?

A car flies up the on ramp, misses my nose by inches as it jets across in front of me, then keeps merging left into the path of the eighteen-wheeler coming up on my left. I see brake lights. If the car didn't scare me enough, the trucker laying on his horn right beside me did. We are at a dead stop for five minutes before moving. I am still going slow in the right lane so I can stop if needed. People are flying around me. There is a pickup truck merging onto the interstate up ahead and people are not moving very fast. He swerves in front of the cars ahead. People are slamming on their brakes and swerving around him. I don't think I can stop in time. I am literally standing on my brakes. The smell of brakes and pavement burns my nose. My heart is pounding. I made it this far without an accident, and on my last day of this incredible journey, it's going to happen.

I watch my mirrors. First left, but there is a semi at my back end. To the right, there is not enough room on the shoulder. I concentrate on not closing my eyes. With both feet on the brake, I push back against my seat with my whole body, try to relax my arms and brace for impact. I hear part of a Bible verse in my head: "He will command his angels concerning you to guard you…" I had to look it up later to find that it is from Psalm 91:11.

"God. I need those angels now!"

The last car between me and the truck swerves left just in time. I stop about five feet behind the guy who almost caused a massive pile-up. Thank God the others swerved, or I would not have been able to stop.

I am on I-77 South now. It's eighty degrees outside and rain clouds are ahead. Crossing the South Carolina state line, the roads are better. The speed limit is 55 mph, but people are driving 70 mph. I stay in the right lane at 55. Up and down hills, some steeper and longer than others. The highway gets bumpy around I-20. It's like a mechanical bull ride on a rollercoaster. It gets smoother on I-26 East. When I see the signs for Spartanburg, I think of graduating high school and Converse College. If life had been different about thirty years ago, this is where I would have gone to college. I wonder for a minute what it would have been like. Life would have been different. I had a choice at that fork in the road, get married and have children or go away to college. I don't know if it would have been better, or worse. I just know I would probably not be on this incredible journey if I had chosen the different path. My life may have been a struggle because of the choice I made, but it is why I am who I am. I am glad I made the choice that I did, grateful for the lessons learned along the way, and the opportunity to do what I am doing right now.

As I am reminiscing, the skies turn blue and the sun bright. It's ninety degrees outside as I take Exit 139 for gas at the Pilot. It wasn't easy getting in and making the turn for the pump (thank goodness for long hoses!), but it was easy getting out.

I am not back on the interstate for long when I glance in my mirror and notice that my awning is loose at the back. Bumping and jerking down the road, I pray it does not come completely undone. I just want to get home.

Workers are mowing the side of the interstate as I merge onto I-95 South and the constant bumpy patches in the right lane get my attention. I move left, then back right when someone is behind me. It is ninety-nine degrees and raining when I pass the Savannah, Georgia exit. The wind is picking up, the sky is getting darker, and I can see lightning ahead. I drive through the massive thunderstorm and am just an hour away from home when I am treated to the familiar sight of flapping rubber seals behind me. I slow down and plan to stop at the next exit. I keep checking my mirrors. I glance just in time to see one end of the awning frame on my passenger side break free from the Wildcat. Forget the exit—I am pulling over on the shoulder of the road! I am able to pull one of the seals completely out and put it inside the camper. I am tying the other to the door handle when I feel like my feet are on fire. Before I look down, I already know. I am standing in an ant bed. I kick off my flip-flops and dance around on the side of the road, getting the evil creatures off of my feet. That accomplished, I dig out some bungee cords and my pink duct tape. I climb the ladder in back to my roof and cat-crawl across to where the awning frame is now disconnected. I lay down on my stomach and inch closer to the side as trucks fly by, shaking my rig. Looking over the edge, praying I do not plummet face-first onto the ground below, I notice that the replacement screws are missing. The bumpy highways have rattled them out, and now the holes are stripped. I manage to tape and bungee everything back together and get off of the roof without killing myself.

I go through one thunderstorm after another. As I merge onto I-295, I am praying my patches will hold. It's almost five o'clock when I make it home to Flamingo Lake and back into my spot. I am drenched but am un-hooked, level, and have power.

I read something by David Avocado Wolfe today: "Travel while you're young and able. Don't worry about the money, just make it work. Experience is far more valuable than money will ever be."

I know that I will find a way to travel more.

CHAPTER 10

NEVER GIVE UP

Hurricane Irma is getting closer to Florida and no one knows which direction she will go. This hurricane is not going to miss us. Will she hit the West Coast, East Coast, or go right up the middle? I have Plan A and Plan B. There is a mandatory evacuation by noon Friday for me. If she comes to the East Coast, I will pull the fifth wheel to Spirit of the Suwannee Music Park (SOSMP) in Live Oak. My neighbor Rex will follow me. I call my sister-in-law to see if she can book a hotel room for Daddy in Live Oak. She tries, but nothing is available. Everything is booked. I call SOSMP to see what they have available. We booked two RV sites and a cabin for Daddy. If Irma goes west, I will head north. It will be an adventure either way.

Irma is going to hit the East Coast. Rex decided to leave this morning, but I have a lot to get done before I can leave. How did I accumulate so much stuff in my new simple life? It's hot and muggy outside with no breeze. I get all of my solar lights out of the yard and into a bin that will go into my storage building out back. They are so pretty at night, but I have way too many. I get my flags and other yard art into the shed as well. I need to get rid of more stuff. I fold up my grill and struggle to get it into the storage compartment under my fifth wheel. It's bulky and has to tilt a certain way, but I am bent over and keep bumping my head on the storage compartment door. It seems like an eternity before I get it inside, fold up my chairs, put them on top of the grill, and shut the door.

I pile all of my deck furniture in a heap on top of the deck and up against the doors of my storage building, then climb into the back of my truck to dig ratchet straps out of the toolbox. I use these to wrap around my storage shed and tie the furniture pile to the deck. The heavy, thick hot air is making this harder than it should be. I climb on top of the picnic table to remove the top from my gazebo. I tug and pull, pull and tug, and I can't get the darn thing off. Maybe if I have leverage from higher up?

I have to undo all of the ratchet straps and move stuff so that I can get my ladder out of the storage shed. I had help putting this thing together. Now I remember that it took two of us to stretch the canvas top over the last corner. I get the ladder situated where I can use it and the table simultaneously. Probably not the safest thing to be doing by myself, but I don't want to ask for help. Everyone else is racing against the clock just like I am. Up the ladder I go. One side starts to sink in the soft dirt and the ladder tilts to the right. I put my left foot down one rung to balance the weight on the ladder. I am leaning left and stretching right. I am getting frustrated and the tears are threatening to fall. Just as the corner of the canvas starts to slip over the edge, my ladder starts to fall. I lean back the other direction and keep pulling. As the canvas comes off, the ladder falls backwards, and I jump forward.

"Dear God, don't let me hit my head on that table! I have too much to get done!"

I land on my feet on top of the picnic table. Three more corners to go, but they are easy with the tension gone. I put the ladder away and secure everything with ratchet straps once more.

The only thing I have left on my site is to move the big storage bench out away from the fifth wheel. I am dripping with sweat, covered in dirt, and now I have to move something heavier than I am. I push and push. My feet keep sliding out from under me in the crushed concrete and the storage bench is not budging. I put my welcome mat on the ground beside it and kneel down to push. Still nothing. And here come the tears. I sit on my steps with a bottle of water and have a pity party, tears rolling down my face. Dang, I wish there was a man in my life to help me. I can't do this by myself. Then I remember my daughter believing I could fix the watermelon she dropped at five years old. I can move mountains. I've just gotta have faith.

I get up to try again. I decide to open the lid and pull it instead of pushing it. When I do, it registers how stupid I was. The bench itself is not heavy. It is made of plastic. It's the crap I have in it that is heavy. In less than five minutes, everything is out, the bench is moved, and everything is safely back inside.

I get a cold Rose Lemonade out of the fridge and sit down on my steps again to watch the gorgeous sunset. It's the calm before the storm. I realize how blessed I am. While many people in Jacksonville are moving their belongings to the highest place in their homes and boarding up windows, I can take my house with me.

People are worried about coming home to nothing. For me, home is where I park, and I have everything.

It's evacuation day. I am up early and go for coffee with Daddy. I need to make sure he has remembered to pack everything he might need. Once I am satisfied he has all of the meds, clothes, and toiletries he will need, I load everything into his truck.

I drain my tanks and fill my fresh water tank, pull in my slides, and disconnect everything. I grab my purse, load Emmi and her bed into the truck, and call Daddy, telling him we will be on our way in five minutes and to be ready to pull out behind us. Using my pink duct tape guides, I hook up to the truck on the first try. We are headed west on I-10 towards Spirit of the Suwannee Music Park for another adventure.

I call Rex to let him know we were on our way. He had already picked up his golf cart rental that we would share and toured the park. He loves it. He told me the spots I had reserved were really steep. He wasn't even sure my fifth wheel would fit between the trees. He had found better spots and would be waiting for us when we arrived. I feel like I am surrounded by angels.

People started evacuating from the Keys and South Florida earlier in the week. Hotels and campgrounds were booked all the way past Atlanta. Traffic is slow, but not as bad as I expected it would be. The slowest places are near rest areas. People are lined up to get off. As I pass the rest areas, I notice they are overflowing with people who are running for their lives. Many are sleeping on the ground.

I pull into the park and ease through the Live Oak trees with their moss swaying in the breeze, and the same magic as always happens. I feel like I am in another world. One where worries disappear and life is lighter.

I stop at the office to get checked in and pick up the keys to Daddy's cabin before we are escorted to my site on River Road. With Rex and my escort guiding me, backing into my spot is easy. But life can't always be completely easy. I cannot get the fifth wheel to release from the truck hitch. I try dropping the jacks a little, but it still won't come off of the truck. I can see the pin that is stuck. I break out the hammer. One tap and it's released, but the pin is rusted and breaks. Not good. I cannot pull the trailer without all of the pins in place. It's too dangerous. Rex comes up with a temporary solution that I pray holds.

I take Daddy to his cabin and get him settled before setting up camp down the road. With Rex's help, it's just like home in no time.

Now to go pick up Daddy's golf cart and get some lunch at the café. It's a clear, sunny day, so we sit outside at a table with an umbrella shading it. I see lots of familiar faces and get lots of hugs from people. Even Daddy is enjoying himself. He talks and talks and talks with a big smile on his face. It has been a long time since I saw him be this social and this happy. I sit back with the warm sun on my face, breeze blowing through my hair, and enjoy watching him. I feel safe in my happy place tonight.

This morning, I am taking Daddy on a golf cart tour of the park. I can't wait to show him why I love this place. We ride for hours. I show him the entire park. We ride around the lake where Hope and I have camped every spring and fall for years. I tell him the story of my first experience tent camping here with Hope, how I was afraid to leave camp after dark. I take him through the woods and show him the airstrip, the flip-flop tree, and the old horse stables. I share story after story of my experiences here.

As we wind through the woods, the river appears ahead of us. We turn right to drive along the edge high above the river. We wind along through the narrow path trying to stay away from the edge. All of a sudden, we stop, stuck between two trees. We cannot go forward or backward. I get off the cart and Daddy gets in the driver seat. I am going to push from the front. I tell Daddy that he has to push the gas, but be ready to stop fast. If he doesn't stop quickly, he and the cart will tumble off the rocky ledge and plummet into the river. He promises me that we can do this. I push as hard as I can as Daddy hits the gas. He flies out backwards and my heart is hammering. He stops just in time. We find a path that is easier and laugh all the way back to camp. He talked about our near-death experience for days. I am so glad I brought Daddy with me.

I drop Daddy off at his cabin for a nap and head back to my site. Rex has just returned and says someone told him that the hurricane was now headed west. They are probably going to evacuate the park. He hooks up a TV outside so we can watch the weather and decide what to do. Someone from the park on a golf cart just pulled up at our site with a notice. We have to be out of the park by 5:00 p.m. I have no idea where we are going to go. I think of all of my friends down the west coast of Florida who decided not to evacuate because Irma was headed east. Now it's too late. I am seriously worried about them.

We don't have a lot of time. Rex and I need to break camp and hook up both campers. I need to also get Daddy packed and loaded with his dog, Scruffy, then return our golf carts. I don't have time to call places for us to park. I call Hope and ask her for help while we get everything together here. We are almost finished and Hope calls to say there is nothing as far north as South Carolina. Everyone is booked.

We are moving out of Irma's path again. Rex decides he is just going to drive north as far as he can. I call my sister and tell her we are driving back to Jacksonville for the night. I will park the fifth wheel in the street and Daddy will sleep inside. We can figure out where to go once we get there. If we leave Jacksonville by morning, we have time to head north.

Headed back the direction we came from on I-10 East from Live Oak, the traffic is horrific. Then it starts to rain. As we get close to Jacksonville, traffic is stop-and-go, bumper-to-bumper. If all else fails, there are about twenty Emergency Disaster Services and Demand Support Services Mobile Sleeper Unit Semis around me on the interstate. There are several wrecks along the way. One of them causes us to change lanes just before I have to change back for our exit. Someone lets me over and I get onto 295. I continue glancing in my mirror, but I can no longer see Daddy behind me. I slow way down, thinking he will catch up. Daddy gets lost if he goes anywhere other than Walmart or to see his doctor. I try to call him, but he never answers his phone when he is driving. I call Rebecca and David to see if they can try to find him.

I get through Orange Park and then to the Buckman Bridge as the wind starts to pick up. This bridge is over three miles long and sixty-five feet above the water. I slow to a crawl and fight to hang on, talking to God all the way across.

"God, you got me this far. Please get me across this bridge in one piece!"

Thank God, there are not many vehicles on the bridge with me. I am all over the road as one blast of wind after another slams into my side. And then I am on the other side. Only a few more miles to go. As I am getting off of the interstate, my sister calls to say they found Daddy and are talking him through directions to their house.

I am safe. Back in Jacksonville for at least the night, parked in front of my sister's house. I still would not have changed going west. It was such a great relaxing weekend and I was not sitting in bumper to bumper traffic with angry evacuees.

Irma made landfall with 125 mph winds as a Category Four hurricane in the Keys this morning. She is tracking up our west coast then expected to turn northeast and expected to make landfall again somewhere around Naples. There is still too much unknown regarding the direction and strength of Irma. Traffic is still horrendous because people from further south waited to evacuate. There are no campgrounds or hotels with openings for hundreds of miles. We decided to stay put at my sister's in Jacksonville.

I back the Wildcat into the driveway as close to the garage as possible without hitting the house. Her nose is facing northeast, so wind doesn't hit her broadside. We are tucked in around branches of the giant tree in my sister's yard with slides out. I hope I made the right choice.

Irma made landfall again in Marco Island, south of Naples. Hurricane-force winds are extended up to eighty miles from her center. Naples is reporting 130–142 mph gusts. Like a giant chainsaw, Irma is carving a horrendous path up through the state of Florida. It's too late to leave now.

My brother-in-law is grilling, and we are emptying the refrigerator for dinner. We expect to lose power any time. The wind is starting to blow, and we are getting some of the hurricane rain bands.

The radar maps and pictures from space show Irma's reach covering almost the entire state of Florida now. The wind is getting worse, but no rain. Nervous, I decide to go to bed early. Emmi and I are in the Wildcat to weather the storm. It's hot and humid inside with no power and I cannot sleep. I need some air. I open the hatch in my room and sleep with my head at the foot of the bed under it. When it starts to rain, it should wake me up when my face gets wet.

It's two in the morning when I wake up to water splashing in my face. I close the hatch and pray that God will keep us safe. I doze off again. It's three now, and the wind is raging, and branches are falling on my roof.

"Please God, don't let that giant tree fall on me!"

I try for an hour, but I can't go back to sleep. I open the door of the camper to a war zone. Limbs are everywhere, and the rain is coming down in sheets. I scoop up Emmi and we run to the garage to watch from what I hope is a sturdier roof over our heads. A large branch falls, barely missing us, but we make it inside.

I go inside and make a cup of coffee then pull out a camp chair to sit in the garage, my theatre seat for the show. It's crazy outside! I try to find a weather update on my phone but nothing will load. No internet and no cell service. I have no idea where Irma is, how big she is now, or where she is tracking. I don't know if the family and friends not with me are okay. I can't do anything except watch, wait, and pray.

The sun is up and the streets all around us are flooded but we are safe. The rain is gone, but the wind is still blasting. I join everyone else on the back patio. In the daylight, things are not as scary. We watch the trees being bent one direction, then back the other direction. Someone notices a red cardinal holding on to the branches. No matter how hard the wind blows, this guy never lets go. He is being ferociously tossed back and forth, up and down, yet he hangs on. The cardinal is our bright spot to focus on. He hangs on until the wind subsides. He never gave up.

My sister, niece, and I put on rubber boots to go see how the neighbors fared. In some areas, the water is over our boots. There are only a few trees down here, but limbs, leaves, and debris are everywhere. I also want to see if I can get a phone signal. We walk out of the neighborhood, up towards the school where I am able to reach people to make sure they are okay.

We are about four hundred miles north of Hurricane Irma's first landfall in South Florida. Now Jacksonville is being swallowed by water, with heavy rain and a record storm surge turning streets into churning rivers and wind-whipped waves crashing through windows.

I am so grateful to be safe and to know that my family and friends are as well. Just another reminder of what's important in life. No matter how crazy it gets over the next days and weeks, I will take time to help my family, friends, and neighbors clean up the city.

Irma headed out of Florida, leaving a lot of water behind her. Other than limbs and debris everywhere, the only damage at my sister's was the back fence. Several panels were blown off into the lake behind them. My brother-in-law had to go to work. We got wet from the high water, had a bit of blood and a whole lot of ant bites, but us girls got all four of the fence panels repaired and the yard cleaned up at their house.

I got word that Flamingo Lake RV Park experienced some flooding, but no major damage. We can go back tomorrow. I am glad I took my home with me.

Daddy and I are both back at Flamingo Lake and getting settled. It is so sad. Our once-beautiful city is a mess. I have been volunteering all over town. helping people with clean up, and could never have imagined the devastation from a storm that didn't even hit us head on.

CHAPTER 11

IRMA

I met with the insurance adjuster last week and she said I needed an estimate from an RV shop. I have an appointment today at Dick Gore's RV World for them to give an estimate for repairing the damage caused by Irma. I pull into service and they tell me I need to be across the street for body work. I wind my way around other RVs and pull up across the street. It's nothing big, just some scratches and a tiny crack in the fiberglass at the corner where my living room slide is.

The guy in the body shop tells me he thinks that it is not such a minor thing. I will be homeless while they coordinate insurance adjusters to decide.

I get a call from the insurance adjuster, who does not recommend repairs. I call my sales rep, Bob at Dick Gore's and tell him I want a used Class A. It just so happens one that checks all of my boxes has recently been traded in.

Oh yes I did! Just bought a Class A motorhome! It is perfect for me. The used 2014 Newmar Canyon Star 3810 has three slides. I have a queen-size sleep number bed, a bunk house that I am going to use as a closet, and a washer/dryer. The kitchen has a residential stainless-steel refrigerator with double doors. I can fit a monster cake in it. My new home even has an office space with laptop/ printer trays and a file cabinet.

As soon as I hand them a check, I drive it over to the Wildcat so I can transfer all of my things. The guys here already have the slides out on the fifth wheel so it's easier to get to everything. I pull the coach door even with the fifth wheel door.

Driving and navigating around things was much easier than I thought it would be. It's hotter than blue blazes. Thank goodness for my friends Hope and Lynne, who are here to help me move everything over. With the built-in generator, I have power in the coach, which means air conditioning, but no power to the fifth wheel, which means it is stifling hot.

After two hours we are all melting, but we are almost done moving everything from inside. I am astounded by how I accumulated so much stuff in such a tiny space. I call Shelly, a fellow Class A owner and friend from Flamingo Lake, who is going to ride home with me. My co-pilot just got here, and we are still emptying the storage under my fifth wheel. It takes us another hour to shift everything over.

We are finished and ready to roll. I am so thankful that these three women love me so much. I could not have done it without them.

I am in the driver's seat with Shelly riding shotgun. The first challenge is to find a way out of here and not hit anything. I am feeling pretty good when I pull out of Dick Gore's in my new home. We are going to take back roads the four-and-a-half miles to Flamingo Lake RV Resort. I turn right out of the dealership, then left before I can speed up. It seems easy until I hit 35 mph.

Shelly saw it happening before I did, warning, "Watch the side of the road."

Too late. There is no shoulder and I am bumping off the road. I get back on, but I am white-knuckled and having a hard time keeping the coach on the road. I have made a huge mistake. I want to travel, but this is way more than I can handle. What have I gotten myself into?

Shelly was surprisingly calm as I kept veering off the right side of the road all the way to the RV Park.

We get on the interstate, and I just have to make it to the next exit. I crawl along, trying to keep the coach on the road. This is scarier than the mountains I faced out west. I make it to the park and am now faced with the challenge of backing into my spot, way different than backing up a trailer. RV neighbors see me pull in and come to assist. With everyone's help, I get into my spot, put down the jacks to get level, put out the slides, and plug in. The only thing I am unpacking tonight is my chairs. I have to sit down and stop shaking. Well, maybe my table, plant, and flying pig so I feel like it's home.

Tomorrow I will try to figure out the mess I have gotten myself into.

I should have taken a test drive before buying a Class A motorhome. I thought since I pulled the Beast from Florida to Oregon, driving a motorhome would be a breeze. It's *not*. It's a disaster waiting to happen. Although I think I made a mistake, I am determined to keep traveling. Shelly connected me with the RV Driving School, and I have booked a two-day private lesson for Friday and Saturday. I have to drive down to Flagler Beach and meet my instructor, Chuck.

I wake up nervous but manage to get everything disconnected and slides in without breaking anything. I have Bulow RV Park programmed into my RV GPS, glad I only have to drive straight forward to get out of my site. This part is easy since the speed limit at Flamingo Lake is only 5 mph. I very slowly, pull way out into the road and turn right out of the park gate. So far, I have not hit anything, although I am scared half to death. I make it up around the curve ahead and stop. I wait until I cannot see a single car before pulling out onto the road and drive way out across both southbound lanes before I turn the wheel right. My coach rocks violently. The crashing noises all around me, things sliding and banging around inside the cabinets, make my fear even worse. I know I am going over, and I'm not even completely out of the park! I brace, ready to crash over on my side, then breathe in relief when the back tires are up on the road with me and the coach stops rocking.

The entrance ramp to I-295 South is mere feet in front of me. I start up the ramp, heart pounding and not sure how I am going to get over since cars are flying by. The trip is only eighty-six miles, but my hands are gripping the wheel so tightly my fingers hurt already. I can't do this by myself. I should have paid someone to drive me to the lesson.

Panic threatens to take over when I hear the dirt and gravel under my tires on the side of the road. I see a trucker in my driver side mirror, flashing his lights. He is going to let me over. I am on the interstate and manage to get up to 35 mph. I glance from one mirror to the next, watching the solid line at the edge of the interstate get closer and closer to my tires. I can barely keep the motorhome on the road. My heart is pounding, and my head feels like it might explode. I consider giving up and turning around. Emmi is sitting on the floor beside me and lets out a yip.

I am not a quitter. I am not alone. God is my co-pilot!

My faith gets me to the rest area on I-95 South just north of St. Augustine. What should have been a thirty-minute drive took me almost two hours, but I am not in a ditch and have made it this far. I climb down from the coach to go for a walk with Emmi and call my best friend.

With renewed energy, we are back on the interstate heading south. Every few minutes I hear the alarming sound of rumble bumps when I ease over the line towards the shoulder of the road. The good news is that I no longer hear gravel under my tires before I can ease back into my lane. I am even holding my speed at about 45 mph, sometimes even fifty.

Finally, I am off the interstate. This is not much better. I am not going fast, but in six lanes of town traffic and red lights. My GPS tells me to turn right ahead. I am now on a two-lane road with no shoulder as a buffer. Hang on, Emmi! We could be in for a rough ride.

The speed limit is 45, and I am sticking to about 25, cars lining up behind me. Some even chance crossing the solid center line to pass me. I think about all the times I drove through the Ocala National Forest on back roads to my brother's house in Central Florida pulling the Beast. I remember driving way too fast and losing patience with the campers and motorhomes that I encountered. I am sorry for that now. I send out an apology to the universe and stay at turtle speed.

My GPS tells me I will be turning left soon. Now at a snail's pace, I see that I have to enter Bulow Plantation Resort through a tiny gap in the fence. Even worse, there are rock pillars and flower beds with concrete curbs on each side of my path. There are scuff marks along the curbs and nicks in the rock columns. People with way more experience than me caused this damage.

Waiting for oncoming traffic to pass, I pray, "God, please don't let me be the one to take out an entire column."

I take a deep breath and start my turn. My nose is through with only what seems like inches on either side between me and the rocks. As I crawl through, I need to make a hard right. I am watching my right mirror closely, looking down at the curb and my tires, then back up at the column and the coach. Everything seems good to my right. I glance at my left mirror for just a second, then do a double-take. Now I understand how the previous rock damage occurred and hit my brakes. Another few inches and my back left side would have needed major repairs. I straighten the steering wheel and inch forward before I turn the wheel left for a few inches and let out the breath I was holding. Both rock columns are behind me.

I am following the road along and miss my next left turn into the actual RV Park. It probably would have been easier to back up, but for some crazy reason, that thought did not cross my mind. I take the forty-five-degree turn to my left that was designed for people coming the other direction. It takes one more wrong turn before I pull up to the office. I have a list of suggestions for this park already. The first would be better signage.

I climb out of my coach and down the steps on shaky legs. I wait my turn inside then tell the person at the desk who I am and that I have booked a pull-through site.

She checks a few things then pulls out a map and circles a spot. "You are here." She zips another line down the map and draws another circle. "Follow this road to your site here." She flips the map around as if that all should have made perfect sense to me. Then she asks, "What are you driving again?" When I tell her a 40-foot Class A, she says, "You might want to walk down to the site first and make sure you can get in." I wonder if she is joking, but she has already dismissed me and moved along to something else.

I take my map outside and study it a minute to figure out where I am going. A-walking I shall go! The "pull-through site" is part of a grassy field, with a pallet wall covering some electrical in the front and a tree in the middle of it. The tiny concrete patio has a car parked on it. Even if the car was moved, I don't think I can get in.

Back at the office, I explain the situation. The woman gives me a list of three more sites around the unworkable site to look at. Doing my best not to cry, I tell her I am new at this, here for a driving class, and that I need help.

Before she dismisses me again, she says, "I'm sorry, we don't have escorts."

Out the door I go for another walk. Another woman who works there comes out behind me and offers to take me on her golf cart. I gratefully accept and apologize for the tears rolling down my cheeks.

"I'm sorry. I am trying to keep it together, but it's been a long day. This is all a bit overwhelming for me."

"Don't worry about it," she tells me. "You should be proud of yourself for trying."

None of the sites are perfect, but I pick one and go back for my coach.

Some people have a beach house. Some people have a mountain house. I have a road house named Irma that I will soon learn how to drive.

Chuck Urwiller from RV Driving School arrived for my first Class A driving lesson. Before we hit the road, he goes through maintenance, set-up, and disconnect. He shows me how to sit in my seat and how to hold the wheel. We drive down two-lane back roads for him to witness how I struggle to keep Irma on the road. He never flinches, just calmly tells me to pick a spot further ahead and keep my eyes there. In less than half an hour, I am getting better. We hit city streets with traffic lights and choose a place to get gas. It's a small station, but simple with his guidance. After we get gas, Chuck directs me to a movie theatre where I learn about tail swing and how it is different from my fifth wheel. He teaches me how to make tight turns, how to back up, and how to parallel park. Irma takes up six spots. Give me seven and I'm in!

By the end of the day, I am exhausted but more confident.

I am up bright and early, ready for day two of my lesson. I am disconnected and ready to roll when Chuck arrives. We head straight for the interstate. He teaches me about roadside and truck stop weigh stations, then we head north to the St. Augustine Factory Outlet Mall where I learn to drive up and down the parking lot rows full of cars and people. By the time we are back on the interstate going south, I am doing well enough to drive 55 mph. My lesson is complete. I have not hit anything, not even a single curb. When I get parked, I ask Chuck if it would be crazy for me to drive Irma to Oregon for Thanksgiving in a few weeks.

"Not at all," he tells me. "Just look at it as practice every day instead of a long trip. Drive only as far as you feel comfortable, and you will do fine."

It's official. I graduated. Chuck Urwiller was an unbelievable instructor.

Heading home, I know these are the moments dreams are made of.

Did you know you should secure your refrigerator when traveling? I didn't. When I bought my coach, the person doing my walk-through forgot to mention that. As I was preparing to take the coach for pre-trip service this morning, I worked through the breakdown and discovered I am getting fast at this.

I bumped (more like banged) down the highway, listening to blinds banging, dishes rattling, and pocket doors slamming open and closed. Emmi sat shaking in the passenger seat afraid to move, terror in her eyes. She had her leash on and was attached to the seatbelt, so she couldn't get into trouble. I was tense and white-knuckled, working hard to keep my new coach on the road. I was certain a cabinet would fly open and dump its contents at any moment.

Bang! Crash!

I have no idea what happened.

Bang! Crash!

Afraid to take my eyes off the road, I take a quick peek behind me.

Bang! Crash!

My refrigerator door is flying open, banging against the wall and dumping its contents all over the floor. Those chicken enchiladas I prepared for dinner tonight, thinking I would just pop them in the oven for a nice meal, are now a cheesy mess all over my floor. And then out flies a jar of pickles. Each bump opens the fridge, spits something out, then the next bump closes it. I make it to an exit and find a place to park so I can survey the damage and clean up the mess. I find a bungee cord and strap the refrigerator door handles together.

This is a huge flaw on the manufacturer's part.

CHAPTER 12

MY HUSBAND IS LOST

I am taking my first big adventure with the new motor coach. Five months ago, I was headed north on I-75 from Florida, pulling my fifth wheel behind me. Even with taking the loops around, Atlanta traffic got me, and it wasn't even rush hour. If that wasn't bad enough, the roads around Atlanta beat the crap out of me. I wrote in my journal, "Remind me to *never* do that again." Then what do I do? Today I am taking my new Class A motorhome on its first big trip. I let someone talk me into going straight through the city in the late evening. They told me there wasn't any traffic that late in the evening and it was the easiest way to get through.

Ummm…they were wrong. People want to be in front of me when there isn't enough room for them, then they slam on their brakes. Dude, you better be praying as hard as I am that I can stop before you become a bump in the road.

I get out of Atlanta and stop for the night.

It's not yet daylight when we head west. My goal is to make it to Oregon by Thursday for Thanksgiving. It's six in the evening when we arrive at Sallisaw/Ft. Smith West KOA in Oklahoma just off of the interstate. I have a lovely, long, level site with a patio and am excited to see the fire pit and gas grill. I eat a dinner of grilled chicken and fresh vegetables. I definitely want to come back here for a few days and explore the local sights.

The sun is coming up, my checklist is complete, and Emmi is ready.

It's early evening when we arrive at the Albuquerque KOA east of the city. The site is long and wide, but not so level. At least it's clean, and the staff is friendly. I cook dinner inside and clean up. I was asleep before my head hit the pillow.

These long days are exhausting. I don't want to open my eyes when I hear my alarm. I get up anyway, feed Emmi, make coffee, and go for a quick walk. I am out of the park early and back on the road. The sunrise is a stunning sea of pinks and blues in the partly cloudy sky, just what I needed to remind me how blessed I am to be making this first trip across the country in my coach. It is absolutely gorgeous as we get close to Albuquerque, New Mexico.

In Mesita, New Mexico, population 776, I start seeing large rock formations, with mostly flat tops and green brush growing in the rocky soil. The contrast is beautiful. It makes me think of miracles. It is my first reminder today that life can flourish where it should not.

Going through Gallup, New Mexico, I pass incredible murals painted on the overpasses highlighting local culture. Just outside of the city, the mountains jut out of the earth. I am amazed at the beauty of the rugged terrain and its broken, jagged rocks that form these mountains. It reminds me of the westerns that I watched on tv as a kid with my daddy.

I have driven about another hour and now I know I am in the Wild West. I see Indian teepees scattered around. In rest areas, I am getting quite the history lesson. In the late 1800s Holbrook was known as "the town too tough for women" and in 1914 was said to be the only county seat in the U.S. that didn't have a church.

In Flagstaff, Arizona, the mountains appear softer. They gently roll to tall peaks and back down again as they lead me through the Coconino National Forest. Here, the bright blue sky serves as a backdrop for swells of gray and brown mountains with a sea of green cascading down at their base. The trees give way to a swath of cream that spreads across the suddenly flat land. At its edge is another line of dark green trees where the colors seem to fade from green to sand as if water ran down the painting, making it lighter and lighter until it reached the edge of the canvas.

The mountains in the distance are part of the Kaibab National Forest. They drastically rise up before dipping down and slightly back up again to run flat. The mesas seem out of place, rising out of the flat cream-colored plains below. I am approaching the exit for Devil Dog Road and wish I could take this detour or find the Beale Wagon Road that so many women in one of my adventure groups talk about. That's *not* going to happen in my motorhome! I will have to come back and find them both when I have a car.

I am getting close to Kingman when the landscape changes. At first, I am not sure what I see ahead. I only know that I *have* to stop and take pictures. As I make my way off the road and onto the shoulder, I think this is probably not the most ideal location to be stopped, but there are only occasional vehicles passing by and I cannot be the only person who has done it. From my vantage point, the ground dips down off the shoulder in front of me leading to massive cottonwood trees in so many shades of fluffy yellow and cream to almost white. They stand tall over the sea of junipers in shades of green ranging from dark to bluish-gray before the rocky terrain, scattered with what I think are mesquite trees in different shades of green, rises back up. The contrast of soft yellow against the dark greens is what had caught my attention. Before today, I had never seen a cottonwood tree in person. From a distance, it looked like the artist randomly decided to add a softness to their finished mountain forest landscape. It's so peaceful that I could stand here for hours, but I will never make it to Oregon if I don't get back on the road.

It's not long before my view dramatically changes again. There is nothing but gray and brown. It is void of the beautiful colors from just moments ago. The flat-topped mountains look like someone took a sharp knife and cut straight down in some areas. Others look like a giant sledgehammer smashed the top, causing massive boulders as big as a house to tumble down and lay scattered in their new resting places. It is an exquisite sight to behold.

In this short drive, I have witnessed all four major types of landforms as well as many of the minor types. The huge array of colors honestly takes my breath away. Driving along, I wonder why people stopped driving across America on family road trips. How did getting somewhere fast replace the allure of taking time to enjoy the scenery? I don't know the answers, but I intend to enjoy life this way, as often as possible, for as long as I can safely drive.

After I cross the border into Nevada, I start heading north. I wind through, up and up, then down before climbing again. The sun is reflecting off of the mountains' different shades of gray, brown, and orange. When the mountains open to the Colorado River, Lake Mead, and Lake Mohave, I am mesmerized. Then there is the Hoover Dam. It is one beautiful vision after another. I am like a kid in a candy store. I make a note to someday visit Willow Beach.

The sun is beginning to set as I drive through the Amargosa Valley. The bright blue sky gives way to pinks, reds, oranges, and gold through the light clouds hovering above the mountaintops, an incredible show. There are no words to describe just how amazing this view is.

There are few choices for places to stay out here. I stop for the night at a campground in Tonopah that I found online. The "RV Park" at Tonopah Station isn't quite what I expected. It is actually an old, run-down hotel and casino with twenty long, narrow parking spaces in the back paved parking lot. There is barely enough room to put out the slides and walk through. They added water, sewer, and electric to each. It isn't well-lit or marked where one should drive. I may have driven over a water line as I searched for the most level spot available. I did not see the gushing water until I went in search of a place to check in. I am hoping someone else is responsible. I find the back entrance and wander through, finding RV registration at the hotel check-in desk. I am greeted by the sweetest smiling woman who is standing behind a sign that reads:

Dogs are welcome in this hotel. We never had a dog that smoked in bed and set fire to the blankets. We never had a dog that stole our towels and played the TV too loud, or had a noisy fight with his traveling companion. We never had a dog that got drunk and broke up the furniture.... So if your dog can vouch for you, you're welcome too.

The Management

I get us checked in and take Emmi for a walk before dinner and then enjoy the comfort of my own bed. Today was such a wonderful drive. Everyone should do this at least once in their lives.

It's Thanksgiving. The days have been long and I am tired. We are not going to make it to Oregon in time for Thanksgiving dinner today. When I venture outside with my coffee in hand, I discern this was probably not the safest place for me to have walked Emmi in the dark alone last night. Across the street behind us is a poor, sad-looking neighborhood. I realize how blessed I am to be able to choose a simple life. I have a sturdy roof over my head and food to eat. I choose to have fewer things because only so much will fit in my coach.

Rounding the corner, I look out away from the broken-down cars, drab houses, and hotel/casino, to see the mountains. This morning's view totally makes up for what the night lacked in beauty. The sky is bright blue, and the entire mountain horizon is a drab brown and gray, except for one side of one tall mountain. I am rooted where I stop. The sun is shining on it revealing exquisite shades of gold and orange. It only lasted a few seconds before the sun ducked behind the clouds.

I thank God this morning for these moments He gives me.

I am having a smooth drive, with incredible views, when I am interrupted by a loud alarm going off. It takes me a minute to figure out what it is—it's the brake alarm. I am in the mountains, doing 65 mph! Does this mean my brakes are going to fail? I need to stop and call someone. I touch my brakes. They seem to work, but the alarm continues. I see a Walmart off of the interstate to my right, take the next exit, wind my way back to it, and park.

I pull out my owner's manual (it's a box of books) and start reading. This could take all day. I start googling, posting on my Newmar Group, a women's RV Group, and my own Facebook page. It's the Newmar Group that comes to my rescue.

"Check your parking brake. Is it engaged?" someone asks.

I don't think it is, but I check it anyway. That's not the problem.

"Check your hydraulic fluid."

Okay. Where the heck is that? Hood is open. I think I see where to check. I turn the cap and hear what is about to happen but it's too late. Fluid sprays everywhere. I turn my face away and tighten the cap as fast as I can. If that was the right place, I am not out of hydraulic fluid.

I call Good Sam Roadside Assistance. I tell the woman who answers my situation and she asks, "Are you in a safe place?"

I tell her that I am in a Wal-Mart parking lot in a town I am not familiar with.

She responds, "That is a safe place. This is Thanksgiving and our vendors are only making emergency calls. Stay put and call back tomorrow."

I don't want to stay in the Wal-Mart parking lot. I want to get to Oregon for Thanksgiving with my son. I am already going to be a day late. I don't want to be two. I start the engine again and the alarm is not on. There is still plenty of daylight left. I can make it to Cave Junction tonight, so I set off. Along the way, the alarm goes off several times. I turn music on loud to drown it out. I keep testing the brakes and keep driving.

I am nearing Siskiyou Summit just north of the Oregon-California state line. From my app, Mountain Directory West, I know the descent is seven miles of steady 6 percent grade. I make the steady crawl to the top. I have learned that you should go up at a lower speed than you want to go down. However fast you are going when you hit the peak will be increased as you go down. If I want to go down at 50 mph, I need to hit the top at about 35 mph. I see signs telling me there are two runaway truck ramps. If I have to use one, my rig is wrecked and I am probably dead, but I won't hurt anyone else.

I am at the top and my heart is pounding. If my brakes are going to fail, it will be here. I cannot depend on my brakes, I need to rely on my engine to do the work. I crest the mountain at 30 mph. In seconds, I am at 35 mph with a downhill curve looming in front of me. I put my foot solidly on the brake pedal and release it. Irma roars in protest but holds me at 35 mph...for a minute. When I pass the first runaway truck ramp, I am up to 38 mph. That's fine in a car, but when you have twenty-two thousand pounds shoving you down a mountain it is frightening! Much faster, and I won't be able to maneuver the curves. Irma is trying to hang on, but she is no longer roaring, she is screaming. I am going too fast.

I pray out loud, "God, we have made it this far, please don't let me miss Thanksgiving with my son."

I push hard on the brake again and release it. Irma is like a living, breathing, mama bear protecting her child. She roars again and I feel the coach pull back. The only thing I can compare it to is when you first pull your parachute cord. I continue to talk to God and go through this exercise a few more times. As I pass the last runaway ramp, I am at almost 50 mph. There is only a mile left and no ramp to stop me. This last mile seems like one hundred. I pray and try to hang on. I take a deep breath and exhale slowly. I have handled harder situations in my life. I can do this! My racing heart slows. I feel like I am on a cloud, floating. I no longer hear sounds. I remember wondering, "Did I wreck and miss it? Am I dead?" And then I am at the bottom, on a flat stretch of road.

I have four more mountains to cross before I reach Grants Pass: Sexton Mountain Pass, Smith Hill Summit, Stage Road Pass, and Canyon Creek Pass. The good news is, though they are curvy and have steep 6 percent grades, they are only two to three miles long. We are gonna make it!

It's late by the time we pull through the gate. Tyler, Andreea and all of their friends are waiting to help me get parked in the dark. I will deal with the brake alarm later. I have cooking to do. We will all celebrate Thanksgiving tomorrow.

Tyler and Andreea's friends from Oregon are here, along with friends who flew or drove in from other states. The kitchen is packed with people preparing the mouth-watering menu Andreea has put together. The guys are all outside watching Tyler fry his first turkey. Every surface in the kitchen is covered with platters and dishes of the meal we will all share. Although the house does not have enough seating in one spot for all of us, it doesn't matter. This is what life should really be about. I am so grateful the Oregon crew waited for me to arrive and have Thanksgiving dinner a day late. This was truly one of the best Thanksgivings ever!

The best part of waking up, is the gorgeous sunrise I see through my front windshield. My brakes have been thoroughly checked and no one can find the problem. I am going to rely on the belief that it's just an issue with the alarm. I will get it checked out when I get home. Today, we are headed back to Florida before winter storms can take over the roads. That's one challenge I am not ready to tackle yet.

Before I pull out of the drive, this is my thought:

"I am thankful for yesterday and the things I have learned. I am thankful for today and the parts of the country I will see. I am thankful for tomorrow and the opportunities to spend more time with my family. I am so very blessed!"

Heading south, I make it back through the treacherous mountains. It seems much easier today. I am not sure if it is because I have more experience or just that I knew what to expect. Mount Shasta is covered in snow as usual and it's stunning. I don't get to see much in the Trinity Mountains because I am rolling down the road above the clouds.

Imagine a shady, forty-acre grove in Bakersfield where you can park your motor home between row after row of trees loaded with ripe oranges. That's exactly what I found at one of the most unique full-service RV parks I have ever visited. The pull-through sites are long, level, and extra wide. Getting parked was a breeze.

There are indoor and outdoor game areas and a nice gym. They have three dog parks, a pool, clean laundry facilities, bathrooms, and even an RV wash area. And the oranges? The sweetest I have ever tasted! I am taking a bagful home with me.

This is the life I dreamed of. The morning started with me having coffee outside. My view was of orange trees and oil wells silhouetted by mountains. The sun is rising but still behind the mountains and the sky is filled with more shades of pink and blue than I ever knew existed.

When I get on the road, heading east on Interstate 40, the landscape constantly changes. I go from flat desert land to high mountain deserts. The colors change from one hour to the next. I stop and get out as often as I want, like at the place that was obviously once a large riverbed, but is now dry as a bone. I stop in a valley with majestic trees in every shade of green you can imagine. Though they were beautiful, this is not what makes me stop. It's the two massive trees whose branches are filled with three different shades of yellow. Along my journey today, I see everything from prickly cactuses to delicate wildflowers.

I meander through the country, taking another week to get back to Florida. Other than my brake alarm being a pain, there are no challenges. At the day's end, the sunsets across our country never get old. Sometimes I wonder if this is just a dream.

"You have been assigned this mountain to show others it can be moved."

When you decide to live tiny, you choose the things you will keep very carefully. For me, one of those things was a small sign that says, "Give me a place to stand, and I can move the world." It is placed where it is the first thing I see every morning. If you believe and have faith, you can do anything.

I fussed at Daddy early in the week because he did not want to turn his heater on in his camper or drip water. He said the lines would not freeze. Guess what? They froze. Oh! Don't forget to follow your own advice. I turned my dripping water off yesterday when it got above freezing but forgot to turn it back on before I went to bed. I woke up this morning and needed to get a shower before a meeting. Guess what? My water pipes had frozen. I didn't have time to thaw it so had to tell Daddy what I had done and borrow his shower. Of course, I had to listen to him giving me a hard time.

It has now been freezing for a week. My water has been dripping for a week, except for the day I forgot. This morning I wake up and groggily head to the bathroom in my Christmas pajamas and fuzzy socks. I step into the bathroom and onto the rug. The shock almost makes me pee my pants. The rug is soaked and now, so are my fluffy socks. RV bathrooms are far from being large, so I only had to glance left to see that my shower was full of water and spilling over the edge. Crap! My gray water tank is full.

I still need to use the bathroom, now even worse because my feet are cold and wet. There is no time. I race from the bathroom to the kitchen, leaving puddles of water behind me. I turn off the water, run outside in the freezing temperatures and around back. As I open the hatch to the drain valves, I remember that I need to pee. Now as I stand here shivering in my PJs and wet socks and have an "aha" moment. I was so flustered I opened the black tank valve and not the gray tank valve. I close that valve, open the gray tank valve, and run back inside to check out the damage and sop up water. Luckily the water had not been overflowing long so I got the water up before there was wall, cabinet, or floor damage. I turn around to see if all of the water has drained out of the shower and see that my favorite hair dryer is sitting inside. I probably cannot save it after it has been submerged in water. I take it out and set it aside, just in case. Lesson learned.

✧

Today I am headed to Wekiwa Springs State Park outside of Orlando. Ever put an address into your GPS and have it take you to the wrong place? It happened to me today. This was my first state park, and I decided on back roads to avoid Orlando traffic. You may have to drive at a more moderate pace, but I love them. Some I am familiar with, others…well, I am at the mercy of Siri. It should take me about two hours. The first hour or so is easy going. Once I get off of 19, my route becomes turns every few miles, so *really* slow going.

Siri says I am five minutes away and tells me, "Turn left then stay right." I do as she says and find myself on a single-lane road with no streetlights. Now I am dodging tree limbs in the dark. I navigate curves and corners and get deeper and deeper into a dark, wooded area. I come around a corner and I can see the lights of a main road up ahead!

Siri says, "Take the next right." I breathe a sigh of relief and make the right turn.

I drive a few miles thinking, "What happened to five minutes?" Surely, it's because I used my phone that does not know I am driving a giant motorhome. Then right again, and it's too late, I am back on that same dark, single-lane, winding road. I should have used my new RV GPS, but I totally forgot about it. I just went in a huge circle.

Siri said I was only five minutes away half an hour ago. Did I miss a turn? I stop in the middle of the road and look at my GPS to figure out what I did wrong. I realize Siri has led me to the locked back gate of the park. I didn't plug an address in, I typed the name of the park. I try to find an address or see if I can figure out on the map where the entrance might be.

I send up a request for God to show me something. A man in a truck pulls up beside me. I open my window and he says, "Ask me why I know where you are going."

I am thinking it's because I am driving a forty-foot coach on this tiny dark road in the woods? Instead, I tell him, "I am guessing it's because many others have done this before me."

He laughs and says, "Wekiwa State Park, right? And yes, it happens all the time. It's not hard to figure it out when a giant bus is on our road. There is no way anyone would attempt this during the day, much less in the dark, unless they were lost."

I just smile, waiting for him to tell me how to get where I am going. But he just keeps talking, "Did your husband get lost? Where are you and your husband from?"

My first thought is, did God plant a man in my passenger seat? I turn my head to see. Only Emmi is there. I look back and say, "Maybe you can find my husband for me." He didn't get the humor. So I smile again and say, "My dog and I are from Jacksonville and are completely lost."

His expression is that of shock, and it takes him a minute to find his voice. "You do this by yourself?" I nod. "Aren't you afraid?"

I tell him what I tell everyone else. "I am afraid every time I try something new, but with God as my co-pilot, I am not afraid to try."

He is still shocked as he asks, "Why are you doing this by yourself?"

"Because I can. Now can you tell me how to get out of here and to the park entrance?"

He tells me that I have to follow the same road as last time because there is no way I can turn around. I want to tell him that if he would just get out and guide me, that I *could* back up and turn around. Though I have faith, he obviously does not. So I listen to his list of instructions (like I am going to remember all of those right, left, left, right street names). Knowing I won't remember them all, my mind is already preparing for another long crawl of low limb-dodging in the dark.

I thank him and he wishes me luck then drives off ahead of me. I creep through the trees with only a few close calls, certain I will hear a huge *crack*, resulting in a gaping hole in my roof. I make it back to the main road again without any major damage.

I still have to figure out where I am going. I turn right, merge all the way over through traffic to the center turn lane, put the coach in park, and breathe. I look at a map of the area on my phone. The man said something about turning left at the road leading me through the trees, instead of right. I can see the park on my map with roads all around it, though I still cannot figure out where the entrance is. I pick a road that it might be and plug that into my GPS.

I turn on my blinker and merge back into traffic. I make the left turn as suggested by the man and soon find myself winding through a neighborhood. A few miles up, I see a place where I can pull over. I call Barbara for some better directions. She tells me the two additional turns I need to make, and I am on my way.

Just when I think I will never find it, I see signs for the park entrance. I ease off the gas, ready to make the left turn across traffic into the park. Relief! I made it! And then my excitement plummets. The gate at the entrance is closed. I pre-booked my site and have a confirmation email. I put Irma in park and pull it up on my phone in hope of some instructions. There is nothing about closing times or late arrivals. I look for a call button at the gate. If nothing else, some instructions. I climb out and walk up to the gate. The only sign I see says, "Park closes at dark." But there is a keypad with a call button. I press the button and a phone on the other end begins to ring. Relief! But again, only for a minute. The phone rings and rings and rings, with no answer. Deflated, I walk back to Irma, praying for some wisdom.

I consider the narrow entrance behind me. I am going to have to back out across traffic. The biggest problem is that I won't be able to see past the rock columns on either side of the entrance until I am in the road. There are cars coming from both directions, there is no way to turn around on this narrow road, and backing out into traffic is not an option.

Now I am tired, hungry, and near tears. I beg God for help. I call Barbara for suggestions on a place I can park for the night. She is only a few minutes away. She says she will come block traffic for me and lead me to her neighborhood. As we hang up, a couple in a truck pulls up behind me. They cannot get around me since I am blocking the entrance. I go back to explain my situation. They tell me the park closed at six and no one works the gate after closing. I had planned to be here before dark, but I spent two hours hiking through the woods in my coach. Lucky for me, the couple in the truck has a code. And I know my site number. I'm in!

I find Site 3 easily. Like most state parks, there are no lights. I pull Irma just past my site and get out to assess how I am going to back her into the spot in the dark. There is a post I can set my flashlight on. It's not much, but at least I may not hit the fence. The only other challenge is a massive picnic table at the back of the site. I try to drag it out of the way, but that's not gonna happen. I am pretty much going to do this blind. It will mean a lot of getting in and out of the coach to investigate. God hasn't let me down yet. I can do this!

I get back in and pull forward before starting to back up. That's when a see a couple in a fifth wheel sitting by their campfire watching me. I open my window and call out to them. The man comes over and asks, "Is your husband guiding you from the other side?"

Why does everyone assume I have a husband with me?! Why do they think that a woman can't do this? Or wouldn't do this? Would they even give a second thought to a man traveling alone in a forty-foot Class A with his dog? I think of a man I watched take almost an hour backing his fifth wheel into a spot. (I offered to help but he declined.) I remember the man that took out the cable line and almost a power line too.

I muster every ounce of patience I have left, smile and say, "I do not have a husband on the other side guiding me. Could you just walk along beside my window and keep me from hitting the fence?"

He looks stunned, "You are doing this alone?"

Here we go again. "No, sir. My dog Emmi is with me and I have God as my co-pilot."

He just shakes his head and calls his wife over. Remember, he pulls a fifth wheel. I did this too, and it's different than a Class A. Steering is opposite when you are backing up. I know this. I just want him to keep me from hitting the fence. He starts telling me which way to turn my wheels. I figure out quickly that this is going to be wrong.

My good friend Barbara pulls up and I ask her to join the guy's wife at the back with her flashlight to keep me from hitting the picnic table. I proceed to ignore the man, who is certain I am turning my wheels the wrong way, and start backing up.

"You're gonna hit that tree in front of you! Stop!" he shouts. I continue to ignore his directions and calmly ask him to focus on what's in the dark behind me since my headlights are showing me what's in front of me. In I glide, smooth as silk.

The old man is still shaking his head as he and his wife walk back to their site, "I can't believe she did that. I thought for sure she was going to hit those trees. And she even backed in straight!" It cracks me up when people are surprised I can back my rig in straight and not hit anything.

Mission accomplished! Maybe next time I will use my paper map. Or maybe not. The adventure is part of the fun!

Emmi and I are up and going for a walk before daylight. I leave my flashlight, thinking that the moon is bright enough for me to see the road. Halfway around the loop, she freezes and starts growling. I try to pull her along, then hear rustling in the dark bushes to my left. Now the ferocious barking starts. It spooks me for a minute, but I decide it's probably just an armadillo. I scoop Emmi up so that we can get away faster.

Back at the park this afternoon, I get to see it in the daylight. My home for the week is wonderful! The sites are all large and mine is dead level. They are all surrounded by nature, making them seem even larger. Each cleared area along the road is fenced on three sides at the back. On our walk, I also read signs warning campers that the park has a lot of bears, giving instructions on what you should and should not do to be safe and at the same time, protect the bears in their natural habitat. I thought of the rustling noises and Emmi's growling response from this morning's early walk before daylight. I will bring a flashlight on the rest of our night walks.

I am sitting outside eating dinner as the sun is setting, Emmi lying on the ground at my feet. I hear an owl hoot a little way off and smile. I love the sounds of nature. When the sound gets closer, I marvel at not just one big owl, but what sounds like several responding to each other. I am thinking how peaceful it is until I notice Emmi is no longer lying down but standing stiffly and growling. The hooting is no longer calm and soothing. It's dark so I cannot see them, but now they are loud, more urgent in their communication with each other—and *really* close. I encountered one barn owl several years ago in the yard of my beach house. She was about three feet tall. When I got too close, she opened her wings—a wingspan of over three feet—and dove toward me in an effort to protect her babies. If these owls are as large as she was, Emmi could be their dinner. I spring into action, scooping an increasingly agitated Emmi into my arms and tucking my body around her. She is now wiggling and barking ferociously as I hear the flap of wings taking flight. We make it up the steps, inside, and I close the door behind us. My heart is pounding, and Emmi is shaking. I will never know if they were flying at us or away. Either way, I am grateful for this incredible moment.

So many people work their whole lives, stockpiling money and things, then retire, only to die not long after. Take time with people around you. Live your dreams before it's too late.

I keep watching for bears but only find flamingos. The pink plastic kind. Traveling alone, I never really considered staying in state parks. I thought I needed a phone number to call if I had problems, and people that worked in the park were available 24/7 just in case. After this week, I know better. There are plenty of campers, from tents to small trailers, to fifth wheels, to coaches larger than mine, who are happy to help. Spending mornings with my coffee watching birds and wild turkeys, spending evenings in my fenced yard listening to the owls hoot and wondering what the rustling in the brush was after dark were great. The level, long, wide spaces are perfect at Wekiwa Springs State Park. I will definitely be back.

I am headed home today in the rain, taking a different route up I-75 North. It is one of those days that I am aware of fear. I see a toll booth ahead, pull in a deep breath, and hold it. How tight will it be? Will I be able to reach the toll attendant? My fear is unfounded. It was a breeze. At the second toll booth, a young girl is working. She looks completely bored. When she glances up at me, a huge smile spreads across her face. She says, "Wow. Aren't you afraid?" I tell her I am afraid every time I tried something new, but the only thing that I am not afraid of is trying. I pay my toll and drive away. She leans out of her booth, waves, and yells, "Get it, girl!"

It made my day. It's the little things that excite me and get me through.

It's twenty-five degrees in Florida. I *love* my Class A and would not go back to a fifth wheel. However, there is a challenge when you are sitting still for a few weeks of freezing weather. I have had frozen pipes, a busted water hose, and learned those lessons.

CHAPTER 13

REST AREA ROBBERY

I have been planning a trip that could take me into some nasty winter weather. I spent a week planning the route across I-10 so I could stay south of the potential northern snowstorms. And then snow blanketed the south, shutting down several stretches of I-10. Still, no snow further north, so I plan a different route. I am too nervous, so I wait. I consider traveling between these routes. I'm just not ready. I plan and wait, watch the weather and worry. Then I realize I am far too smart to be the only thing standing in my way. I stop planning and start praying. This morning, I wake up with a new plan. I will get on the road and head west, then north at some point. I will just drive. No reservations, no detailed plan. I am going to wing it.

I feel much better.

It never fails. When I decide to go on a trip pulling an RV or driving a Class A, people want to know my schedule. The truth is, I probably just decided a few days ago (like this time) to leave for somewhere and don't have a schedule set in stone. I have a general idea of when I am leaving and my final destination, but that's it. For me, it's part of the fun. Drive as long as I feel like safely driving, stop and see whatever I want to see along the way, and find a place to park for the night. If you want to know where I am, follow me on Facebook.

Last night, I was talking and laughing about everything that has gone wrong in my travels. I tell the story of my refrigerator spilling its contents. After several trips with my bungee cord, a friend says, "You know there is a lock on your refrigerator, don't you?"

I learned something new.

This morning I am up early and ready to go. As I go through my "pre-flight" checklist, I notice one tire is slightly low. Everything else is good. I will just get air on my way to the interstate.

I stop at the RV park office to let them know I will be gone a few weeks. I meet a sweet woman from Boone, NC on my way out of the office. When I reach my coach, she stops to ask, "Do you drive this by yourself?" When I say yes, she tells me how brave she thinks I am. She says she is afraid to even back her husband's big truck up. "There's no way I could pull our fifth wheel!" What she doesn't know is I prayed this morning that God would do the driving because I am still a bit afraid. Her kind words gave me strength and took today's worry away. I told her about my Facebook journal, *Climbing Mountains and Bumping Down Highways.* I hope she finds it so I can hear about the first time she tries.

What would one of my adventures be without a little bit of drama? One of the tires was a little low, so I stopped for air before leaving town. The man putting air in said that all of the tires were good. That one tire had just as much as the rest. I couldn't understand why, but he used my gauge then showed it to me. The gauge said I was good.

It's forty-four degrees and sunny by the time I hop on the interstate just outside the park and head for I-10 West. Driving down the interstate, I can't stop worrying and wondering why when I checked the tire it was low. Maybe the cold temperature this morning? I still didn't feel right. Then it hit me. The man must not have thought about the *two* tires and only checked the stem for the outside tire. Off the road I go to check myself. That is exactly what happened. Lessons learned: One—just because it was a man that should have known what he was doing, doesn't mean he does. Two—a woman can know as much as or more than a man does, and three—trust your instincts!

I get the air I need and head back out.

I start calling around for a spot to spend the night in, but there is nothing available nearby. It's seven o'clock at night when I make it to Gautier, Mississippi. I am tired and decide a rest area is good enough. I feed Emmi and we take a walk. I fix myself a hot dog and settle in for a night of Netflix.

I am leaving today in the rain. At least it's a warmer sixty-one degrees. I am driving along the highway at 60 mph when a gust of wind blasts me from the side. It hits me so hard I veer right towards the shoulder. I know not to overreact, but it's hard. Over the white line I go. I hear the rumble bumps and then am over the lip of the pavement into the grass. I have to get back on the road but know that the wind is blowing so hard it isn't going to be easy. I let off the gas, my heart pounding. I look in my mirror to check the person beside me and say a quick prayer. I am coming in. I know I've got this, but that guy beside me does not have the same faith. When I start over, he swerves left onto the shoulder. I am back in my lane and never crossed the dotted line into his. Now

I am worried that he will overcorrect and hit me. I can breathe again—he is back in his lane. The entire episode was only seconds, but felt like an eternity.

Watching the truckers drive easily around me, for a moment I think perhaps I should marry a retired truck driver. I am in awe of their skills, especially those guys pulling tandem trailers. Wow! Then I witness the truck ahead of me get blasted by a gust of wind. I watch him go through the same drill and I know that even with only a few months of experience under my belt, I did just as well as he did. Now, being the smart woman I am, it's time to take a break.

Bumpy roads are uncomfortable, but we often learn the best lessons from uncomfortable situations. Today was one of those bumping-down-highways kind of days. Literally! I decided to try the interstate today. I think I must be on the roughest road in the country, besides the portion of Route 66 that took me an hour to go ten miles a few years ago. I hit several bumps in a row, then hear something fall. The crash is followed by the sound of glass breaking. I find out after I stop that this road is so bumpy my medicine cabinet's mirrored door flew out of its track and shattered.

My best friend calls to steer me out of the path of a major storm and guides me to a rest area. I pull in just as the rain begins to fall. I recognize Dave and Irene Carey's from their YouTube channel, *Carey on Vagabond*! Someone else brave enough to ditch "normal" life and enjoy life while they can. I am so proud of them and grateful for another day of encouragement. It seems I may be stuck here for a while. I fix something to eat, check out my map, make some calls, and decide where I will stay tonight.

It is still raining, but the storm has passed. When I stop at the next gas station, I check the air in my tire. It is low again.

The weather? The bumps? I don't know, but I ask Siri if there is a Camping World anywhere near me. I need to have this checked out. I find the place I am searching for.

I wander through a short maze and find a counter. I tell the young girl I find that I have a problem with a tire. She says, "We have to charge you thirty-seven dollars and forty cents to look at the tire." Like I am going to say no? I must take too long to answer her because she says, "Well, if you decide that you want us to look at it, let me know," and goes back to her computer. I am dumbfounded. Every other Camping World experience I have had has been perfect. I want to respond with a smart answer, but as I stand shivering and dripping wet, I put a smile on my face.

"I am fine with the charge. Could someone please look at the tire?" Without saying a word, she gets up from her seat at the computer and walks through the door behind her.

When she returns, she tells me, "Drive back past the garage door that has an air pump outside it. Turn around and park by the pump. Someone will be with you in a few minutes." I keep telling myself not to complain. I wander back through the maze, splash through the mud, drive further back, and find the air pump. I wait while the man gets through adding air to all of my tires. When he's finished, he goes back to the problem tire. It has not lost any air. I am at a loss, but I thank him and get back on the road.

I decide not to take the extra time for the loop around Houston. I have faith. I am driving straight through it. The slow traffic doesn't worry me at all. It is after I get through downtown when I get into trouble. Someone literally has just stopped in the middle of the interstate in front of me. I put my foot on the brake, afraid I am going to slide on the wet road. I let off the brake and check my mirrors, but there is nowhere to go.

"Oh God. Please let me stop."

I press the brake again. I am going to hit him.

"God, he is in a sportscar. If I hit him, I am going to run over him. Please God, don't let me kill this idiot!"

I stop inches from his back bumper. My heart is pounding so hard I can hear it. Now, he waits to get over so he does not miss his exit. Does he have any idea what it takes to stop forty feet of metal on a wet road?! Of course, he can't see around me, and I am so close I can't go around him. As I reach for my horn, he darts out across traffic to the exit almost parallel to us, three lanes away. I sit stunned, while people lay on their horns and hit their brakes. I wait for the sound of crushing metal. It was a miracle no one wrecked. When he makes it off the highway, I can breathe again.

I call Houston West RV Park to tell them I am running late. Peggy says she will wait for me. As I exit, my GPS says to turn left. I make the left turn, but after a few minutes, my GPS tells me to make a U-turn. Knowing I have not passed my road, I call the campground back and Peggy says I should have turned right. I scope out my options and there are no cars in either direction. I have four lanes. I am making a U-turn in the middle of the road. Now I am headed in the other direction. She tells me to turn left on Cooper Road after the lake in just a few miles.

"We are on the left. Don't worry, I will wait for you."

This road turns into two lanes. It's dark and I strain to read signs as I watch for my road. I come to a crossroad and am sure I have gone too far. I call again and tell Peggy where I am. She gives me more directions with landmarks and tells me I may have to go a ways to find a spot to turn around. "Don't worry though. I will wait on you." While we are on the phone, I tell her, "I will just turn around right here in the road. I will be there in a few minutes." I use the cross road in front of me to make a wide loop and am at Houston West RV Park in less than five minutes. A man meets me at my door in the rain with an umbrella and points to my spot. It's a pull-through site directly in front of me. They may treat everyone the same way, but I feel like a queen.

Texas is full of wonderful people and places. Their rest areas are amazing with water and electricity available. I met two marvelous women this morning. Peggy, who helped me last night, and Candy, who is a bus driver who plans to hit the road in a year when she retires. I can't wait to hear about it. They both promise to keep in touch. I head out of the park in misting rain.

Blessings are sometimes disguised as annoyances. I had planned to visit a historic fort this afternoon, but the road is closed because of an accident. I had planned to get fuel five miles up the road, but that is not happening now. I find a gas station along my detour. I fit, but have to take up the sidewalk along the edge of the town street. I climb down, fuel up, and go to climb back in…when I find my hydraulic steps are swinging. It's a good thing I am not afraid to get dirty. Here I am in a gas station, lying on the ground under my coach with my shiny red toenails sticking out trying to figure out what is wrong. Then I see cowboy boots.

"Ma'am, are you okay?"

Then there are two of us laying on our backs under my rig. Bumpy roads severed the bolt. I have everything anyone could imagine to fix anything, except a bolt that size. So, for today, it's ratchet straps and bungee cords. The good news is it happened when I was stopped and not when I was driving down the road.

It's mid-day when I call Junction River South for a reservation. They have plenty of room, but tell me I should ignore my GPS and take another exit. Not far off of the exit I am warned of a steep descent ahead. Immediately, here it is, with a sharp curve right after it. As I am simultaneously trying to slow down and not run off the road to my left or crash into the mountain on my right, the GPS says turn left. I feel like am taking the turn on two wheels, sliding in sideways. I have arrived. This is a small, nearly-empty campground on the river. Lucky me! My site has a direct view of the water. I get set up and spend the rest of the evening sitting under a tree on a river enjoying the sunset.

My life rocks!

When I wake up, my leg muscles are killing me. Then I remember why. I am climbing up three feet every time I get in my coach because the steps are broken. It's a chilly twenty-eight degrees but clear this morning. After a lazy morning of coffee by the river, I pull out and head further west.

I am getting off the road for fuel and get this text message, "Welcome to Mexico!" I am in a total panic thinking that I must have made a *really bad* wrong turn somewhere. It is afternoon and the sun is on my left. That should mean I am going north. There is no way I am in Mexico unless I have been here for a long time.

After filling up my gas tank, I nervously go inside and tell the cashier, "I have to figure out how to get out of Mexico."

She looks at me like I have two heads, "Excuse me?"

I keep trying to tell her I somehow got turned around and crossed the Mexican border by mistake. "I just want to get back on the American side." She now looks like she is ready to call the guys with straightjackets for me. I show her my text. She laughs so hard that everyone in the store stops to stare at us. Between her bouts of laughter, she tells me that I am close, but not in Mexico. I am relieved, but now red-faced with embarrassment and just want to get out of the store.

Have you ever been in love? Felt that heart-pounding excitement? That adrenaline-induced awe? The knowing that there is nothing more wonderful? It happened to me today and it will never get old. It happens every time I crest that hill and see the first mountains of a trip spread out before me. I start thinking, I start analyzing, because what else is there to do when you are driving a forty-foot coach by yourself? I start thinking about love and beauty. Whether it's a place or a person, there is always a cost. I am not thinking of the financial cost, but the life cost. To live life in these mountains means hard winters and struggles. But would it be worth the cost to experience such beauty and peacefulness for part of the year? It's the same question relating to people. No matter how amazing the person, no one is perfect and we all have our moments. Would it be worth the cost to know that you could spend the rest of your life with the people who give you such joy most of the time?

I stop at Pilot at the first exit across the New Mexico border for gas. It's six thirty and getting dark. I think I will just spend the night at the next rest area. As I pull back onto the interstate, I see the sign, "Rest area, next exit." It's a great rest area and the perfect spot for us to spend the night. Emmi and I go for a walk. As we are walking back to the RV, I see a bright, full moon over my coach.

In the wee hours of the morning, with coffee cup in hand, I open my door. It's freezing outside! I close the door before even stepping through it. In a few minutes, I emerge dressed for a blizzard. *Wow!* The white moon I usually see off in the distance is a bright copper orange. The massive sphere in front of me is so close I can see the shadows of its craters. I am in awe as I take it all in. The blood moon to the west this morning is gorgeous, totally worth the early wake-up and cold.

I am thinking about getting on the road, but I hear my Daddy's voice saying, "The faster you go, the behinder you get. Just slow down." And I wonder why I was in a hurry. Because I might hit traffic in some city? So what? I decide to wait for Her Majesty the sunrise! I snap photo after photo as she begins to wink over the mountains beside me. I am glad I stayed here for the show.

This morning it was twenty-eight degrees. Now it's a balmy eighty degrees. I am at a rest area and taking Emmi for a walk. Signs for the pet walk area lead us to an open gravel area. Emmi appears to be reading the sign posted here, looks up at me, then turns around heading the other way. The sign reads, "Poisonous snakes and insects inhabit the area." I guess she decided to wait until the next stop. Standing in my flip-flops, I am suddenly aware of the ground around me.

I'm with you, Emmi, let's get moving.

I am up at 4:45 a.m. to watch the lunar eclipse. It's stunning! I am trying to take pictures and record videos as it's happening, but nothing does my experience justice. I am wide awake now, so decide to drive further. As the sun starts to rise, I stop at another rest area to witness the spectacular scene. Both the sun and the moon are sharing the sky over me.

Almost daily, someone says I am brave when they first learn I am driving my coach on journeys alone. I don't think of myself as brave. The woman who finds the strength to leave an abusive relationship and starts over on her own is brave. The people who quit their jobs to start their own businesses are brave. The child fighting an illness or disease, who still somehow finds the strength to laugh, is brave. The person battling cancer is brave. The woman who donates a kidney to her husband so she doesn't lose him is brave. I have watched people I know and love do all of these things and I admire their strength.

I do not feel much bravery as I head north and get a glimpse of the mountain I have to face. It is thirty miles of 5 percent, 6 percent and 7 percent descents. What if my engine overheats as I coax this beast to the top? I am afraid!

"God, give me strength. Show me what to do. Better yet, you drive!"

I hit the road thinking there will be a rest area or gas station just before the mountain to stop at and be ready. That isn't going to happen. All of a sudden, the road splits with a sign overhead saying, "All trucks take this route." This is the beginning of my forty-mile journey over the Tehachapi Mountains. There is no turning back now.

I slow down to 45 mph, get in the line of trucks, turn on my flashers, turn off my air conditioner, and start the straight-up climb. My engine is growling. I see signs telling me that there is water available on the way up for my radiator if I need it. Oh crap! I don't even know where my radiator is, much less how to put water in it!

"God, best plan in this situation is that you don't let my engine overheat."

I watch my gauges. I see the signs about reducing speed to 35 mph and runaway truck ramps as I near the top. Now I really start worrying. What if a runaway truck is behind me? What if *I* am the runaway coach behind a truck? I envision piles of tangled metal. I give the task back to God and start down the mountain. When the engine really begins to growl, I wonder when this will get scary. Then I become conscious of the fact I am no longer afraid. For thirty miles, my engine does the work with only a few pushes on the brake to keep me between 35 and 40. I enjoy the wondrous view all the way to the bottom. I am not brave, I simply have faith!

It's late afternoon when I pull into Lost Hills RV Park, but the office is closed. A sign on the door says, "Be right back." I wait. And wait. No one shows up. I call the number for the park and a woman answers. I tell her who I am. She gives me directions and she tells me to pick any pull-through site, that she will catch up with me later. I hang up thinking, "How strange, but okay, I like picking my own spot." I find a site near the end and get parked. It's big and level. I get everything connected and put my flamingos out to graze. This will be home for a few days.

I left later than I had planned and spent a lot of time checking out the sights along my way today. It's still daylight at eight thirty in the evening when I stop at a rest area in Corning, California. I had no idea it was this late. My goal today was Mount Shasta so that I could wake up tomorrow and see snow. That would mean I will be crossing a mountain in the dark. I should just stop somewhere for the night and make the rest of the drive in the morning. I try, but can't find a park nearby with availability. I will just drive as far as I can and sleep in a rest area if I have to.

I am driving along in the dark and have no idea where I am. I know what road I am on and where it goes, but if I have a problem, I could not tell anyone how to find me. The only thing that I know is that it's a two-lane road. There is a mountain jutting out of the road on my left and a cliff dropping to who knows where on my right. It's so dark! Suddenly, a steep curve catches me off guard. Slow down. Keep looking straight ahead. I climb up and try not to fly down. The curves are crazy. A minute after I think it was a mistake for me to do this in the dark, I see a sign for a rest area ahead. I pray there is an empty spot for me to park.

The exit is ahead, but I am going downhill faster than I should be to take it. For some reason, I think of a bowling alley. Irma is the ball careening down the slick alley, with pins that resemble cars being tossed left and right. It's not a pretty picture. I have seconds to decide—keep going or get off this mountain road? I am getting off! I put my foot hard on the brake and release it. Irma roars but pulls back as I take the exit. Crap! It's a short ramp! Brakes again! Another roar as the engine downshifts and reins us in a little more, though we are still going too fast. I may have to speed right through. One more time. I tug hard on the reins. It's enough! There is one parking space big enough left.

My breathing is back to normal. Now I need to decide if I will sleep here tonight or keep going. I have my paper maps, my mountain app, and google maps open on my phone. If I can just know what's ahead of me, I can do it. I figure out that I am at the O'Brien Safety Roadside Rest Area. I am at the southern end of the Cascade Mountain Range. There are some steep climbs, but the satellite pictures don't show anything worse than what I have already done in the daylight. I'm going for it!

There are a few spooky spots, but I make it to my destination.

Today, I see snow! The big, fluffy white pillows blanket the landscape. We have just started a walk and Emmi hops off the trail thinking she is going exploring. Then she is gone. The leash in my hand looks like a fishing line that disappears in the snow. Laughing, I pull her out. I have to carry her for the rest of the hike.

We came, we saw, and we are on our way back to Florida. It's February, so I am hugging the coastline all the way through California. Instead of spending several days in different locations, I am going to try something new.

I "boondocked" in rest areas and at scenic overlooks. You can't stay even twenty-four hours in these places, but I figured out how to make it work—pull in just before sunset and leave by noon. My flamingos wouldn't stand on the pavement, but I pulled my chair out to watch many a sunset. Imagine waking up in the morning at a scenic overlook. Your door opens just ten feet from the ridge of a canyon. I watched the sunrise here. It was amazing!

I pull off at a rest area near Salome, Arizona. Emmi and I take a walk and enjoy lunch outside. When I parked the coach, I left several spaces on either side of me. As we walk back, I notice that semi-trucks have parked in those empty spaces beside me. The one on my door side is close. Emmi and I squeeze between the truck and Irma. A man comes around the back of my coach towards us. I am guessing that he's the driver of the rig running next to me. Then another man appears behind him. Why would two men get into their truck on the same side? The hair raises on the back of my neck. I turn around to walk back the way I came. I only take about four or five steps and three more men walk around the front corner of my coach. I am trapped. If I scream, no one will hear me over the noise of the semi engine running next to me. All five men are cleanly dressed and appear to be in their sixties. I am afraid, but trying to memorize everything about them that I can. Average height, average build, though a bit on the thin side. I realize this description could fit anyone.

I silently call out, "God?" just before the first man says, "We broke down and need money to get our RV fixed."

"We were just taking a break and I don't have any cash on me," I tell him.

Another man says, "That's okay. We can just go inside...."

My mind is reeling. This can't be happening. Then I remember I had this jacket on a few days ago at a street fair and there is cash in my pocket. More than I want to give them, but I don't want them in my coach. "Wait. I forgot about the cash in my pocket." I put both hands into my pockets and feel the money and the cold, hard metal of my gun. If I pull it out, will they run? Or with men on either side of me, will one try to take it from me? I always wondered if I could actually shoot someone. At this moment, I am so afraid I know I can pull the trigger. But if I do, will the rest run or attack me? Even if I hand them the money, they may still kidnap me or steal my coach. I hand them the money and am ready to drop on the ground and roll under the semi out into the opening. It all happened so fast! I hand the bills over and hit the ground.

Before I am halfway across, they are running. When I come out the other side, they are gone. They have blended in with the rest of the road-weary travelers.

I get back in my coach as fast as I can and lock the door behind me. My whole body is shaking. I sit down in my seat and cry. I keep reminding myself that I am okay, I am not hurt. Yet the tears won't stop. I thank God that I am alive. I want to leave, but I can't drive like this. I have to calm down. I close my eyes and take slow, deep breaths. In and out, in and out. I tell myself this situation has nothing to do with traveling. It could happen at the mall or grocery store. It could happen anywhere.

After I get my wits about me, I put Irma in drive and we are on the road heading east again. I am climbing a fairly steep grade through the Dragoon Mountains. There is a man on a bicycle loaded with stuff who has gray hair, a scruffy beard, and his clothes are a bit rough. He resembles one of the lobster fishermen I remember from my childhood visits to Maine. My first reaction was to feel sorry for the homeless guy. I prayed for his situation to improve as I drove on down the other side of the mountain. I start to think about how hard it must have been for him to climb that mountain on his bicycle with possibly all of his worldly possessions. Then it hits me like a ton of bricks that I just judged this man. While I pride myself on not judging people, it was so easy to quietly judge him. It's possible this man was on an adventure that he planned and trained for. Perhaps he chose to live a different life unencumbered by society's traditional things. Or perhaps he just went camping for a few days and was enjoying nature. I will never know. But I do know that it took a lot of strength and determination to climb that mountain on his bicycle. If he had been dressed differently, would I have judged him differently? Life is full of uphill battles. Homeless or not, it was a good reminder to not judge others or to assume something you don't know as fact.

The rest of my day is fabulous; I just won't be sleeping in a rest area for a while. I stay at some of the same campgrounds and RV Parks I stayed in on my way west. It makes me feel safer knowing my surroundings.

I am almost through Texas. It is a sluggish, rainy, windy day. This adventure is almost complete. Every time I pass a Cracker Barrel sign, I dream of their vegetables. After a long, cold day of wind and rain delays, I could drive another hour to my spot for the night or call and ask if I could spend the night in their parking lot.

A huge shout out to Cracker Barrel in Slidell, Louisiana for giving me my own parking lot, with lights all around it and also asking the police to keep an eye out tonight. I have an awesome dinner, unbeatable service, and sleep like a baby.

In just a few more days, I am back in Florida. Many people thought that I was crazy to sell everything and buy a Class A motorhome with plans to travel the country alone. Even with the challenges, I love my life. I am already planning for the next trip.

CHAPTER 14

IN THE MEN'S ROOM

I am giving up my home base site at Flamingo Lake and I am nervous about coming back in the middle of the busy summer. Ken and Steve both assure me that they will always find room for me. I love my Flamingo family!

I am supposed to be in North Carolina mid-week for my daughter's wedding. My friends Sandy and Ronnie stopped by last night to drop off the beautiful cups she made for the bride and groom. It is Sunday, and I decided to add a stop to the beginning of my trip. Before I go north, my first stop is Spirit of the Suwannee Music Park for a few days with my best friend, Hope.

I turn in, the excitement I always feel here immediately evident. I pull up to the office and they tell me there is a festival next weekend, and that I cannot come in without a ticket. I know about the festival, but I am not here for it. I tell them that I will be gone way before people start setting up. After several calls to people here I know, they decide I can stay.

We find our way to our spot and I expertly back Irma in around the trees. We get tents set up, tarps hung, and a campfire crackling. Captain Brian stops by for a visit, and we cook burgers over the fire. I am spending a few days in the woods with my best friend. The days are filled with book reading, a trip to Lake City to get wood from our friend Ralph, and listening to birds sing as the sun comes up after a thunderstorm.

This is my amazing life. I am sitting in the dark early this morning with Emmi in my lap and coffee in my hand, listening to the cool wind blowing through the live oaks and pine trees.

Friends encourage us to try things we can never imagine doing. Thanks to my best friend who took me tent camping at this exact same place on the Suwannee River so many years ago. Back then, my idea of camping was the Red Roof Inn with no room service. I fell in love with the peace it brought me. After spending the last three days here with her, I love it just as much today as I did over ten years ago. That first trip, I was afraid to leave the campsite alone. It was the beginning of what gave me the courage to travel the country. Thank you, my best friend, for helping me step outside of my comfort zone.

Today, I am heading north. If you ever find yourself traveling through Pooler, Georgia in an RV and are thinking about stopping, you should keep going. I saw a Camping World and needed a few things so thought I would take a break here. They only have room for cars to pull in and are at the end of the street. I had to turn around in the middle of the road. I parked on the side of the road for just a minute to use the bathroom when the honking and yelling started. I get back to my seat and there is a man who barely speaks English blocking the road beside me throwing a fit, telling me I can't park here. I open my window to tell him that I was only parked for a minute. He continued to jump up and down yelling, "You no park here! My business! You no park here!" This poor Indian man needs to learn some social skills.

Love can give you more strength than you ever knew you had. My daughter is getting married this weekend and I told her that I would arrive today. Nothing is going to stop me. The wind at 18–25 mph, with gusts even higher, is worse than any I have experienced since driving a Class A. It just won't let up. It knocks me sideways and back again. It's blowing so hard that my windshield wipers came away from the windshield and they were not turned on. I spend the day just trying to hang on to the steering wheel. I am not giving up!

As I cross the border from Georgia into South Carolina I see brake lights. Slowing down, I can see logs in the road. I think a truck has lost his load. As I creep closer, I can tell that the wind has snapped at least one giant tree in half. It has hit one car and pieces were sticking out of the front of another. I keep going, thankful to still be alive.

I snug in with the semis when I can. They're getting tossed around as if they are mere toys. One honks his horn as he passes and gives me a thumbs-up sign. I am not giving up! I will not let my daughter down.

I am settled in Clemmons at Tanglewood RV Park. Every muscle in my body hurts and my hands feel like they are on fire. My palms look like they have been sunburned. How did I not notice until now? I don't know the answer. What I do know for certain is that love, faith, and determination can do anything.

I made the seven-and-a-half-mile journey from Tanglewood RV Park to my daughter and son-in-law's house. In an RV, no trip is complete without noticing a problem of some sort. One of my slides won't lock, and as I raise the electric visor, I notice that the tiny windshield crack that appeared when I was making my trip to North Carolina last week has grown. I am not sure if my auto insurance will cover it but will call to see about getting it replaced or repaired before heading further north in a few weeks.

Driving along, all I can think about is rounding a corner and my slide flying out or hitting a bump and my windshield splitting in half. Is the slide heavy enough to flip me over on my side in the middle of the road? If my windshield splits in half and falls out as I drive through the rain, do I keep driving? I turn onto the two-lane residential road and my GPS warns me that this road may not be suitable for my coach. I have seen worse. Besides, I am really good at backing up. I am watching tree limbs and power lines as I crawl down the road. Just before I get to my daughter's neighborhood, I see an extremely low drooping line. How did I miss this before when I was driving a car? Dang! Dang! Dang! Not sure I can make it under, I get close and notice a fire station just past the line. If the fire trucks can make it, surely I can too. I hold my breath, keep looking up, and inch along. I can't see it anymore. I don't hear anything hit or scrape along the roof. I must have made it. But what if it hangs up on the a/c or satellite? Inch, inch, inch and finally it is behind me.

Now to navigate this neighborhood. I make all of the turns except the last one. As I approach, I see lots of low-hanging tree limbs stretching out over the street at the corner. I assess quickly and decide whether to keep going, park right here, or try to back all the way out. I think I can pull far enough ahead and make a wide turn, avoiding the limbs and not hitting the Mustang parked in the street. I round the corner with no scratches or dents and I am here.

It's been two weeks since a rock flew up and cracked my coach's windshield. The crack continued to grow as I waited for a new windshield to arrive. They said that it could take days, or it could take weeks Not so long ago, I would have completely stressed out. I lived in the "it's gotta be right now" world. I was patient and didn't worry. I got the call yesterday and it had arrived. Pfaff's Auto Glass will install it today. Not one part of my plans was hindered.

Now to get there. I start the engine so it can warm up, organize a few things that could fly off of the counters, and climb into the pilot seat. I am on a dead-end street. At the corner is a small circular turn-around. I think it will be easy to turn around there. I put Irma in drive and hug the curb to my right. I would have preferred going further, but a car is parked in front of the neighbor's house. I make the wide swing and start to turn left, then I have to stop. I now have a street sign directly in front of me on my right corner. If I had only had that extra foot in the turn-around. No problem, I will just straighten out and back up a bit. I put Irma in reverse, check my mirrors and back-up camera. I don't have enough room to both straighten and back up. That car is now behind me.

Plan B...keep my wheels turned, back up the way I entered the circle, and drive to the cul-de-sac around the corner at the dead end of the street. I am out and on my way. As I drive through town, stopping at this red light and that, making right turns and left turns, I am aware how far I have come. I am not afraid. I can do several things at once and check mirrors automatically. Then the GPS says, "in one mile, make a U-turn, then your destination is on the right." I watch for Pfaff's on the left as I pass it, I need to judge the entrance. I remember the part of my driving lesson where Chuck had me drive through a mall parking lot. I can do this!

I have an intersection and two lanes to work with. Using the crossroad in front of me, I pull as far up as possible. I wish you could see the expressions on the faces of those people ahead of me at the light. They look extremely worried. I cut sharp left, watching all of my sides through the mirrors as I roll around the median without bumping over it. In just a minute, I am parked straight in front of the building. My new windshield is installed, and I am back at my resting spot a few more days before my next journey.

It's fifty-seven degrees and cloudy when I leave North Carolina for my trek north this morning. I was expecting to run into rush hour traffic, but it was smooth sailing. About twenty miles from the Virginia border, I start seeing signs for construction. The interstate drops to just a two-lane road...soft shoulder to the right and concrete barricade as a divider for oncoming traffic to my left. A warning sign reads, "Narrow bridge ahead. Wide loads take next exit." Am I considered a wide load? They must mean those trucks with signs saying wide load. I don't have one, so I should be fine. Right? I pass the exit for wide loads. It's a bit bumpy but pretty easy. I cross a small bridge with plenty of room, round a curve at about 50 mph, and then see what the big deal is. There is the narrow bridge less than one hundred yards in front of me. Dang it! It may be too tight. Maybe I *am* a wide load. I know Irma isn't going to make it through this. All I can do is hang on tight and keep the wheel straight, no matter how much scraping of metal I hear. More than a little spooked, I grip the wheel and tell God I am sorry, but I just put us in another predicament that he has to rescue me from.

I forge ahead, and in a minute, I am through without a scratch. Good thing I have Wonder Woman driving skills and God as my co-pilot. I am now out of the construction area and in Virginia.

The rest of the drive to Pennsylvania is easy and I enjoy the sights along the way. I make it through the narrow streets of Port Deposit and under a questionable overpass less than an hour from my aunt's house.

I see the farm up ahead on my left. My aunt won't be home yet, but she said she would leave the electronic gate open. As I get close, I see the gate is closed. I can't turn in. There is also a truck pulling a trailer with a tractor on it behind me. I make a left turn just ahead on the narrow gravel lane that runs alongside my aunt's property so the guy can pass me, only to find out he is turning here too. He waits while I try to back out. I can't go back the way I came in because I will still be in his way. I need to back up in the other direction. If I was pulling a trailer, this would have worked. On either side of the lane is a ditch. The blacktop road behind me is only about eighteen feet wide, with a big ditch and a berm that runs along the other side. My big girl doesn't bend very well. I have to back into the road far enough for my front wheels to clear the ditch on this side before I turn my wheels right. Although I am not worried about an automobile hitting me, the truck and tractor are a different story. Watching my back-up camera, I ease backwards. I can't make the turn without hitting the berm with my left hip.

I pull back into the lane, looking ahead for a different option. The only one I see is the field along the right side of the lane. It appears to have been freshly plowed, but there is a patch of grass that runs down the field's length. I don't know how solid the ground is there, but if I could pull up and over, the tractor could get past me and I could try again. I open my window and yell out to the guy, "What do you think about the grass on the right? Is it too soft for me?" He won't commit. "Is there room for me to turn around at the end?" All I get is a "maybe."

I think about his response for a minute. The last time I got a "maybe" response was just last August, and I took the chance. It wasn't easy, but I was rewarded with the most amazing stop on the entire trip. I am confident I will figure it out and drive on down the lane.

When I reach the end, I am on an Amish family's farm. The farmer is out in his field working with a team of mules. I am sure he sees me, but he pays no attention. The man in the truck who went around me gets out and goes to the farmer. So much for someone offering to help. There are trees on my left and a driveway to my right. I cannot turn into the driveway because there isn't enough room to back up around the trees. I pull forward some more so I can back into the driveway. I put Irma in reverse, check my mirrors and my back-up camera. I have to keep an eye on the big boulder sitting on the other side of the driveway. I slowly ease back, turning my wheel right, and keep watching the tree now in front of me. I think, *I've got this.* Then there is a slight bump and my back passenger side dips down. I try to pull forward immediately but my tire is spinning. I try reverse. Same thing. I put my coach in park and climb out to investigate.

I discover there was a small hole beside the driveway. I should have gotten out to look before I backed up. I did not see the hole in my mirrors or camera because it had the same soft grass as the area around it. Now there is slippery mud around my back tire. I try to think what I might have onboard to put under the tire but it won't matter; I can't be in the coach backing up and outside the coach putting something under the tire at the same time. I have got to ask for help.

I don't usually mind asking. People always help me when I need it. This time is different. The farmer and the man in the truck are ignoring me. It's as if they were waiting for me to fail. I don't want to ask them. I ponder my situation. If I keep trying, I will only make it worse. I *have* to ask for help. I go traipsing across the yard and through the field in my flip-flops to meet the farmer and his team of mules, sure God must be chuckling under his breath. I am sure the farmer has never seen such a sight.

I reach the two men and they stop talking, waiting for me to say something. I apologize and explain my predicament (like they didn't already know) and ask, "Could you please help me?" The farmer must have taken pity on me. He just starts walking towards the house, then comes back to my coach with a concrete cinder-block. He tells me to back up some so he can put the blocks in the hole in front of my tires, and that once they are in place, I can drive over the blocks onto level ground.

It worked! I am out and facing straight up the lane. I open my window to apologize again and thank him. He just nods once as if in greeting. Or perhaps, it's just, "Fine. Now get off my land and stop keeping me from my chores." Either way, I am grateful as I head back up the lane.

My aunt is home and heading up the driveway and to the gate. When I am even with the driveway, I stop to tell her I am going to pull up, then back in through the gate. I don't tell her I just failed that task a few minutes ago. It doesn't matter that her driveway is just as narrow or that there is an actual fence for me to hit on either side. That was just practice. Besides, I have her watching my back. She will stop me before I get into trouble...I hope.

I pull forward and into the left lane until my back tires are just past the driveway, turn the wheels sharp right, and start easing backwards, thinking this is going to be perfect on the first try.

"*Stop!*" my aunt yells. I stop, put the coach in park, and climb over to the passenger seat to ask what's wrong. I don't see anything in my mirror or back-up camera I will hit. She is worried about how close I am to the gate controller. I assure her that I can see it and won't hit it. I can tell by the worry on her face that she doesn't believe me. I climb back in my seat, foot on the brake, put the coach in reverse again, and check my mirrors. She has her hand on the controller between it and the coach, like that is going to protect the controller. Now I am worried. God, don't let me crush her hand. I move backwards as I turn, watching how close I am to her hand. She keeps telling me I am going to hit the controller. I don't tell her that it's the fence on the other side I am more likely to hit. I straighten my wheels, and in a minute, the needle is threaded.

I have to back down the driveway around the center island and *not* drive over my uncle's grass. For some silly reason, I am more afraid of this than I was hitting the fence. With my aunt's guidance, I manage and am glad to turn my engine off.

It has been a wonderful few days. I decided yesterday that the wind, ice, and snow is too bad. I am skipping Niagara Falls for now and headed south. It's forty degrees and raining when I pull out of the gate from my aunt's farm, keeping an eye out for the horse-drawn Amish buggies along the way.

I am in a 50 mph zone, probably driving 45 mph. I crest the hill and see a sign saying 12 percent grade. That's not so bad if it is stretched out over five miles, but this one is straight down for less than a quarter of a mile. It even flattens out at the bottom, but there might be a bigger problem. There is an intersection and a traffic light at the bottom of the hill. It's green now. Hoping it stays that way, I tap my brakes, pressing them on and off trying to reduce my speed in case it turns red. I am not that far away when the light turns yellow. I am only going about 35 mph, but the roads are wet. Then it turns red, and I'm not sure I can stop. I consider laying on my horn and blowing through the light. I press the brake and downshift. Irma's roaring, but she does as she was designed, and we stop a foot over the line.

I am getting close to Port Deposit, where I have to go under a train track that only has a 13'6" clearance. Even though I made it through when I came in, it still makes me a nervous. I am 12'10' tall and only have eight inches to spare, and that's only if my tires are inflated exactly the same as when I last measured. What if the road is higher coming in this direction? As I come around a corner, I spot road flares ahead. The left side of the road is blocked. It appears a man had misjudged his height when he tried to pull a boat through. Said boat is now being lifted up off the road by a wrecker. I go a little slower and make it through without hearing scraping metal noises.

It has continued to rain off and on. I have no idea where my next destination is. I only know I am headed south far enough to pick up a westbound interstate. It feels quite liberating to have this much freedom. I see a sign that says "6 percent grade, three miles." I experience mild panic when I recall the first 6 percent grade I encountered eight months ago. I roll through it as if on any Sunday drive and laugh.

I have come a long way.

Merging onto 81 South, I see an incredibly old, very high, incredibly narrow bridge ahead. The Potomac River is a long way down below. The bridge needs to be replaced, and people are driving across it in the wind and rain. Really, God? I am supposed to drive this giant across it too? It's raining, the wind is blowing, and it's two lanes with a concrete barrier down the middle. If there was an exit before it, I would take it. In my heart, I know I can do this. Part of me knows it is safe, or they would have closed the bridge. I try to relax, knowing it's only dangerous if I panic. If the wind hits me and I go over the side, I am dead. I am trying to think of a Bible verse that will calm me.

"Hello, God. I am about to have a panic attack. I could use some help here."

When I hit the first big pothole on the bridge, I flinch. I take a deep breath and try to relax my grip on the steering wheel. I don't know which is worse, the wind or the massive bumps. It's so bad that Emmi gets out of her seat and lays on the floor.

We are halfway across, moving at a snail's pace and causing quite the back-up. Deep breaths. Just look straight ahead. Ignore your mirrors. I am almost there when a big gust of wind hits me. Breathe! I pick a spot to watch after the bridge, bump off at the end of the bridge, and am in West Virginia. It has not been long since my last break, but I know there is a rest area ahead and I am stopping.

I park in the rest area, turn off the engine, and climb out of my seat. the roller blind over my couch has fallen on one side. The bumpy bridge was so bad the screws were bounced right out. I roll the blind as best as I can, then get the screws out on the other side and set everything on the floor behind the couch before heading outside.

As I am walking back inside, I notice the emergency latch is open on the big window now missing its blind. One more big bump and the whole window would have fallen out on the road. I almost didn't stop. I am now thanking God that the blind fell and I stopped. I never would have noticed it. I close the latch, secure the emergency exit window, and get back on the road.

I am staying at the Shenandoah Valley Campground for a few days in search of different waterfalls. It's a few miles off of the main road down a winding, tree-lined two-lane road. "Down" being the key word. The trees open up and the park below comes into view. The road goes straight down with a ninety-degree right turn at the bottom. I make it without flying off into the lake and get checked in. It's a pretty place set down in the valley along the Middle River.

The sites are mostly pull-through, gravel, and fairly level. Mine backs up to the clear, lazy river. I am hooked up and make it home. My flamingos are staked in the ground, my chair is out, and the side table with my travel plant and Wilbur the flying pig is set beside it. My welcome mat is at the foot of the steps and I pull my awning out when it starts to rain.

I am under my awning watching the rain and the lazy river run along behind me. My Zen is interrupted by the jarring weather alert emitting from my phone, a thunderstorm in the vicinity. If the wind picks up, I will bring my awning in. While I am listening to the thunder and watching the lightning off in the distance, my phone goes off again. This time it is a tornado watch. The alert says a tornado was spotted in some town and is moving north at 50 mph. I don't know the area, so I try to pull up radar maps but can't get them to load. I open my maps and type in the names of towns in its path. It appears I am about fifty miles northeast. I try to get more info on the storm, but cable and internet are out. I text my best friend to see if she can tell me more.

She calls and talks through what she can find. Looks like it's going to miss me. The rain gets heavier, but there is no wind.

An extremely loud noise is emitting from my phone again, this time it's a tornado *warning*. It's now thirty miles away. I turn on the radio and the first station that picks up has the same alarm then a recording, *"This is the National Weather Service. A tornado is on the ground in your area. Seek shelter immediately!"*

I'm putting my shoes on when there is a knock at my door. The man standing there in the pouring rain asks, "Are you watching this weather? We are from California. What are you going to do?" Honestly, I don't know. I don't have time to disconnect everything and I am not staying here. As people are loading into vehicles to leave, we ask one full of people where they are going. They are headed to the bath house up behind the pool.

I rush back inside to retract my awning, grab Emmi, a blanket, and make sure my phone is in my pocket. I am literally running from a tornado in the rain on foot, trying not to slip and fall as I run uphill. I see the pool and now the bathhouse. There is an open door with a light on. I move faster in that direction. I am almost there. As I start to go in, I see the sign, "Men's room." I cannot go in a men's bathroom! I turn around to see where the women's bathroom might be, and feel stupid when a man yells, "It doesn't matter! Get inside!"

Emmi is shaking, and we are cold and soaking wet. The first thing I see is a urinal. My life is in serious danger, why is this so hard for me? I need someone to know where I am. I call Hope but can't hear her. I send a text. "It's coming here. In bath house men's room behind pool." My phone is ringing. It's Hope. She stays on the phone with me as I stand shaking and dripping in the men's room. Then it's quiet. The noise is gone, leaving a light, steady rain.

I peek out the door. A man comes up to say that the tornado has passed, and they will drive me back to my coach. We laughed about me worrying about the men's room. He apologizes for not taking me when they left and promises to grab me if anything else happens. As I walked in my door in search of warm, dry clothes, another warning alarm is blaring from my phone. Flash flood warnings.

It's going to be a long night.

I get up and check the river level behind me throughout the night. This morning, I go out to check again and explore the park after the storm. The clear lazy river that was behind me yesterday is now a raging, muddy mess, downing trees and collecting trash from the banks. Yesterday, the river ahead of the waterfall was so shallow you could wade across in rainboots and not get wet. Today it would be impossible to not get swept away. Entire tent camping sites are under water at the lower end of the park. You can't even tell that there was a road between them and the river yesterday.

On my last day in the valley, just as it is getting light outside, I open the door and see white things floating through the air. I assume they are campfire ashes, then I notice it's thirty degrees and that's snow. I am so glad I remembered to drip my water last night. I decide to get packed up and on the road before the weather gets too ugly.

I get everything stowed, slides in, and disconnect sewer, water, and electric. I start the jack auto-store system. It seems to be taking forever. The cold must hinder them. Eventually, they are up. I start my engine, then go through my final pre-flight checklist.

I wind my way up out of the valley and when I reach the top of a hill, my heart starts to beat faster. I can see the Blue Ridge Mountains. On this cloudy, cold day, they *look* blue. Wow! I want to stop right here and just stare at the beauty of them. But that's probably a bad idea since I am in the middle of a winding two-lane road with cliffs on either side.

I go back through the town of Verona and merge onto I-85 South. Just as I get on the interstate, my "jacks down" light comes on and the alarm starts screeching at me. I stop to check it out and get fuel at the Pilot. Pulling in, I am facing the truckers getting diesel and need to turn left to the gas pumps. One of the truck drivers starts flashing his lights at me and motioning with his hands. It takes me a minute, but I realize he thinks I am coming through the diesel line from the wrong direction. I point to where I am actually going, he smiles and gives me a thumbs up. The row of pumps that I am pulling up to are out of order, but I cannot see that until I am almost to them. Backing all the way out is not an option because there is now a semi blocking my path. I could keep going, exit, and come back in the way I came, but to use the other row of pumps I need to be facing the other direction. I need to pull up and turn around. It will require some fancy three-point turn maneuvers, but I can do it. It is as if everyone here stops what they are doing to watch the crazy woman driving the giant motorhome. I get to a point where I can make the left turn back. I am on a tremendous slope sideways and wonder at what angle will I no longer be able to stay on all six wheels. What if I fall over on my side? It strikes me as funny how I automatically lean my body right to balance the weight, as if that would help. I make the turn without tipping over and get in line behind another RV.

At the pump, I press the "jack auto-store" button (because this always works to pull the jacks back in) and go inside to pre-pay for my fuel. When I come back out, I see that the one jack that was down did not go up. I now have three jacks partially down. It's *cold*, *windy*, and *snowing*. I get fuel and try to get the jacks to come back up. The system is struggling, making all kinds of noise. It will bring two up and another down. Nothing I try is working. I still have three jacks partially down. The man next to me pulling a fifth wheel says he thinks I have enough clearance to at least find another spot to park. I turn the wrong way out of the station. It's too late. My jack alarm is screaming, and I am on a two-lane country road with no place to turn around. At least I am going slow enough that if the jacks keep going down, I won't get in a massive wreck and start flipping across the interstate. Just as I am imagining this, I see a sign for truck parts, tires, and repairs ahead on my left. Surely, they can help me.

I pull into their lot and get as close as I can to their shop. There are two regular trucks outside running. None of the doors have windows or signs and I don't see anyone outside. I have my hands on my gun in one coat pocket and mace in the other pocket as I try doors. One is unlocked and there are lights on inside.

A few semi-trucks have parts on the floor around them suggesting they are being worked on inside, but I still don't see people. I cautiously enter calling out, "Hello? Anyone here?" No one answers, but I find an office with windows on the other side. Moving across the garage, continuing to call out, I reach the door and see a man inside on the phone. When I open the door, he gives me a dirty look and goes back to talking. I step back and wait. And wait. And wait.

Finally, he is off the phone and comes out to ask what I need. I tell him the problem. He asks several questions, which I answer, and says he doesn't know anything about RVs, but will look at it. We walk out the door into the snow, he sees the coach, and immediately asks where my husband is. This could go two ways. One: he laughs at me and thinks I am crazy. Two: he is an ax murderer and will kill me once we are inside the coach. It's the first time I pray that someone thinks I am crazy.

I tell him that it's just Emmi and I, with God as our co-pilot. He shakes his head and reminds me that he knows nothing about RVs.

We all climb in. Even with instructions, he cannot figure out how the buttons work. I tell him I want to try the manual override. I show him one button to push and hold, while I go out and see what that jack does. I go outside and check. Nothing. I go back in and ask if he can check the hydraulic fluid, wondering if it has a leak or is too cold.

He tells me, "That is not the problem. I'm sorry, I can't help you. Try a camping place. There is a Camping World about an hour away." He is out the door with it closed behind him before I can respond.

Listening to the jack alarm and praying that the jacks don't go down any more, I find my way back to the interstate, stop at the next rest area, and try the auto-store button again. Nothing. But the good news is that they have not come down any further. I get back on I-81 South and then merge onto I-77 South. I stop at the first rest area and try again. I have driven one hundred miles with this alarm going off. The jacks go up! Feeling relieved, I am back on the interstate, hoping I can outrun the snow before it gets heavy. The peace and quiet was not meant to last. Twenty-five miles up the road, the alarm is back on.

I am now making a steep climb over the Blue Ridge Mountains and there is no place to stop. I see warnings of construction and that one emergency truck ramp is closed. The wind is blasting and there are cops all over. I climb, climb, climb. I get to the top and see the sign that tells me, "steep downhill grade next twelve miles." I don't experience an ounce of fear over this, and can't help smiling.

I make it to the rest area at the bottom to look at my jacks again. The snow is gone, and the sun is shining. I press the auto-store button and the jacks are up. The alarm goes off. Slightly later than planned, I make it to my daughter and son-in-law's house.

✧

After a few days of rest, I am on my way south. I expect a four-and-a-half-hour drive. Five and a half at the most, depending on stops. I plug the Mount Pleasant / Charleston KOA address into my RV GPS and hit the road. My journey starts out easy with smooth roads and no wind. I take a series of south and east turns, driving some interstate and some state highways.

My road is closed ahead because of flooding and I have to take a detour. I have no idea where I am, so I ignore the GPS and follow the signs that take me on one two-lane country back-road after another through North Carolina. I drive past miles and miles of houses on lots of acreage, then the occasional big new house sprawling out with land. At times, my GPS warns it isn't sure my coach can maneuver these roads. I can do nothing else but keep going.

On another two-lane road I pass several dilapidated old mobile homes. They might be rentals or homes for farm workers. It makes me sad and at the same time feel so very blessed. How, in this country, do people live like this?

I am elated when the detour ends. I am on a four-lane highway and start following my GPS again. Now according to my GPS, I am supposedly twenty minutes from my destination. Yippee! Then I see a sign. Problem! I am in Myrtle Beach, not Charleston. I find a spot to pull over and review my paper map. I am two and a half hours from where I need to be. I ask my British male Siri for help. This could be bad since he does not know what I am driving, but I chance it. It guides me to US 17 and I follow the directions, praying it will get me there in one piece. After a few question-able turns, I eventually see KOA signs. A little after five o'clock, I arrive at my perfectly-level spot by the water and get set up for a few days.

On my last day in Charleston, I wake up with no plans. When other people are going to work, I am sitting in the sun with my coffee, enjoying my view of the lake and watching the birds. I am not fighting rush hour traffic, I am going for a walk through the woods by the lake with Emmi. It's late morning by the time we leave the park.

Taking I 526 to loop around Charleston, I encounter my first challenge of the day—the Wando River Bridge. I am a little spooked when I see how tall it is. The wind is already whipping, and I know that the higher I get, the worse it will be. I take a deep breath, decelerate, and place both hands firmly on the wheel with elbows firmly planted on the armrests to keep us steady. Don't look down, left or right. Look up and out.

I am over! I was so focused on hanging on I forget to be afraid. Now the Cooper River is ahead of me. I made it over the last one alive, and this bridge does not seem as bad. Again, I am safely on the other side. Now the Ashley River. This bridge appears even less daunting. I don't know if it's a smaller bridge or if I am just more relaxed, but this one is easier. Third time's a charm!

I get gas at the Exxon just before I-95. It's easy getting in, but not so easy getting out. I thought I had a clear path, but some idiot flies around my right side and parks in front of me as I am turning right leaving the pump. *Brakes!* They are only about three feet in front of me and I still have to make this turn. I glance in my left mirror and check my rear camera. There is no room for me to back up without hitting the gas pump. I still am not a good judge of the distance in front of me. I turn the wheels sharply and inch forward, watching my back-end swing. It's very close to the pump. Inch forward a little more, put my foot on the brake and stretch up out of my seat. Maybe I can see the back of the car in front of me. I keep inching forward, listening for the sound of crunching metal.

I did it! I can breathe!

I merge onto I-95 South and fight the wind all the way back to Flamingo Lake RV Resort in Jacksonville, Florida. I am home and sitting still for a week.

CHAPTER 15

EATEN ALIVE

I have wheels again! This is not as easy as one might think it should be. I wanted a vehicle that I could tow with all four wheels on the ground behind my coach. I knew the weight limit and thought, *I just have to find a vehicle under that.* Not the case.

I considered Honda CRVs and learned they were only towable until a certain year. Then I looked at other all-wheel drive SUVs and learned all of the things you had to do each trip to tow it, like remove fuses ten and eighteen, disconnect the whatchamajig, put it in park, turn ignition one click left then two clicks right, then put car in neutral. Really?

I found information that said if it was four-wheel drive, I could tow it, which isn't necessarily true. I picked out a Subaru but learned that my warranty would be voided if I towed it. Someone told me about the *Motorhome Magazine* Tow Guides. They come out with a new one every year. It gives you every piece of information you could ever need to make the best decision on your tow vehicle. Once I had all of these for the past seven years in hand, I started talking to people with the same type coach towing the car I am interested in. Today I bought a 2014 Jeep Cherokee Trailhawk.

It feels good to have my own wheels again. It feels even better to know that when I travel in the coach, I can see more sights.

I have gone through just as much research on the tow equipment and braking systems. I am calling Dick Gore's tomorrow to order and schedule the install.

I am doing something new today and honestly, I am nervous. I will drive the coach over for the final piece of towing equipment and pull my new car back to Flamingo Lake. Not only am I driving my massive coach, but I will also be adding to its length with another moving thing. I am definitely scared.

At Dick Gore's, Harry is being so patient explaining everything to me, even with my million questions. He walks me through doing everything myself. I must look nervous, because at one point he stops and asks me if I am okay. I tell him I'm scared, but not afraid to try. There is just so much to remember!

I spent my last evening at Flamingo Lake playing bingo and visiting with my newly made friends here. This morning, Ron rolled by in his golf cart to give Emmi one last pet and Pam waves as she drives by. All connected and rolling out! The backroads at 35 mph gave me some time to get comfortable with turns before getting on the interstate. Thank you to the person following me. I really appreciated you merging and waiting for me to merge before you went around me. It's way easier than I thought it would be. The only time I feel the car behind me is when I hit a bump. I feel the pull just a bit like when I was pulling the fifth wheel.

I disconnect the car and back into my site like I have been doing it all of my life. It is now safe for everyone to get back on the road.

My next big adventure begins on Tuesday. I will be checking out East Coast beaches all the way to Maine!

It's six o'clock, cloudy, and already a steamy seventy-eight degrees when I wake up. My goal is to stay off of interstates as much as possible and hug the coast for most of this trip. As I get everything situated around the driver seat, it dawns on me, this will be my first trip pulling the car. I hope I hooked it up right.

I make it across the South Carolina Border and the Trailhawk is still behind me. I've waited as long as I could, but I need fuel. There is a Pilot fuel stop about two miles ahead. It's hard enough navigating forty feet into a station for gas, and I have added the Trailhawk to my overall length. I exit the interstate, turn left, and see Pilot just ahead on my right. I scope out the pump layout before I make the turn. My heart is racing. I need to make it all the way over to the last island of pumps, then make a sharp left. How sharply can I turn without jack-knifing? Will my tail swing be even bigger? Will the Trailhawk hit the cars parked behind me? I crawl in, watching my mirrors and cameras. I make the turn without hitting anyone or wrapping myself around the pumps and causing an explosion worthy of the evening news.

Filling Irma up takes a while. Will I be out of everyone's way with this extra length? I inch forward, watching the pump on my left and the cars parked behind me. I climb out and walk around my rig, shocked at what I have done. This is the best pump line-up I have ever made. I am straight, the gas pump is perfectly even with my tank, and there is plenty of room for people to get around me.

I make it out without incident and pull into the Myrtle Beach KOA not long after with the Trailhawk still behind me. My escort kept saying, "You're such a little lady driving this big rig. I have never seen such a little lady park like that!"

Thank you, Marc, for boosting my confidence!

This morning when I first walk onto the beach, I see miles of umbrellas in both directions. The parasailing is just beyond, the boats right on the beach. I am going parasailing courtesy of Ocean Watersports, located blocks from Myrtle Beach KOA. Two young women joined me on my parasailing adventure today, Nicolette and Michelle. We all agreed that Captain Hudson rocked this trip.

While I wait for our pictures to come through, I spend some time getting to know two other young women who work the booth. One even dreams of RVing across the country. Thank you, Sarah and Brianna, for the great pictures.

On my last night, the city put on a firework display close enough for me to watch from my RV. My first stop on this East Coast adventure was in Myrtle Beach, not because I wanted to come here, but it was as far as I could drive in a day. I would definitely come again.

I am packed, stowed, and ready to roll. Everything worked as it should. Next stop, New Bern, North Carolina.

New Bern KOA is home for three nights. Thanks to Jen in the office for all the suggestions on places to see. My escort winds through the park's tight turns with me navigating along behind him. I am concerned when we pull into a muddy site. When I step out, my escort is waiting for me at the door and I tell him this must be the wettest site in the park.

He agrees and suggests I ask the office if there is another spot available. I am going to give it a shot first. I plug in to power and connect the water, push the auto-level button, and my jacks sink in the mud. This is not going to work.

I walk back to the office to inquire if there is another site. Nope. I have the last one available that is large enough for me. I am let down and consider moving on after a night's rest. Instead of being short with me, the manager, Pat, calmly starts looking for solutions. She asks, "Would you mind moving for a bit and so we can put down more gravel?"

"Of course not," I reply. "I am flexible and would love to stay."

While she is talking about this with my escort, he suggests, "Why don't we try putting something bigger under her jacks first?"

I agree to give this a try and head back to camp.

He shows up within minutes after me, bringing long two-by-eights that would stretch the width of my rig. He climbs down in the mud to put them in place under my jacks with my rubber pads on top. I try my jacks again and this works! I am happy as a clam at high tide, super excited that there was room for me.

Not once did anyone grumble. In fact, several people stopped to see if I needed anything else. The New Bern KOA may have muddy, bumpy roads and sites, but they have the best people. I am enjoying my stay. If you own or manage a campground, just remember, your customers are supposed to be enjoying a vacation.

If they have a challenge or complaint, kill 'em with kindness and most will be okay.

By late afternoon, it is pouring and my site is majorly flooded, with water running down the road. Sometimes you've just got to wait for the rainbow. I sit inside and watch. I didn't get a rainbow, but I do get an incredible sunset as the storm moves across the water. There is a cool light show now that the storm is across the river from me.

I meet Phil taking sunset pictures. He is sleeping in a hammock under a tarp while he waits on boat repairs. He is from Upstate NY, got divorced, sold his house, and bought a houseboat with zero boating experience. We talk for hours and promise to keep in touch. It's nice to meet people willing to step outside the norm and try something new.

I make the hour drive to the beach. There is only one parking area with public beach access. It takes me twenty minutes to find an empty parking spot. You have to pay at a kiosk to park here. Credit only, no cash. I step onto the sand and even with my flip-flops on, my feet are burning! The beach is crowded, with umbrellas and chairs everywhere. I spread out my beach blanket, read a book, have lunch, and walk along the water's edge.

It's not "my" Atlantic Beach, but not bad.

I pulled into New Bern KOA two days ago. The women in the office who checked me in, were some of the most personable I have met doing this job. There isn't much to see or do nearby, but if you are looking for a family camping vacation, it's great. This KOA also has some cool stuff, like the pier in pristine shape and the giant checkers and chess games. Emmi loves the clean, grassy Kamp K9 space and I loved the fenced pet bath area. Overall, it was a great visit.

On this day three years ago, I brought home my first camper. While preparing to leave this morning, I think of how far I have come. It's 8:45 a.m., sunny, and eighty-five degrees. Jacks are sluggish, but in. As I pull out, the awning to my left is really close. A couple ahead of me stop what they are doing to watch. They look worried. The man looks concerned as I drive by them. The woman says, "You go girl!"

Just like that, I am on the road again. Next stop…Chincoteague Island. GPS says 259 miles. The biggest fear I still face is large bridges. Today, there is a big one on my route.

Speaking of my GPS, it is struggling to keep up with me. It does not tell me which way to turn as I exit the KOA. There are people behind me, so I choose right. As I make the turn, it says, "make a U-turn." I have obviously chosen wrong. I drive on, searching for a place where I can turn around. Just before each crossover, I hear again and again, "make a U-turn." I know! I know! This is a lot of monstrosity to turn around!

There's a spot ahead with a left turn lane and a wide street entrance across from it. Turning my blinker on, I merge into the turn lane and pull forward as far as I can without landing in the ditch along the median. I wait until there are no cars coming. This is going to be a challenge and it's going to take a minute. Actually, a few minutes, if it's even possible. What's the worst that can happen? I could get stuck with Irma and the Trailhawk stretched across the entire two lanes. Since I cannot back up, I will have to get out and disconnect the car and move it before backing up and turning Irma around. I am so far forward in the turn lane that I can't pull forward and move on to a better area. This has to be the one.

I have turned Irma around in two lanes before, but not with the added length of a car behind me. I hear that voice in my head, "Have faith." I take a deep breath and turn left, aiming for the far right side of the road straight across from me. I make it across and turn sharp left again. This road looks smaller than it did from the other side, and I'm not sure there is enough room. I am not only stretched across part of the road behind me but am now headed straight for the stop sign in front of me.

Guardian angel to the rescue again! I finish the turn without even running over the grass and feel triumphant when I drive back onto the road, going in the right direction.

This is the exact drive I wanted. I am traveling along two-lane roads lined with tall, shady trees. I take in the sights of cornfields and occasional white farmhouses with perfectly manicured front yards. It reminds me of living on the farm in Tennessee. There wasn't a homeowners' association, and yet the grass was always mowed, the flowers always blooming, and never a weed in their beds. It's the same along these back-country roads. I wonder what happened that so many no longer take pride in their home?

I also notice the many volunteer fire departments and churches along this route. Both build community bonds that are often not found in the city. Men with jobs to do and farms to work are often awakened in the middle of the night to put out a fire in someone else's home. They are not paid to do this dangerous job but are still committed to it. The country churches always have "church ladies" who visit the elderly and the sick. They cook, and cook, and cook, always ready to feed a crowd. Everyone knows what everyone else is doing. I think our world needs more of that.

Up ahead to my right there is a large field. It has one massive old oak tree in the entire field, shading a tiny graveyard. The straight rows of the crop are interrupted as they circle around the outer edges of the tree canopy. I know someone still visits this place because it is so well kept. I wonder how long this has been here and about the family lovingly placed under the shade tree. In most places people are paid to take care of the plot where our families are put to rest. It feels good to be in this place where time seems to have stood still.

I am cruising along, enjoying the scenery, totally relaxed. A sign ahead says the speed limit is increasing from 45 mph to 55 mph. I press the gas pedal, speed up a bit, crest a small hill, and there is a traffic light. It's yellow! I am at 50 mph and there is no way I can bring Irma to a halt in this short distance! Who decides what speed limits should be, where they change, and where signs should be placed? I put my foot hard on the brake and release. Then again. My engine kicks into a lower gear. There are cars on both sides of the crossroad, waiting for their light to turn green. The light is red! I put both feet on the brake. If the cars move, I will hit them. I let off the brake a second and push hard again. The engine kicks down even lower. Repeat. Irma roars and comes to a stop, just barely over the line. The best part is the people in the cars were paying attention to their surroundings. They knew I was coming and might not be able to stop. They waited, even though their light was green. No one honked their horn in agitation. They just waited to make sure I was able to stop.

While we are on the topic of speed limits...I see a sign that says, "Slow moving farm equipment use this highway." A few feet beyond is another sign that announces a 70 mph speed limit, and then a bridge. This seems so crazy. I am laughing out loud, thinking they must be joking. Is it like a real-life video game? Fly across the bridge, dodging slow-moving farm equipment? Do you get points for not falling off the bridge? Lose points when you knock slow-moving farm equipment off the bridge? Maybe bonus points for *not* bumping them off the bridge? I slow down, keeping my eyes peeled for slow-moving farm equipment. I never see any, but I see the same set of signs several times over the next hour. I laugh each time.

I crossed the many bridges through North Carolina without incident. Actually, I felt pretty good. I go through the toll just before the Chesapeake Bay Bridge and that's when my heart starts beating a little faster. I make it okay until I reached the base of the tunnel. It's two-way traffic with no divider and no shoulder. The speed limit is 55 mph, minimum 45 mph. They are just gonna have to give me a ticket…I am going 35 mph! I make it out the other side and speed up to fifty across miles of water.

Now there is another tunnel. Same scenario. I am about halfway through the tunnel when a semi-truck comes across the center line toward me. I am going downhill with the Trailhawk pushing from behind. I flash my lights; he's still coming. I push my brakes hard to let the engine downshift. He's still coming over the line. I only have seconds to decide. I move right and hold tight to the steering wheel to keep steady in case I hit the wall. He's right here! I want to close my eyes. It takes every ounce of willpower to keep them open.

God, help me.

I have to take one hand off the wheel to lay on my horn, and he flies by so close I think his mirror is going to catch mine. I hear the scream of tires braking on the road and an incredibly loud noise, then brake lights from the cars behind him in my side mirror. The fronts of cars approaching me dip hard as they too hit their brakes. I have no idea what happened behind me, but I see light at the end of the tunnel! As I climb up and out onto the bridge, my mouth is so dry I can't swallow. I need water, but first, I have to pry a hand from the steering wheel. Thankful that I am okay, I pray there are no more tunnels.

I am close to Chincoteague KOA when my GPS tells me to make a right into the park, beside a giant water park. Either the GPS is wrong, or this is going to be way too touristy for my relaxing week. Driving past the water park, I find the guard station for the KOA. The young guy that greets me completes a form, then tells me to pull forward and take it into the office to check in. He tells me to park just past the golf carts. I tell him I will be blocking the parked cars if I do that. "It's okay," he replies, "they are employee cars."

I pull forward, park, and climb down. There are visitor tags on the cars; they are not employees' cars. Hopefully, I will be out before they want to leave.

The office feels like a car rental place. There is a line and high counter with several employees working the desk. When it's my turn, I walk up to the desk and hand the woman my slip of paper. Before I can say hello, I am asked for my name, which is irritating because it's already on my slip of paper. She tells me what site number I am on and then gets excited because I have one of their premium patio sites.

My escort waves from his cart in front of my rig. I am ready to roll. On our way through the park I see a bunch of adorable tiny houses. The pavement turns to dirt when we hit the back side of the park. Then I see the view. Wow! We have reached my home for the next few days, Site 245. My escort pulls straight through and I follow. I totally ignore his directions because I know my rig and where I need to be when I make the turn. I know where I need to be positioned to reach water, sewer, and electric. When I climb out to see how everything looks around me, my escort says, "You must be a truck driver; that was impressive."

"No," I tell him. "Just a Class A driver."

The spaces are small, and the rock pad is quasi-level. The deluxe patio is concrete and clean with brightly colored furniture on it. I have a table with four chairs, a patio glider, a potted flower, and a chiminea. I am in my spot, but my car is still *way* in the road. They advertise max pull-through, sixty-five feet. I know my tow equipment and car are not an additional twenty-six feet long. I tell my escort this is my first challenge. There is not much room for me to put my car once it is disconnected. He is so nice. He heads back over to the office to see if any of the sites around me will be vacant. He is back in a few minutes and says that I can park my car in the site next to me.

Now I have another problem. While my escort was gone, I plugged into power. When I went inside to turn the air conditioner on, everything blew. I checked my breakers inside. Nothing works. I checked the breaker at the plug outside. Still nothing. My escort calls maintenance, and Ben shows up in two minutes. He checks the breaker at the pole and says it has power, then goes out of his way to investigate where power comes into my rig. My surge protector is flashing a warning light. He goes back to the breaker and notices someone has installed it wrong. The fifty-amp breaker is installed on a single pole and is only pulling thirty amps. He reinstalls it correctly and plugs my cord back in. Still, I have the warning light and no power. I ask if there is a local mobile RV repair company.

"Yes," Ben replies, "but let's try to fix this without costing you anything." I go inside to check breakers again. I turn both main breakers off then back on. I have power!

I finish getting connected, level, and put my slides out. I had to manually level, but I made that labeled diagram this time. As I finish up and sit down to enjoy the view, my escort drops by again to check on me and see if I need anything else. The people on the ground here are as amazing as the view I have of the sun setting behind the lighthouse across the water from me.

After a peaceful morning on my patio, I am excited about taking a kayak trip today. I drive over to Memorial Park a few minutes away and easily find my kayak guide, Shane, from Assateague Explorer Cruises, by the launch ramp. A family of four has arrived before me and is getting checked in. I tell Shane I am kayaking alone.

When he asks if I am okay with a single-person kayak, I tell him I paddle board, but have only had limited experience on a lake in a kayak. He decides I am fit enough to handle a kayak by myself. I grab my water shoes and leave my flip-flops in the car while he checks in two other single women, one from California and another from around the Boston area here on a day trip.

Everyone is wearing their life vests as we go through a quick lesson. When Shane points out my kayak for the day, I am a little anxious. It's a narrow, enclosed, touring kayak. I have only used a "sit on top" wider kayak. Nervously, I tell the group I will be the first to flip my kayak.

It's a team effort getting our kayaks in the water. I help California and she helps me. I make it into my kayak without flipping it with Shane's help. First challenge met and conquered.

It is a sunny, calm day on the water. We start out across the Assateague Canal on our way over to the Chincoteague National

Wildlife Refuge. Our guide, Shane, is perfect. He is able to keep us all, with different levels of experience, corralled. Just as I am getting the shoulder roll paddle down, a pod of dolphins swims playfully through our group. Everyone stops paddling to watch. They are all sleek and shiny gray and effortlessly slip through the water around us and move on. What incredibly graceful creatures!

Our guide shares a ton of interesting history about the area. My favorite is about the wild ponies. The Chincoteague Pony, also known as the Assateague horse, is a breed living in a feral condition on Assateague Island. They are grazing right beside us. Shane points out a majestic bald eagle perched in the trees watching us. We stop paddling to enjoy the sight, then make it all the way up to the bridge and rest a few minutes in the cool shade under it.

As we paddle back, I watch a seagull pick up a small crab. Immediately two others swoop in, diving and screaming at the holder of this tasty meal. I am quietly rooting for the guy who worked hard for his lunch, but the two others are determined to steal it away. He is no match for them. He drops the crab and one of the others quickly snatches it in mid-air. The fight is over. I know this is nature, but still I am sad. We make our way back across the channel to the ramp after a great adventure. Best part? I didn't flip my kayak!

Today, I am taking the short ten-minute drive over yesterday's kayaking bridge to the Chincoteague National Wildlife Refuge. The Lighthouse Trail is my first stop, but the parking lot is full. I drive a little further to another parking lot. Exchanging my flip-flops for sneakers, I set out on a connecting trail. Even on the shady trail, it's *hot*.

It's almost noon when I reach the base of the lighthouse built in 1833 and re-built to 142 feet in 1867. It rises twenty-two feet above sea level and is further inland today but was originally near the end of the island. The moving sand since 1870 has stranded the lighthouse almost five miles from the inlet. This brilliant beacon has guided so many people through the night. I begin climbing the 175 steep, winding steps. I won't lie, two sets left, and I am starting to feel the burn in my thighs. The climb was worth it though. The view is astounding. Good thing I did this first. They are closing the lighthouse in thirty minutes because of the extreme heat.

I return to where I parked at the Visitor's Information Center to get more water and a hiking trail map. The inside is air conditioned, so I take my time browsing through the exhibits and learn more about the local history.

Once I make it through everything, I sit in a rocking chair to look over my trail map. In this heat, there's no way I can manage all of the trails, so I will take the two where I have the best chance of seeing the wild ponies. I hop in the car to find the parking lot between the Woodland Trail and the Black Duck Trail. On my way, I stop to see a big herd of ponies off in the distance.

When I get to parking, there are only two cars in the lot. I guess everyone else chose the beach over hiking. I park, apply sunscreen, and coat myself in bug spray. With water and camera in hand, I set off on the 1.6-mile Woodland Trail first. It's a nice, easy, paved trail with patches of shade along the way.

I start out by seeing a bumblebee tasting the sweet nectar of a honeysuckle. After ten minutes of being totally enthralled, I laugh. I came all the way here to spend time with a bumblebee? It's pretty awesome to have the lifestyle that allows me to do this, but I am going to melt before I finish the first trail. I only get about a hundred yards and I see wild blackberries. I think of so many Father's Days picking blackberries with Daddy. With the thought of the resulting blackberry cobblers, my mouth is watering. Most are not ripe yet, but I find a few. I pop the first one in my mouth, hesitant to bite into it since it could be sour. Gently, I bite down, totally ready to spit it out, and oh man! A gush of sweetness floods my mouth. I close my eyes and remember picking these as a little girl in East Texas. I am in heaven! After a few more, I get going again. I look across the trail and see dragonflies everywhere. Mesmerized, I am stuck again, trying to get a picture of one being still.

Another few yards up the trail I watch a gray Delmarva fox squirrel. My kayak guide yesterday told me that these were once endangered, and because of the Chincoteague National Refuge, their population is growing. I *have* to get a picture of him, which is easier said than done. He scampers to and fro, stopping every few seconds to scratch. After about fifty snaps in rapid succession, I hope there is a good picture.

As I move on, I spot more squirrels and dragonflies, and stop at wet areas and wait quietly for something to move. I come across a wooden pier and take the detour. At the end, I am rewarded with another group of wild ponies.

Back on the paved trail, I see another path ahead. It's not marked, but I head down it anyway. I have made it to the end of the path and think I see three white pony faces watching me from the trees. I really wish I had a pair of binoculars. A little further along the path I notice where the grass is laid down. Someone or something rested here. Suddenly there is a flutter of wings and screaming. I stop, stand totally still, and wait until everyone settles down before I turn and look. Only one bird is left on the log. I have spooked the rest.

I come across the Bivalve Trail. It's one I did not notice on the map and isn't paved. I pull out my trail map to see where and how far it goes. It goes to Tom's Cove, only a half-mile to the water and back. I start down the trail and through the trees. It's cool and shady here. It feels good. About halfway down the trail, I hear what sounds like a swarm of bees. It's loud, and I am under attack. It's not bees, it's monster mosquitos! I feel like I am being eaten alive. I can see sunlight and water ahead, so I make a run for it. As soon as I am out of the trees, they are gone. Although I am melting in the heat, I have never been so glad to see hot blazing sun. I take my time exploring along the water, and when I'm done, I check my map to see if there is another way out besides through the fierce man-eating swarm. There's not. The only way out is back the way I came in.

Hoping the swarm has passed on, I set off back along the sandy, shaded path. It's only minutes before I hear the loud buzzing noise again. Every mosquito who lives at the Refuge must be here. Mosquitos don't usually bother me, but these monsters have apparently decided my blood and sweat would make a great buffet. I worry about not being on the main trail. I can just see the headlines tomorrow, "Woman Found Dead in Refuge, Eaten by Monster Mosquitos" It doesn't matter how hot I am, I want sunshine now. As I hurry along the path, there is another squirrel. He's miserably trying to scratch and run at the same time. The minute I am back on the main trail and in the sun, the beasts are gone. I have big red welts all over my exposed skin, but I am going to make it out alive. Forget the other trail.

I make it back to the car and find my way to the beach at Tom's Cove. They advertised: "One of the most gorgeous beaches found on the Atlantic Coast is the one at Chincoteague National Wildlife Refuge. The white sands of this windswept barrier island are a major reason for visitors to flock to this area." I disagree. The sand is brown, not white, and it's *hot*! It's also crowded and steep. My beach in Florida is much better.

The best part of this beach is the water. I run and dive in like a kid. The cold hits me with a shock that takes my breath away, but oh, it is incredible! My body temperature slowly reduces to normal and it soothes my bitten skin. To get back to my car, I have to run through the sand again. I am sure my feet are blistered. By the time I get through it, I am I search of water to rinse off. I don't see any nearby. I don't love the idea, but I use the rest of my drinking water and get in the car to head back to my RV.

I am back at my site, relaxing in the shade on my glider with Emmi laying at my feet when in pulls a gorgeous new Airstream. Our new neighbors are from Maine, and we chat about the route I should take going up and where they are headed next. Emmi loves playing with their cute Labradoodle puppy, Molly. They will both sleep well tonight.

CHAPTER 16

WILL THEY FIND ME?

I am up at seven. It's already a sunny eighty degrees. I take my time visiting with the people I have met here, saying good-bye to Bosco the Boxer and his family. I say good-bye to Joyce and Ken, and we promise to connect again. I make it out of my site and up the narrow road out of the campground, car and all. I pull out of the park, headed for Cape May KOA.

In Delaware, there are a lot of chicken companies. Now I know why there is so much corn being grown. Little square houses, most are white, with front porches. It strikes me as interesting that none have fences, even if they are close to another house.

I am having GPS challenges. I keep losing satellite signal.

I drive through Historic Georgetown and back out into the country again. Traffic is moving really slow. At noon I am pulling into the Lewes Ferry Terminal. All lined up for the narrow booth and there are still a few lanes open. I am gonna make the 12:15 p.m. ferry.

At the booth, I present my driver's license and the woman asks if I have a reservation. I don't. "This terminal is by reservation only," she says. Dang! She leaves the booth to measure my length, comes back, and checks her computer. "The first reservation is at two forty-five. Will that work?" she asks. Of course it will. She spends another minute asking how I do this by myself and tells me, "You are living my dream!"

I pull over to my lane, glad I had the faith to live *my* dream.

Emmi and I enjoy the view and have some lunch on the dock. Our server Carla is awesome.

Wow! I thought my rig was big. This captain just turned the ferry around in a tiny channel and backed it in. Now it's my turn to do something astonishing. I am the second vehicle driving onto the ferry. The entrance is narrow and doesn't appear tall enough. The man there keeps waving me forward. I crawl through. They want me to get closer to the wall on my left. I make it on the ferry with no damage to it or Irma. My road house is the talk of the boat and the hour-and-a-half ride was incredible. Meeting the Souto family and hanging out with them made it even more sensational.

I am off the ferry and trying to follow my GPS. I take a wrong turn and end up going over the bridge to Historic Cape May. When I reach the top of the bridge, I realize I am in trouble. The town below is like every historic town in tourist season. The buildings are stacked side-by-side, the narrow streets are clogged with traffic and people, and there definitely is not going to be a place to turn Irma and the Trailhawk around. Even for me, a U-turn would be impossible.

I turn right at one of the first streets I see. My hope is to circle around a block. My heart beats faster and my stomach feels like I just dropped off a cliff. I am on a dead-end street with some sort of waterfront restaurant in front of me. People are everywhere. They don't know whether to stop and watch or run for cover. I make the easy left turn across the dirt parking lot, hoping there is a way out, all the while people are pointing at us and talking about us. I can only imagine they are saying. "Look at that crazy woman!" I am almost at the end of the dirt lot and see a tiny paved street to my left. I feel like I just won the lottery. If I can make the turn, I will be heading back to the main street. I navigate with my mirrors and rear camera, watching my tail swing and the Trailhawk behind me. I can I see the main street ahead. Another anxious moment. How am I going to make that left turn with buildings so close to the street I could reach out and touch them? How am I going to get across backed up traffic with no red light?

I might as well be a dinosaur the way people are watching me. I make it to the end of the street, inching forward a bit at a time. Now with my nose is in the road, someone waits. Perhaps he just thinks this crazy person in a bus is going to run over him, but it's my way in. Cars are still thick coming from the other direction. I keep going. A woman sees me and stops, waving me through. I am across and heading back over the bridge in the right direction. First, I thank God for not letting me hurt anyone, then I send out a thanks to my RV driving instructor, Chuck, for making me drive through a movie theatre parking lot and a packed mall parking lot.

Finally, the Cape May KOA sign is ahead on my right. I drive past lots of seasonal sites in the front. This is totally foreign to me. Not only do they have loads of stuff, but they have professionally built screen patio enclosures attached to their RVs. These RV's are not going anywhere. Why would they do this if they are not going to use their RV to travel as it was intended?

I pull up in front of the office and go inside. The ladies at check-in are so friendly. I had to reserve a back-in site. She pulls out a map and shows me where Site 10 is, just down the paved main road on the left.

If home is where you put your flamingos, then I am here. No escorts, and only a back-in spot on the main road available. I dropped the car in less than ten minutes, parked it, and jumped back in the coach. I am in front of my site. It is long and on a rock pad that is mostly level. Only problem is a tree with limbs that need some trimming, but I backed in straight around it first try. Kinda like I know what I am doing. I get settled before letting my friends from Missouri know I made it.

When was the last time you woke up and thought this could be the best day of your life? I caught up with dear friends I met RVing out west last year. Bev and I made it up the 199 steps at the Cape May Lighthouse to see the breathtaking view of the Jersey Cape, where the Delaware Bay meets the Atlantic Ocean. We are going to the beach at Cape May Point State Park, but about the time my toes hit the sand, lightning strikes. My happy feet scurry right back up to the car.

I am tired today. It could just be the dreary, gray weather. I consider a re-route so I can rest a little. I will skip Bar Harbor and add two days to Niantic. For now, I am going to take a nap.

I am wide awake at six thirty, with a plan to be out by eight. But first, coffee. I walk out the door, coffee in hand, wearing shorts, a tank top, and flip-flops, and am hit by a blast of cold air on my exposed skin. It's sixty-eight degrees! Laugh if you want, but after days and days of near 100-degree heat, this is cold.

People keep telling me to go around New York as I head north toward Niantic, but I have been through rush hour traffic in Atlanta, Houston, and LA, and this is Saturday. I am going for it.

At Highway 9 and 109, I get confused again, just like when I came in. I make the wrong turn and end up on Garden City Parkway. At least I am heading north. Garmin eventually recalculates, and the time to arrive seems right. There is a lot of wind. The tree limbs are waving viciously on the left side of the road as I drive along the coast. The grass in the salt marshes to my right is almost laying down.

Garmin keeps losing satellite signal. I remember I am supposed to turn on 18 somewhere, but have no idea how far north, south, east, or west. I try Siri, but the British guy keeps trying to take me around the cities on a ten-hour journey. I will just wing it, hoping Garmin will find a satellite soon.

I go through my first toll plaza easily. It's six dollars, as is the next. The one after that is three dollars. Each makes comments about bravery and wishes me safe travels. I hand my card to all three telling them to follow my journey. The fourth is six dollars again, and the attendant is a little short with me, telling me it is my responsibility to tell them what I am driving and that I am towing so they can tell me how much. I don't give her my card.

Garmin kicks in and tells me that in ten miles, I will take 18 North, then the battery dies. I make it to 18, knowing the next turn I will make is onto 95 north.

✧

I am on 95 north, and the first toll booth says no cash. What do I do? I pull up and see a button that says press for ticket. Problem is, that button is too low for me to reach from my window. I see a ticket protruding from a slot I can reach and stretch to grab the ticket. Someone must have forgotten it; it's from about five minutes ago. Not knowing what else to do, I take it and roll on down the road. My first toll on the New Jersey Turnpike is $24.55. With all of the lane-changing going on and cars totally ignoring posted speeds, I start out nervous, figuring out that my blinker is worthless. They just keep flying by and around me. I learn that if I just start easing over, they get out of my way.

I pass the exits for Trenton and think of my first train ride. I drive through Newark and right through New York City and experience the "Welcome to Manhattan" sign going over my head. I am following the signs for trucks to go over the George Washington Bridge as they direct me to the upper level. My toll here is a whopping eighty-four dollars! The last toll I pay is five dollars.

I need a bathroom break and gas. Emmi could use a walk too. A sign appears: "Connecticut Welcome Center nine miles." I will stop there but am trying to figure out which side of the road the exit is going to be on. It's to my right. Off I go. My options are, fuel for cars left, and fuel for trucks/buses right. They think all buses and trucks use diesel. I am to go left into the tight short area at the pumps meant for cars. I need the first pump on my left. While I wait for the car in front of me to finish, I am totally blocking traffic, mostly because semi-trucks are parked in the fire lane behind me. The guy in front of me helps by signaling that I can keep moving forward until I am almost on his back bumper. Thanks, dude. When he's finished, I pull up until the pump is aligned with my tank. My front end and back end are both halfway into the driving lanes, but people can get around.

I go in to pay for my gas and ask how I get back around to parking. There is no way. Once you get gas in a big rig, you are forced to exit. I fill up and wind out of the space meant for cars and back onto the road.

As I turn into the Niantic KOA, I am looking forward to enjoying one place for a few days. Everyone inside is really nice. They tell me about the activities planned tonight, but I am going to miss them. I am meeting up with my adopted Uncle John and Aunt Jeannine for dinner tonight.

My escorts, Bill and Bob are great. One of them tells me, "We will be making a series of tight turns to get to Site 107. You will need to make wide turns in these areas." I ask him if he would make wide turns pulling a trailer or driving a coach. He does not understand what I am asking. I explain that, in a trailer, it tends to cut corners when you make a turn. In a coach, when I turn right, it's opposite. My tail swings about six feet left when I turn right. If it was okay with him, I was going to consider each turn and make the best choice for my rig. He agreed and said they would give me a heads up when they were going to turn.

I pull right into my site, a long, level, rock-covered pad. Soft, but good. I call out my window and ask if my car is out of the road. Bill tells me I am clear of everything and starts explaining how far out my slide will come and that it will be clear of the tree beside me. They both ask if I know how to hook everything up and if I need help. Where were these guys when I was new at this?

They do teach me something. This park only has gray water dumps, no sewer or black water dumps at the site. I can dump that tank on my way out. When I look at the tiny hole in the ground for gray water, I tell them there is no way I can drain into that. I show them how my system works. It's one connection going through a large hose. I pull levers for each individual tank. They tell me there is an adapter for that and they can help me, confirm I am plugged in and don't need any help, then they promise to check on me tomorrow. This is the best campground service *ever*!

It's cool and sunny when I walk Emmi this morning. I inhale the sweet smells of nature and watch the chipmunks play. It feels good here. We are sitting outside, and the most shocking thing just happened. Two yellow shirt-clad KOA guys on a golf cart just stopped. One of the men jumps out with a smile on his face and says, "I'm sorry, ma'am, but we are going to take your poop." It takes me a second to understand, that he is talking about the two orange doggie poop bags I had dropped on the ground by my steps. I usually find a dumpster or dog waste collection can myself. This is one of the nicest things that has ever happened to me in a campground.

I am driving over to Mystic, Connecticut for a festival and to do some sightseeing. I am off the interstate and wandering through the neighborhoods set high up on a hill along the water. Turning into town, the streets are packed with people. It's easy to find public parking by simply following the signs. I find a spot and start up the shop-lined streets toward the drawbridge. The first stop that I make is at Argia Mystic Cruises. I want to book the sunset cruise aboard a traditional sailing ship for tomorrow night.

I catch up with (my adopted uncle and aunt) John and Jeannine for lunch at Abbott's Lobster. The food was amazing. If you come here expecting some sort of white glove five-star lobster house, you will be seriously disappointed, but if you recognize you are getting some of the freshest seafood possible and appreciate the gorgeous outdoor setting you are eating it in, you will come away thoroughly satisfied and glad you came.

After lunch, we take a ride over to Stonington Borough. It is a charming seaside village situated on a mile-long peninsula. It has the tiniest beach and tiniest lighthouse I have seen so far. After a wonderful day, I am back at camp feeling wiped out. I am settling in for a relaxing evening.

I am jolted awake. Breathing seems to cause some discomfort. I try to go back to sleep, but it feels like there is a cramp in my chest. No matter how much I try, I can't get comfortable. I toss and turn for hours. I get out of bed. I try walking around and sitting on the couch. I try laying on the couch and being propped up by pillows behind me. Nothing helps. It's getting worse. It feels like something is squeezing my heart. The discomfort is moving up the left side of my neck and across my left shoulder, into my arm. The pain gets worse every time I try to breathe. I wonder if it could be heartburn. I have never had heartburn. I google it. There isn't any clear information, but I don't think that's what's wrong.

Then I start to worry. What if it's a heart attack? It would take days for someone to find me. I call 911 and get transferred, and tell them what's going on. They tell me they will send someone. What if they can't find me? I just want someone to tell me it's heartburn.

It's three in the morning when I call to wake my daughter and her husband up. He's a doctor. He will tell me not to worry. I did not get the answer I expected. He tells me that I should go to the hospital, and I shouldn't drive myself. I tell them I have already called 911, but it's getting worse and I still don't hear sirens. What if they cannot find me?

Still on the phone, I go outside. As I get the bottom of the steps, a police car is shining his light in the distance. Within minutes the ambulance is also here, and they are loading me up. I am in my pajamas, and my dog is inside. I want my purse. "No, ma'am," they tell me. "We are taking you to the hospital."

I see lights, but I don't hear noise. I know we are moving. We stop. Another man gets in. We are moving again. I hear something about a bridge. I hear "this might hurt," but all I am aware of is this incredible pain in my chest.

At the hospital, the ER doctor wants to know where I live. It's hard to talk. I try to tell her about my RV and travels. "You are homeless?" No that doesn't sound right.

"I have a home. It's just different. It's not in one location."

I hear things in bits. Someone says my first EKG shows something abnormal, but almost everything else is good. I hear a flurry of movement and noise. They don't like my low blood pressure. I think I try to tell them this is normal. Maybe I don't say it out loud, because there is another IV and fluids.

"It's not going in fast enough. Move it to the other IV line."

I am admitted and in a room with fabulous nurses running test after test. While they are all negative for a heart attack, I am still in pain. Nurses and aids still panic over my blood pressure. One nurse goes into full code mode. I beg my nurse to please talk to someone. If everything regarding my heart is normal, couldn't we look at something else? She offers morphine. I don't want pain meds, I want to know what's causing this pain. My son-in-law talks to a nurse by phone and suggests trying something, but it will have to wait until morning.

After another long night, the cardiologist comes in to talk to me. He takes time to ask questions and listen, then leaves to review my chart. In a few minutes, the nurse is back with the drug my son-in-law suggested last night. In twenty minutes, the pain is finally minimal.

After two days, I am discharged with a diagnosis of pericarditis. I am thankful it was not a heart attack, because I still have places to go, things to do, and people to meet. John has been taking care of Emmi. He is picking me up and I am going back to camp for some rest and trip re-grouping.

I am awake early, listening to a big thunderstorm. The noise comforts me for some reason. Possibly it's because I am alive and able to continue my journey.

My unexpected delay at the hospital this week caused me to miss the sunset sailing cruise from Mystic aboard the schooner Argia. Though they do not generally offer refunds or transfers to people for cancellations, they offered both to me. I am on the phone with my sister telling her, "This is my last night here and I don't think I should take them up on their kind offer. Maybe I should rest instead." She says, "You should go! The boat and the water will probably be very relaxing. Don't give up the chance to see another sunset." She's right. I have twenty minutes before I have to leave in order to catch the boat. I thank her and call to see if they have room for me tonight.

I am standing in line, waiting to board. Behind me, there is a group of women in their fifties, all carrying sunflowers. They are talking about a book. I ask them what they are reading that is so interesting. The woman directly behind me says, "We are reading *All the Light We Cannot See*, by Anthony Doerr. It's a novel about a blind French girl and a German boy trying to survive the devastation of World War II."

I am hooked and want to read it too.

They are all part of a book club, and two of them have been friends since the first grade. I also learn that the woman behind me has recently lost her husband. Before he passed away, they had talked about taking this sunset cruise, but they never did. Her friends are here with her for a memorial in honor of her late husband. A tear slips down my cheek before I can stop it. I have never met this woman and feel like I don't have the right to shed tears. This is her moment. I apologize as I wipe the tear away. I tell her about my journey and that I am writing a book about it. At the heart of my story, I want to encourage people not to put things off that they want to do. People suggested I should cut my trip short and go home to rest. The heart scare I had this week and her comment affirm that I am doing the right thing. I am going to finish my trip.

Once we are in open water, we set sail. As the wind fills our sails, my mind is flooded with memories. It's like being eleven years old again on my grandmother's forty-seven-foot sailboat. Wind and water have incredible power, yet they can be so soft and smooth. I remember sailing so far out I couldn't see land at all. There was no fear, only awe, when I stood at the bow of her boat in the sun as we blasted through the water.

Before we turn back to shore, I get to witness a very special moment. The book club members each take a turn at tossing sunflowers overboard in memory of a special man. The widow stands at the rail, looking out to sea, deep in thought. Standing tall with her head held high and wind blowing through her long blonde hair, she raises her arm and tosses her own sunflower. It glides to the water below, and unlike the others, it lands face up. It stays that way, floating along in our wake, until we can see it no more.

It's sunny and sixty-four degrees when Emmi and I go outside for one last stroll around the Niantic KOA this morning. We walk over toward the tent camping area at the edge of the forest. Flowers are blooming along the way. There is a tiny breeze, the birds are singing, and the air smells sweet and clean. The squirrels are playing a game of tag, running through the branches and chattering at each other. The sun's rays are dancing through the branches. It's so peaceful.

The power and water are disconnected and all of my slides are in. I am getting the Trailhawk attached to the coach and John, one of the guys who works at the campground, steps in to help. He is worried about me doing this by myself after just getting out of the hospital. With that job done, he tells me if I will drive over to the dump station, he will handle dumping my tanks. I feel like I am imposing, but at the same time grateful. Getting ready to leave was a quite the process today. I am already tired.

It's mid-morning when I leave the park for Maine. I have mostly interstates today. As I begin to merge onto the highway, there is a big buck standing in the grass just off of the road. He watches me all the way up the ramp, like he has been waiting for me. It feels like a good sign.

There are large rolling hills with incredible views. The curves are sharp, but the road is good until about fifty miles in, when it gets weirdly bumpy. I can barely hang onto the wheel. I let off the gas and tap the brakes several times. It's getting worse. I glance at my rear-view camera and the Trailhawk is dipping and diving, swaying uncontrollably side to side. Holy crap! This has never happened before. Brakes! Brakes! Brakes! Still, it won't stop. I turn my blinker on and start for the shoulder of the road. It isn't wide enough, and the grass drops off down a hill, but this will be as good as it gets. Irma is half in the exit lane and half in the grass. My flashers are on and I climb out.

I think I had a blowout. I pray it's on the car and not my rig. I have a spare for the car, and though I have never done it, I could change that. If it's the coach, I might be here a while. I walk down the length of the passenger side, crawling under my rig to check the inside tires. Nothing is wrong. I am walking around the back of the Trailhawk to check the other side. Cars and trucks are flying by on the driver side. I wait and wait then decide to risk it. I walk up the other side. Outer tires look okay, but no way I am crawling under from this side. I face oncoming traffic, preferring to see who's gonna hit me. I go back around and roll under. That tire is fine too. I check all of my connections, all are good. I am at a loss. I get back in the coach, grateful I don't have to change a tire. I get back on the highway. It doesn't happen again. Now I am at a total loss. I later learn that this is what RVers refer to as the "death wobble."

I am crossing a big bridge, feeling pretty confident. On the other side, a truck in front of me is in the process of having a blowout. A piece of the tire is flying up at me and I want to duck.

The huge flap of rubber smacks the edge of my windshield with a loud thump. People are hitting their brakes and swerving as more pieces of the tire sail through the air. I get off of the interstate at the Maine Welcome Center to check it out. I am thankful there is no damage.

I am getting tired. Just north of mile marker thirty-eight in Maine, I see a spot of pink in the middle of brown, gray, and green. It's out of place. As I get closer, I see it is a bright pink flamingo like the ones I carry with me. Someone has placed it between two big rocks on the edge of the forest. It makes me smile.

It's early afternoon when I arrive at the Augusta/Gardiner KOA. I immediately like Becky, the woman checking me in! My escort leads us up a steep hill to my perfectly level pull-through site. I get connected and put out the flamingos. This is home for a few days.

It's cool outside this morning. I am driving miles of back roads to Boothbay Harbor. There's probably a faster way, but this is what I wanted. Abandoned farmhouses, large and small, with mobile homes pulled in next door, houses with drooping roofs still being lived in. People still live on acres of land that serve no purpose other than a view.

Boothbay Harbor has grown over the last forty years, but the residential areas with views of the harbor below are almost as I remember. I wander the streets and shops along the water. This part is nothing like I remember as a little girl. Few things in the shops are made by locals. It is now mostly rows and rows of shops with t-shirts made in Cambodia. I've had enough. I will keep the memory of the handmade ragdoll in a yellow dress my grandfather bought for me here so many years ago.

I am having dinner at Richard's in Brunswick with my Uncle Tom. My mom lived with her family in this area when she was young. Everything I remember looks the same. As I walk from the church parking lot to the restaurant, a man sweeping his sidewalk with an old-fashioned broom catches my attention. The broom handle has straw tied to its base. As I approach, he stops sweeping and greets me with a friendly smile. His name is Jim Burbank and he was born right here in this house ninety-one years ago. Once upon a time his grandfather, Clarence Winfield Pierce Foss, was the town doctor. The office, as was the norm a hundred years ago, was part of the house. He shows me the street-facing door that was once the entrance to his grandfather's medical practice. I am going to be late for dinner. It's okay, slowing down and taking time to listen is one of the reasons I set out on such an adventure. Before I leave, he tells me I have to try the warm potato salad tonight and invites me to come back for another visit. This is what summer evenings should be like everywhere.

The visit with my uncle was a lot of fun and the warm potato salad was perfect. It's almost eleven at night when I get back to the RV park. I have firewood, thanks to my neighbors from Florida last night who left it. I decide that the fifty-five-degree temperature is perfect for a campfire. I change into sweats and snuggle into a chair with Emmi. As my fire crackles, all is quiet except for the soft hooting of owls. I laugh, remembering the owls in another park that wanted Emmi for dinner. These sound much friendlier.

✧

This morning, it is seventy degrees and overcast. The birds are singing and there is a light breeze rustling through the trees above me. I am reminiscing about Frank Hampton. Though I only knew him for a short time, he was truly a godsend for Mom when my stepfather passed away. I am going to drive back to Brunswick and spend the day with his children, Frankie, Steph, and Melanie.

The first stop down memory lane is Estes Lobster House for lunch. I remember Mr. Estes sliding lobsters across the old wood floor towards my brother and I when we were little. One poked Buddy's toe with its banded claw. We saw blood and were certain it had bitten him.

I had such a great day with my adopted siblings. I am glad they are part of my life. My time in Maine was all about childhood memories and spending time with family. My last day here has been one of the best days along this journey.

I am taking my time this morning, doing what RVers do, chatting with neighbors. I am sad to leave, but ready to roll. Upstate NY here we come!

It is a long drive full of crazy bumpy highways and climbing mountains, and still I make it to Herkimer Diamond KOA way before dark. As I turn off the road, I am greeted by beautiful, green, manicured grass, big trees, and large open spaces. I am impressed by the park sprawling out in front of me.

There are no escorts, but I find my way easily through the park to my long, shaded, and level pull-through spot. I get connected and make it home. My flamingos are ready to greet visitors at the split-rail fence across the front of my site. This will be mine and Emmi's home for a few days.

I am leaving the campground, driving the Trailhawk, in search of Judd Falls. I am sure there must be a more direct route, but my GPS sends me winding through back roads, climbing up and rolling down steep, curvy lanes. About every two miles, turn left, turn right, turn left, turn right. I wonder if my GPS loses satellite signal, could I find my way back?

I turn left onto a narrow, dirt and gravel road, and drive along with the dust billowing behind me. My GPS says I have reached my destination. So much for trying longitude and latitude points. I am in the middle of this road with nothing around and no place to park. I check for another option. I am going into Cherry Hill.

In Cherry Hill, I pop into Coyote's Cafe. A wonderful woman tells me when I leave to go left and follow the road until I go under the overpass. The I will see a cleared spot with some big rocks and tall grass. That's where the trail is.

I follow her directions but see the spot as I pass it. It's much easier to turn around in the middle of the road when you are driving a car. I am back, parked in the clearing. I change my shoes and dig out the walking directions I previously found.

"Walk straight back to the woods towards the gorge."

I kind of see what once was a trail. I am heading through the tall grass towards the woods.

"Follow the trail to the right once you are in the woods."

Okay. I see where there are two trails and I take the one to the right.

"The trail is not maintained and can be slippery."

Not to mention steep. I see a tiny trail to my left, but there is a larger trail to my right. I choose the larger trail. Surely, it's larger because more people use it. I walk and walk and walk.

"When you reach the stream bed, you only need to follow the gorge back upstream to get to the fall."

I keep walking. I re-read my directions. I am now circling around the other side of the gorge. I keep walking. Sometimes my trail isn't really a trail. Eventually, I hear what sounds like the trickle of water.

I leave my makeshift path towards, and about a hundred yards ahead, I spot the tiny stream. But there is no path on either side. I step into the cold stream and am momentarily shocked by the frigid water. Am I really going to do this? Climb up a moving stream across the rocks that have formed its bed? I decide I didn't come this far to see a tiny stream trickle over the rocks and forge on, picking my way through the rocks and little pools, climb over some fallen trees and under others, hike up several falls, and hope there is something awe-inspiring ahead.

Now I hear water splashing a little louder. I can't get up the creek in this area. There's too much in my way. I go up the bank to my right, but there's no path. I see a possibility back on the other side of the creek. I just have to climb higher to get to it.

Back over and up I go, holding tree limbs along my way. The narrow path becomes more of a trail. As I come around the bend, I find it. I am sure it is much bigger in the spring, but I found Judd Falls. The hike took me almost an hour, and the trek has me hot and sticky. I walk to the wall so the cool water can splash over me. I climb to the middle of the pool when the fall is raging, and sit on a big rock. I look straight up the rock wall that surrounds me on three sides and imagine the power of the water that gushes over it.

Now I wonder if I can find my way out. Picking my way back to the path, I discover that I took a wrong turn coming in. I think I was supposed to take the path to my left and not the big one. In just a few minutes, I see my car.

I take another path to my right. It goes to almost the top of the falls. Some of the path is merely a rocky ledge that goes straight down to the rocks below. I test every step before putting my foot solidly on the rocky path beneath it. I hold onto tree limbs as I head back to the car.

Next on my agenda today is the Herkimer Diamond Mine and digging for Herkimer Diamonds. These are a type of quartz and not really diamonds. I try breaking the big rocks in the heat, but only get wounds and a tiny diamond still stuck in one of the rocks. The first rock I hit with a sledgehammer breaks and a chunk hits my foot. It feels like every bone has been shattered and leaves a nasty gash. I move towards the edge of the mine where there is some shade where my neighbors, the Parrettie family is mining. They show me how to dig inside the crevices. I get a little muddy, but this is much cooler and easier. They are also kind enough to share a few "diamonds" with me.

My neighbor Danielle invited me to ride the river rapids behind the park with her. She already has tubes, so I don't have to buy one. When we get to the edge, I am surprised. It is not cold at all and not nearly as rough as I thought it would be. I am taking lots of pictures with my new waterproof camera and chatting with Danielle. Then my tube bounces off of a boulder into rougher water. I am trying to not fly off into the rapids and lose my camera in the process. Sorry folks...no pictures. Instead of getting upset, I just hope that whoever finds it enjoys the pictures I have taken.

I wrap up this part of my journey by having dinner with Danielle, Jon, Mackenzie and Peyton Parrettie and their boxer, Sadie. Dessert is campfire s'mores made with fudge stripe cookies. When a thunderstorm crashes our party, we say goodbye and talk about connecting again on the Outer Banks of North Carolina.

CHAPTER 17

A LIFE OR DEATH DECISION

WE are on our way to Niagara Falls, and it appears I'm going to be climbing mountains and bumping down highways in the rain today. It rains the first two hours of my four-hour trip. I am traveling across miles and miles of bumpy roads that I paid a toll to use. It's mostly farmland, with rare exits except service plazas. The exit that leads me to the Niagara Falls KOA puts me on 190, which is almost as bad as the old portion of Route 66 I took a few years ago. It actually has such large cracks and holes that grass is growing in them.

Niagara Falls North/Lewiston KOA is a great KOA. If you want a quiet campground, this is the one. It's easy to get to the falls from there, they have long, level sites and room to park your car, and the owners are wonderful.

My friends from Missouri just so happen to be in the same KOA. I am excited they are staying an extra night to show me around. I tried getting here in April but was stopped by a winter storm. It was one of the things on my bucket list. Bev helps me get settled, and we are on our way to the falls.

The sunset at Niagara Falls is gorgeous. Honestly, I was more in awe of Shoshone Falls. Maybe it's because there are so many people you can't just stand and absorb the beauty, the sound, and the feel. Still, I am glad that I am here. I hope tomorrow will be different from ground zero.

We make it in time to see the incredible illumination and fireworks over Niagara Falls. I lose Bev as I am ducking under people at the rail so I can watch.

Bev and I are back at Niagara Falls again this morning. We just got in line to get our tickets for an up-close and personal Maid of The Mist boat tour. We expected to wait an hour, but in minutes, we have our boarding passes. When we make our way down to the boat, we are handed blue rain ponchos. I guess this means we should expect to get wet.

We board our boat with about two hundred other blue-clad tourists, and climb to the upper deck. From our perch along the rail, we are guaranteed to get soaked, but we will have a perfect view of the falls. The sun is bright overhead and the water is an astounding blue-green.

We are already melting under the thin plastic of our ponchos as we approach the American Falls and Bridal Falls. Last night, from the top, these falls appeared small. From the bottom, they're much more impressive. Our captain skirts along the rocks at its base. I had no idea we would get so close; the water crashes over and hits the rocks to our side, and we are showered with its mist carried by the strong wind.

The motor of our boat is vibrating in protest, working against the massive current on our way around the bend to Horseshoe Falls. I alternate between terror and wonderment. Our boat is being pulled closer and closer to the base of the second largest waterfall in the world. I know we are too close. I can feel the thunder of the almost three thousand tons of water per second violently plummeting into the pool of water that surrounds us. I feel it the second our captain puts this vessel we are on in reverse. We are still being drawn further in, closer to certain destruction. My heart is pounding in my chest as waves toss us around wildly. It's like being in the middle of a massive thunderstorm at sea. The only thing missing is the flash of lightning. The roar of the falls is so loud you can hear nothing else. For a moment, it feels like we are suspended in time as water pours over us. It's a feeling like nothing I have ever experienced before. I am brought back to reality when the boat begins to shudder, as if it can handle no more. The captain is turning us around. We head back into the sunshine and calm water.

Today we say goodbye to our friends and head south towards Pennsylvania. My RV GPS is dead and won't charge. I have reviewed maps and my phone for an hour, trying to memorize a route of two-lane back roads. I am going to wing it and pray there are no low overpasses or bridges.

The two-lane roads are smoother than the roads that led us to Niagara Falls. The winding climbs and drops aren't even bad. The mountains are a verdant blanket of green. It's like a painter took every shade imaginable and blotted them all on a canvas with a brush.

It's a good thing I wrote directions from the last highway. Siri wants me to go a different route that would have taken me somewhere else. That alone is the reason I make it to Williamsport South/Nittany Mountain KOA without getting lost.

It's a beautiful park, another one with no escorts. The young girl checking me in actually laughed when I asked. My site is back the other way. Laughing Girl hands me a map with my route drawn on it, which has me making a U-turn out of the office. I stupidly ask if other people make a U-turn here. Her answer is yes, all the time.

I walk past my coach and out to the road in front of me for a look. I don't see how this U-turn is going to happen, but I am going to try. I swing wide right, then turn sharp left. The road is pretty narrow. I keep my wheels turned and inch forward, watching the Trailhawk in my rear camera. I am still several feet from the trunk of the tree in front of me, but the low branches are almost at my windshield. I can't make the turn. Now I am stretched across the entire road. I have been warned many times that I cannot back up when flat towing a car. I will have to disconnect it.

I put Irma in park and climb out to see that I am already blocking traffic, although stressing over it won't speed up the task. I have to go through the two-minute process of getting the Trailhawk out of neutral first, so it won't roll down the hill behind me when I disconnect. Then I have to pull the pins that keep the Blue Ox arms connected to the front of my car, except I can't get them out. I have made such a tight turn, there is too much pressure on them.

My friend Dolly gave me a lovely new hammer for my recent fiftieth birthday. It's about to get used for the first time. I just have to find it. By the time I am back with my hammer and a screwdriver, the line of vehicles waiting has gotten longer. I quit worrying about them a while ago. If any one of them was in a hurry, they could have offered to help. Three times I swing the hammer, and solidly hit the first pin. Each time, it moves. On my third swing, the pin lands flush with the metal pole protruding from the front of the Trailhawk. I still cannot pull the pin out by hand. I expected this. I line the screwdriver up on the center of the pin and give it a good whack. The pin flies out and lands across the road. The tow bar still does not release. A blast of WD-40 and a solid kick does the trick. As I am bent over the other side, hammer in hand and my hair in my face, a woman comes up to ask if I need any help. "Thank you, but I think I've got it now."

With the car disconnected, I put my tools inside and park it out of the way. I back Irma up, complete the U-turn, and get to my site. I leave her engine running in the giant, almost level, pull-through site. I now have to walk back up the hill to get my car.

Back at the site, I plug in the electric, set pads, get level, and connect the water. I start to open the cover for sewer and the pressure built up inside causes it to fly off like a missile. A poop explosion follows right behind the missile. I stand here a minute, totally shocked. At least nothing is on me and I keep a box of Kimberly-Clark pink nitrile gloves in my water compartment. I connect the sewer line, then clean up the mess. All for a sleepover!

Emmi and I are ready for a walk. We meet a guy from Florida with his kids. They live close by and just bought a new camper. They are having challenges with their slides and getting level. The new owner opens his outdoor kitchen compartment to get a drink. The refrigerator is not locked. The refrigerator door flies open and starts spitting cans out like a winning slot machine. Can after can explodes as it hits the ground. I feel bad for him, but am glad I was not the only one with challenges today.

I am leaving for Aunt Cackie's. The closest campground with full hook-ups I could find is Tucquan Park.

Again, with no GPS, I am winging it with maps. Highway 441 and this long stretch of River Road was not on my researched list of roads, but somehow in construction, I ended up on it anyway. I start out going through a narrow town street in a 25 mph zone. A semi coming up the other side, so that's encouraging. I am out of town but it's actually getting worse. Narrow switchback roads climbing up and going down. A lot of semis are traveling on this route. Why they would choose this road, I have no idea. I am going around these sharp curves at 10–15 mph, sometimes less.

I am on the outside lane coming around a curve and hear brakes locking up. A truck pulling a trailer was swinging too wide, too fast and had to stop. I am watching all my mirrors, my back camera, and the road ahead of me. I see a narrow bridge ahead just before I curve left. There's no shoulder, only a guardrail to my right, and a semi-truck is coming around the corner, partially in my lane. I only have seconds to make a decision. Do I stay in my lane and leave it to the trucker to save my life? Or take control myself? I know if I move over, I am going to scrape the rail. I don't trust the trucker not to slam into me and knock me into the rail and over the side.

"God, help me hang on!"

I push on the brakes and scoot right. I am not afraid, I only feel sick when I hear the scrape of metal on metal. A voice in my head says, "Don't panic. Let it scrape." I make it around the curve and am still on the road. There is nowhere to stop; I have to keep going. I peek in my right-side mirror and can't see any dents.

When I arrive at the campground and can check, I find there are no dents, but a heck of a scrape down three compartments. It's only paint, and I am safe.

I spend the next several days relaxing on Cackie and Dean's lovely new deck, baking a cake for Dean's birthday, roaming back roads, visiting with friends, spending time with my family, and having fun.

Before getting back on the road, I need to drain my tanks and would like to stow things in preparation for leaving tomorrow. I know Pennsylvania needed the rain, but I am over it. It stops for five minutes, then pours all over again. Roads are washing out and everything is a muddy mess. Just as I am having a woe-is-me moment, a rabbit hops up next to me and cocks his head as if he is wondering why I am so upset. It stops raining and he hops away. There isn't another drop of rain until my tanks are dumped.

I love my guardian angel and my life.

I went to bed early, but barely slept last night—about three hours total. Weather alarms warning of floods went off most of the night. This is not a good way to start a long, tough drive. At least it isn't raining so I don't get soaked finishing the outside breakdown. Still, I am covered in mud by the time I am ready to roll. I totally forgot to add water to my fresh water tank. It's a good thing I keep a tub of baby wipes for occasions such as this.

I go in search of bigger roads, praying none are washed out. My biggest challenge may be getting out of the campground. I make it out of my site without hitting the motorcycles, abandoned golf carts, and other stuff in the site to my left or the trailer that appears to be permanently parked on the edge of the hill in front of me. There is a steep, muddy gravel hill in front of me. At the bottom, there are trees blocking my view, where I have to turn sharp left for the campground exit road. I make it without sliding down it or plowing into anyone. The campground tractor is already out grading the road. I can only imagine what it looked like an hour ago. Parts of the road have a river running through them, while others have soft, newly spread gravel. It takes fifteen minutes to maneuver up the half-mile road.

At the end of the gravel road is a steep downhill section that immediately dips back uphill to the main road. I can see the deep grooves where others have scraped their campers getting out. I have to turn left here without getting stuck. I can just imagine the picture. My coach nose and rear are stuck on each side of the hill, wheels off the ground and water running under me. To make it worse, I cannot see right or left beyond the boulders and bright pink echinacea they have worked so hard on at the entrance. I inch forward and feel like the horse and cart I saw earlier this week trying to get out into the road. Whoa! There is a car flying in my direction! I stop and the car swerves around me. On the next try, I make it out. It's a bit bumpy, but I don't get stuck on the hills.

I am Virginia-bound back through winding climbs and falls on my way to an interstate. My camp neighbor, Michelle, tells me to ignore my GPS and turn left after the big barn being built on River Road. It will detour me around the worst of this road then back onto it further down. I take her advice. Up a hill, around a curve, and a long steep drive down to water flowing across the road before I climb back up. If this is easier, I definitely did not want to stay on River Road. Along the way, I encounter more tiny new rivers and rocky red mud that has washed out of the fields and across the road. At least the curves are not as bad as they were coming in.

I am still on those winding two-lane roads when the first tractor-trailer is coming toward me in the other lane. My chest tightens, and I grip the wheel harder in panic. The next truck coming at me is in a curve. My heart starts to race.

"God, I don't like this."

I have flashbacks from a few days ago when a truck almost ran me off the road. I can hear the screech of metal scraping against metal, but I am nowhere near the guardrail. Still, I cannot shake the fear of thinking that the truck is going to hit me. I talk myself through it. "This is the result of a trauma. Face it now." I am in my lane and so is he. "Stop worrying. Just look ahead and drive through it."

It takes an hour and a half of traveling these back roads, but I am really excited to see I-83 South headed toward Baltimore. Even in the blinding rain, four to six lanes of merging traffic are a relief. As I merge onto the interstate, there is a big groundhog sitting up on his hind legs off the shoulder of the road to my right. He looks like he was waiting for me. Like he is saying, "I knew you would make it. Congratulations!"

I love these signs that appear along my journey. I just hope he turns around and goes back into the woods and does not try to cross the highway!

It's still raining when I merge onto I-649 West, then I-70 West. As my aunt suggested, I ignore Siri when he tells me to exit

I-70 onto Highway 15. I want to stay on this interstate all the way to 81 South.

I see a sign for South Mountain, then another just after, "6 ½ percent Descent Next 3 Miles." I recall my first mountain experience and how much it scared me. This one is easy. Not because the mountain is easier, but because now I know how to do it. Respect the mountain, get to an appropriate speed, and don't worry about how slow you are going. Others can go around you. Keep your foot off the brake. In tow/haul mode, your engine will help you. Your speed will continue to increase, but as you increase by 4 or 5 mph, press solidly on the brake one time, then let go. It's like a parachute slowing you down. I love the sound of my growling engine when I do this. Just keep doing the same thing until you get to the bottom.

I am on 81 South and the blinding rain is one solid waterfall cascading down my windshield. I reduce my speed and push through for a while. After the second or third large puddle of accumulated water, I decide I do not want to drive through more puddles. There is a Virginia Welcome Center ahead. I am going to stop and wait for the weather to pass. I get parked and lay on the couch, and Emmi snuggles in with me. Listening to the rain on the roof, I close my eyes and drift off into a peaceful sleep. I slept for an hour and now feel great.

There is a lot of traffic when I get back on the road. After a short driving distance, a semi-truck ahead is going off onto the right shoulder. Then I see lots of brake lights in front of me, and him trying to merge back into traffic. More trucks are going to the shoulder. As I get closer, I understand why. I quickly follow suit and all sixty feet of Irma and the Trailhawk are heading for the shoulder to dodge a huge tire in the middle of the interstate.

Siri pipes up telling me to exit the highway in one mile. I thought I had further to go. What do I know? I take the exit off of I-81. I wind through towns, turning left and right for about twenty minutes, then Siri says, "In one mile, use the right lane to merge onto interstate 81 South." This was a detour onto Highway 11 then back onto the same interstate. Totally crazy.

I am down to less than a half a tank of gas when I see a sign for Pilot. I love Pilots. There is usually plenty of room for me to maneuver and they have yummy pizza. I take the exit and turn left. Approaching the station on my left, I discover it is very small. I consider just looping back through the big trucker area and finding another place. As I turn into the entrance, a big rig is backing up to turn around. With my tow vehicle, I cannot back up. Back to Plan A.

I change course and turn into the car area, simultaneously scoping out all of the pumps. I decide on the island to my far right. There are two pick-up trucks already getting gas at these pumps. There is no other option but to block traffic. I wait until the guy directly in front of me finishes and start to pull forward. The man in front is super nice and guides me to within inches of his bumper so I can reach my tank at the pump. It's a stretch, but I am close enough.

While my tank is filling, I scope out an exit. The pump is taking forever, and I have about sixty gallons to go. I walk through my options. People are watching me, but I don't care. There is room for me to pull up towards the store and turn left across in front of it. I am not sure there is enough room for me to make the narrow left turn at the end of the last pump island, because there are also cars parked there. I would have to get really close to the cars before making the turn. Then I have to turn left again to circle back to the exit. On that last turn, my tail swing could take out one of the cars that would be to my right. The next option is to pull up as far as possible without hitting the curb, then turn right without my tail swing taking out a gas pump. I see two challenges here. One, it's a tight U-turn out; two, it's also the truck lane I will be exiting through. If I can't make the U-turn and block traffic while I disconnect my car to back up, there are going to be some mad truckers.

I choose option two after looking at both several more times. It's not easy, since I first have to get my car around the back end of the pump island. I have to be near-perfect at judging how close to the curb I can go and still make the turn without hitting it. Inch by scary inch. If I get too close, the curb is too high for me to go over. I turn my wheel sharp right and press the gas softly while checking my tail swing. Look forward, back down my left side. My back end is so close to the pump I can read the instructions on what to do! "Immediately, get away from the vehicle and go inside. Ask the attendant to shut off the emergency valve." My first thought is that I will have to add a step and grab Emmi. I hope there is enough time. I might be two inches away, but I still have to turn further. I inch along, praying it will not explode. Now my back generator exhaust pipe is so close I cannot see light between it and the pump. Another inch, and I am clear!

My struggle is not yet over. I have to make that tight U-turn. There are two semi-trucks headed up the lane. I swear that when they see me, they speed up. Oh, ye of little faith. Waiting for them to pass, I chant "God is my co-pilot! God is my co-pilot!"

Funny thing about faith. When the second truck is clear, I pull out as if it's not a problem at all and make the U-turn like a pro. When I glance to my right, back by the pumps, I get a thumbs-up from someone who was watching. That tiny gesture meant so much to me.

I pull out onto the main road thinking Pilot should hire me as a design consultant. More and more people are buying RVs. Because engines are stronger than they used to be, and gas is cheaper, they are opting for gas rigs. I maneuver these pumps almost daily and could show them how to make their travel plazas more RV-friendly.

It has been a long day of detours and blinding rain, but I make it to Natural Bridge, Virginia. I am checked in to the Natural Bridge/Lexington KOA for a few days. Wow! I wish all parks were this easy! I am level and put my flamingos out in the dark.

I am taking the Trailhawk back out the way I came in yesterday to see Natural Bridge and its caverns. I can't believe I made this drive in the coach. I swerve to miss a tiny terrapin that resembles a pine cone in the road. Winding along a mountain ledge with the river way down below, I don't finish turning my wheels right before I have to start turning them left, then back to the right.

At the cavern, our tour guide Cameron does a great job. I even got cave kisses, which are supposed to be good luck. (I know what you are thinking…they were from the cave, not the boy!) When a drop of water from the cave ceiling lands on your head, it is called a cave kiss and considered good luck.

Next on my agenda is to go see the Natural Bridge. The hike is lovely, but the bridge—*wow!* It all started with a creek running through it wearing down the mountain beneath it. On my way back to camp, I pull off to figure out how to get to the footbridge

I saw yesterday. The effort of picking my way through trails was rewarded with a spectacular view.

Now I am back at the best-laid-out KOA I have ever slept in. Just one more night before I head back down that steep winding road further south. I am sitting as the sun goes down, listening to the birds singing their last songs of the day and the crickets starting their evening serenade. I am being still and taking in how people RV. There is a pull-behind camper and a fifth wheel, both with their big screen TVs flashing through the windows...an older couple sitting outside their camper talking by their campfire... a family laughing as they make s'mores outside their cabin...a woman reading a book with her four small dogs inside a make-shift picket fence. We RVers find peace and relaxation in different ways, and yet we all run to the great outdoors when we want to get away.

I exit the KOA and make a slow, crazy, twisting crawl back down the mountain. Emmi and I are on our way to North Carolina for a few days.

I love back roads, but am thrilled to see the on-ramp to an interstate, even if it is a mountain-scaling highway that snakes through Virginia. I have crossed these mountains before and know what to expect. Up and over I go without a problem and am soon in Winston-Salem.

Three years ago, I was excited about hooking my first camper up by myself. Today, I drive a huge Class A motorhome across the country, towing a car behind me. Anyone can do anything they set their mind to!

The last three days in North Carolina with my daughter and her new husband have been full of fun and relaxation. Now it's time to head further south.

Since my RV GPS died, I open the Maps app on my phone. I contemplate available routes, zooming in and out to make sure my rig can do the route, having learned my lesson about just picking the fastest. I choose the one that says go west on I-40 to 77 South, to I-95 South. I am tired and don't have the energy for two-lane back roads. It's interstates for me today.

I need some sort of guide. Though it doesn't know that I am in an RV and won't keep me from low overpasses, I do not have a choice, I will have to use the Maps app on my phone. I am close to the first interstate and Madam GPS says take the exit onto I-40 east. Maybe it's a loop or something. Since I don't know where I am, I take the exit. A few miles into Interstate 40 East, I see an accident where a car has spun around on the westbound side of the interstate, blocking traffic. It must have just happened. No one is out of their cars and there are no emergency services. I pray everyone is okay.

Then it's a "Route" something, then "Highway" something. Before I know it, I am going east on a two-lane road! Then I hear, "Road closed ahead. Your route has been updated." Next command, "In one mile, turn right onto Main Street." I am in the hood! No way I am stopping here to figure it out. After a myriad of turns, I am on Route 52 going through Society Hill, South Carolina.

Hours later, I see a sign that tells me if I turn right, I will get to the final interstate I had planned to take, I-95 South. Ignoring

Madam GPS, I go that way. Just as I make the turn for the inter-state ramp, there is a sharp curve and I hear a noise. I remember that sound: the refrigerator doors flying open and the freezer below sliding out. I take a quick glance back once I am on the interstate and driving straight. Yep. I cannot believe I forgot to latch the doors. There is nothing that I can do now except listen to them crash to the floor and spew out their contents.

I drive on, take Exit 150, then turn left for gas and to clean up the mess. The Mobil station on the right is near-deserted, but it is a perfect spot for RVers. When you turn in, the pumps are situated so you just drive straight up to them. After filling my tank, it's easy to loop around the back for Emmi to walk, then drive right back out.

Back on 95 South, a highway patrol car is on the right shoulder with his lights flashing. As I approach, I change lanes and see a white truck and its big camper off in the woods. The sight in front of me is both scary and sad. I think it was a fifth wheel, but it's hard to tell. It's twisted and tilted. The only thing from keeping it from lying flat on its side are the trees propping it up. The outside wall panels are off and laying at different angles, belongings and furniture strewn in a path and in the trees. I am reminded of how blessed I am. I had zero experience and no idea what I was doing three years ago when I started this journey. I still don't know nearly enough and have made it through some crazy situations.

Exhausted, I make it to my exit for the KOA Campground. As I circle around the ramp, I find there are two lanes for me to merge into. There are cars coming, but I have my own lane. I am good. Or so I thought! Just as I start to make the merge onto Highway 17, my GPS says, "Turn right." I am not going fast, but a little too fast to do this. I am not ready. I press the brake enough to let a car pass then do it anyway. I can just imagine taking the turn on my left three wheels. The movie will show my rig bouncing back down on all six, and me popping out like, "Yeah, I meant to do that!"

In reality, I make the turn without any drama and drive down to the KOA. It's 1:15 p.m. when I go inside to get checked in.

I give the owner, Jennifer, my name and KOA Membership number, but there is no reservation. I check my phone for the confirmation, and I am at the *wrong* KOA! I had booked Santee, two to three hours behind me, and I am at Point South/Yemassee. Jennifer finds a pull-through spot big enough for me here and even finds the phone number so I can let the other park know I won't be there. I won't have sewer hook-ups, but it's only for a night. I will have fifty-amp power and water. One of the million reasons I love KOA. Just in case that doesn't give KOAs enough brownie points, the originally booked KOA refunds my money for their campground. I never expected that.

I follow my escort to the site and slide in easily. He makes sure I am okay before heading off. I get electric and water connected, am near perfectly level without even using my leveling jacks, and put out my awning mere seconds before rain pours out of the sky in buckets.

I am sitting under my awning, watching the deluge and looking at my phone to figure out where I messed up. It's because my app is set to avoid highways. I looked at several potential stops in South Carolina and booked one. This morning I start typing KOA in my maps app. I was a goofball and chose the first one in my history.

I am going to have dinner with part of my best friend's family in Charleston tonight. To do that, I have to disconnect the Trail-hawk from Irma. I open a radar map to see when this rain is expected to end, but it's not until late tonight, hours after I need to leave. I dig out my rain boots and find a jacket. My hair is all tucked in and my hood is on. It's so tightly tied you can barely see more than my eyes. I think I am ready to tackle the task and step out into the storm.

I bend over to start the disconnect process and my jacket rides up a bit. Within minutes, my attire is worthless. My rear end is sticking out and soaked with cold, wet rain, and water is pouring into the tops of my rain boots, where my sockless feet are soon sloshing in water. I finish the exterior task and have to disconnect my portable brake system inside my car. For a minute, I am excited about getting out of the rain. That was before I opened the door and remembered that I cannot get in until I push the seat back and unhook it from my brake pedal. Not only am I soaked when I finish, but so is the inside of my car.

The rain has reduced to just a sprinkle. I am finally somewhat dry and leaving for dinner with the Smilowitz family in Charleston. I plug their address into my GPS. It's about an easy hour drive straight up Highway 17. Well, it would have been, if it had not started pouring again. Although my windshield wipers are on turbo, you can't tell by my windshield. I can barely see anything through it. I ask God to tell those people driving 30 mph with either their flashers, or no lights at all on, how to drive in the rain or get off the road. Instead, the rain slacks off. I laugh out loud, thinking even God knows it would take too long to fix this for me.

I have arrived in one piece and although I have only met the family twice, I am welcomed into their home as if I was part of the family. It's cool inside, but the aroma of food is comforting and somehow warm. The beautiful woman responsible for this dream ahead of me is in the kitchen. I have never met her, but I know this is Aunt Dot. It was such a treat to sit around the dinner table with this loving family, talking and laughing as the kids bantered good-naturedly.

It is hard to leave, but I have a drive ahead of me and an early morning tomorrow. Before I head back to camp, we say our good-byes and promise to do this again.

It's raining when I wake up around seven. I am not in a hurry to leave, so I get my pack-up chores done between downpours. I don't need my GPS because this is the last leg of my seven-week East Coast trip. I check with Siri to see how long my trip should be. It is 184 miles, straight south on Interstate 95, to Hannah Park in Jacksonville, and it should take just under three hours. It's sprinkling when I am ready for lift-off.

I make one stop at the rest area just north of Brunswick for a snack and potty break. It seems like only minutes before I am on I-295, then exiting onto Merrill Road. I am in the right lane, literally banging slowly down the road. It's horrible! I want to get in the left lane, but everyone is passing me because of my snail's pace. Someone flashes their lights and lets me over. It is the simplest kindness that makes my day.

Do you ever feel so totally blessed?

I arrive at Hanna Park, as the locals call it (officially known as Kathryn Abbey Hanna Park), and get checked in. This is the first park I stayed in with my first RV. I rocked the tight squeeze (because of all the trees and brush) getting in. I am almost dead level without leveling jacks. I disconnect the car, move it, and get Irma hooked up. I open my black tank and smell poop, close the valve, and go to investigate. The park's drain at the ground is put together with electrical tape, and raw sewage is oozing out onto the ground. Oops! Sorry, maintenance guy. I call the office. The camp host, Bobby, shows up and has to call maintenance. Everyone is talking about the scrape on the side of my rig and how lucky I am. Bobby says he can fix it. I offer to pay him if he can. I go to the store for some supplies, and when I return, there are no scratches!

On my last morning at Hanna Park, I am sitting outside at dawn with Emmi laying at my feet. My flamingos are standing sentry at the front corner of my site. The sun is beginning to cast her light through the trees, and I hear the beginnings of a new day. Birds are chirping, cicadas are singing their tune, and squirrels are chattering. I hear the quiet hum of an air conditioner in the distance. I pick up my coffee and inhale the rich, strong aroma. Being tucked in the woods, waking up with nature, is incredibly peaceful and relaxing. Then I am reminded that life can change in an instant.

With no warning growl, Emmi bursts from her spot, barking angrily, ready to attack. I don't see anything and no amount of soothing or firm commands will settle her. An armadillo comes ambling out of the bushes as if he doesn't have a care in the world. Emmi erupts with more fierceness than a mountain lion. Picking her up is like trying to get a giant cat in a tub of water. Scratching, hissing, barking, growling, and squirming, I can barely hang onto her and get her inside. I snap a picture of Mr. Armadillo as he strolls across the road into the woods on the other side. Nature returns to her singing as if nothing happened.

Sadly, between finishing this book and it being published, I learned that Bobby passed away. To you in heaven, my friend, I will never forget your kindness. Thank you.

I filled Irma up at the easiest gas station ever: Raceway. Super easy in and out. I leave and get back on the highway in the pouring rain. My windshield wipers are trying to keep up. I am coming up on a semi parked on the shoulder with his flashers on. No way to get over. Both lanes are packed. I am getting close and he turns his blinker on. Surely, he knows how hard it would be for me to stop Irma and will wait for me to pass. Nope. He's coming in. I am standing on my brakes and looking for a way out. The only one is the ditch. Which would be worse, rear ending the truck at 60 mph or flipping into the ditch? I don't like either scenario. Foot off the brake and back on. Irma growls, kicking into lower gear. I need the idiot truck to speed up. Foot off the brake and back on. Irma roars and pulls me back enough to not land in the ditch. Of all people, that truck driver should have known better. Now I am rolling along like nothing ever happened.

I am off to check on my condo repair status today. Finally, after three years, my condo is rebuilt and livable again, but my journey is not finished. I am putting it on the market and staying in my RV.

With God's help, I survived five decades of life that were sometimes a challenge, but it evolved into something incredible. I did something most women would not do alone. I took five big trips across our amazing country and I only have five states left. In life we often say, "Someday…" and it never happens. I was faced with a challenge and the reminder to make today *the* day.

Is there something you have dreamed of doing but don't because you don't know how? Or because it's too far outside the box? Or maybe people say it's crazy? Don't let fear of the unknown or other people's opinions stop you! Good things come to those who go, not those who wait.

Now I just have to decide how I will tackle those five states left.

ACKNOWLEDGMENTS

First, I would like to thank God for being my co-pilot and having my back, every step of the way (even in my stupidest moments)! Without HIM, none of this would have happened.

Amber & Tyler, I am so proud of the adults you have become (regardless of the mistakes I made as your Mom)! You should know, I got the definition of success all wrong! I wish I had spent more time showing you the idea of enough and the concept of balance. I wish I had taken you on adventures instead of working vacations. Wherever your journey in life takes you, I pray you'll always be safe. Enjoy the ride and never forget that I love you!

A huge thanks to my best friend Hope, who has always encouraged me in every crazy thing I do! Thank you for being the best weather watcher ever and diverting me away from storms.

Thanks to my brother Buddy for giving me the best advice, "What's behind you doesn't matter. It's what's in front of you that does." Thank you, brother, for pushing me to work less and travel more.

I also want to thank all of the travelers, RV park/campground staff and owners I met on the road who invited me to dinner, helped me fix things, shared advice and encouraged me to keep going. (I wanted to list names, but I was told this section was not supposed to have chapters!!!)

The right things happen at the right time. I am so glad that I stumbled on the "little" video by Steve Harrison and Jack Canfield called Bestseller Blueprint and later joined their Quantum Leap Publicity and Marketing Program! They have both taught me so much! The last time I saw Steve he said, "You need to speak about *Do the Thing You Fear*." Thank you, Steve, for tying all of the pieces together for me. Thanks to this program, I was connected with Debra Englander. I was just a woman who wanted something more in life and did something crazy. This amazing woman believed in my story before she even read a single word of what I had written. Her constant encouragement and guidance were the greatest gifts I could have ever asked for! If not for Debra and the talented team at Post Hill Press, you would not have this book in your hands today.

Finally, I'd like to thank all of those people who didn't believe in me, because through this journey, I learned that your opinion doesn't matter. I believed I could, so I did!

ABOUT THE AUTHOR

JENNI climbed the corporate ladder and found success as a businesswoman and entrepreneur. Today, success for her is defined as spending the majority of her time helping other people or trying something new. Some days, it's making it over a mountain in one piece or finding a hidden waterfall.